EYE OF THE HURRICANE

MY PATH FROM DARKNESS

TO FREEDOM

DR. RUBIN "HURRICANE" CARTER, LL.D.

WITH KEN KLONSKY

FOREWORD BY NELSON MANDELA

Lawrence Hill Books

Library of Congress Cataloging-in-Publication Data

Carter, Rubin, 1937–

  Eye of the hurricane : my path from darkness to freedom / Rubin "Hurricane" Carter with Ken Klonsky ; foreword by Nelson Mandela.

    p. cm.

  Includes index.

  ISBN 978-1-56976-568-5

  1. Carter, Rubin, 1937– 2. Prisoners—United States—Biography. 3. Judicial error—United States. 4. Criminal justice, Administration of—United States. I. Klonsky, Kenneth. II. Title.

  HV9468.C376A3 2011

  365'.6092—dc22

  [B]

2010038527

Interior design: Mayfly Design (www.mayflydesign.net)

Short excerpts from this book appeared in an interview with Rubin Carter by Ken Klonsky (edited by Andrew Snee) for The Sun *magazine, August 2003, entitled "Going the Distance: Rubin Carter's Long Journey from Convict to Crusader."*

Published by Lawrence Hill Books

An imprint of Chicago Review Press, Incorporated

814 North Franklin Street

Chicago, Illinois 60610

ISBN 978-1-56976-568-5

Printed in the United States of America

5 4 3 2

To every human being on this earth who
bravely seeks perfection in themselves by looking inward.

In the land of the blind, the one-eyed man is king.

—ERASMUS, 1510

"Kundalini is the force that keeps [us] in a hypnotic state. 'To awaken' for man means to be 'dehypnotized.'"

—G. I. GURDJIEFF, AS TRANSLATED BY P. D. OUSPENSKY,
IN SEARCH OF THE MIRACULOUS

Who you were born to, your social status, where you were born, your religion, the color of your skin, are all accidental, all part of what can be called the law of accident. This level of life in which we live and breathe and exercise our beings is controlled by the law of accident.

—DR. RUBIN "HURRICANE" CARTER

CONTENTS

ACKNOWLEDGMENTS

Dr. Carter would like to acknowledge the following people for their contributions to the writing of this book: John Artis, for his love of Truth which allowed me to live long enough to write this book; Sam Leslie, for standing by me as the best friend I've ever had and for his bravery in taking "the work" out into the world; Thom Kidrin, for being my lifeline to the world by supplying sustenance for the body and food for the mind during my long prison ordeal; Alonzo Starling, former chief of staff at Innocence International, for keeping me on track and for the pure joy of his company; Judge H. Lee Sarokin, for being my King Solomon and swimming against the current.

The authors would like to thank the late Larry Hoffman, former Canadian Ambassador James George, and the late Annie Jacobsen for their invaluable assistance and encouragement. The authors would also like to recognize Morty Mint of the Mint Agency for his diligent work in shepherding the book to its publication. In addition, they would like to thank Verna Relkoff of the Mint Agency for her incisive edit and reorganization of the manuscript. Finally, the authors would like to thank Sue Betz and Devon Freeny of Chicago Review Press for their editing and their patience.

FOREWORD

Nelson Mandela

Rubin Carter embarked upon a journey of reconciliation many years ago. His path was longer and more difficult than others who had preceded him, for Rubin's Spirit was dead. In his powerful testament, *The Sixteenth Round*, written more than thirty years ago, Rubin describes the effect on him of the racism and brutality of the American prison system: "The treacherous years of living in [prison] had done their job to perfection: they killed my poor heart dead."

His self-diagnosis was hardly surprising: twenty years in prison for a crime he did not commit can kill the strongest of men. The lesson he was learning in prison was that "life was capricious...always subjected to someone else's whim." From that analysis it is easy to despair; it is easy to believe, especially as a black man who grew up in a segregated society, that all hope is gone.

It is to Rubin Carter's credit, fighter that he is, that he refused to accept his own death sentence, just as he refused to accept the guilty verdict of the state of New Jersey. Rubin chose to live, and his means of living was to seek out his inner self. In that bleakest and most unforgiving corner of the world, prison, Rubin chose to dream, to dream of life beyond the steel bars and concrete walls, a life of helping and a life of peace. The hate that placed him in prison, the hate that was mirrored in his soul, could never be the means of his freedom.

His first step toward freedom was knowing he needed the help of others, that he lived in a larger world where the possibility of good existed. Rubin communicated with the outside world, he read voraciously, and he began to understand. As he writes in this book, "The more laws we are under, the less free we are. I lived under paternal law, American law, the law of segregation, criminal justice law, military law, and prison law, so I was never any freer than a slave.... No matter who you are, you are born into the universal prison, the world of sleeping people and mechanical laws.... The only escape from the physical, the metaphorical, or the universal prison of sleep is to wake up!"

Rubin woke up in prison and became a free man. Once his freedom became a physical fact, Rubin determined that he must come to the aid of all those languishing in prison for crimes they never committed, the victims of injustice. That has been the life of Rubin Carter since he was released from prison, "giving back the work," as he says. At times, the personal price has been steep, but the commitment to give back has never lessened, never faltered.

I commend Rubin Carter and the dedication he has for others. He has journeyed a long way and has touched the hearts and souls of many with whom he has come into contact. His rich heart is now alive in love, compassion, and understanding.

PREFACE

Ken Klonsky

Highway 209, south and west of Kingston, New York, lined by prosperous villages, farmhouses, and rolling hills, looked and felt on that November morning of 2004 like a bucolic paradise, a gentle road to nowhere. Golden autumn leaves, a blue sky, and a hint in the air of summer past were marred only by the occasional sign to remind us that this was the day after election day, a day on which George W. Bush had won the presidency for the second time.

The closer we approached our destination, the shabbier the villages and the farmhouses became. That destination, Eastern New York Correctional Facility, a gray stone structure built on a disproportionate scale, appeared incongruous in this setting. The width of its frontage gave the impression that the building had no depth, like a movie set for an old-fashioned medieval spectacle. Flanking the prison were two gargantuan turrets shaped like chess rooks. The multi-tiered building with heavily barred windows sent a subliminal message: *Leave all hope behind, you who enter here.* Maximum security. Minimum hope.

Rubin "Hurricane" Carter, Alonzo Starling, and I had set off from Toronto the previous day on a journey of hope. We planned to visit a prisoner at this penitentiary, David McCallum III, the first case for Carter's recently launched organization, Innocence International, dedicated to assisting the wrongly convicted worldwide. After the visit with McCallum, we planned to go down to New Jersey where Carter had been asked to speak to young offenders at the New Jersey Training School for Boys in Jamesburg, the very place where he had been sent as a youth for assaulting a known pedophile. Carter and I were writing a book together, this book, and I could think of no better way to get to know him.

What kind of man is Rubin Carter? There are those who focus on his character flaws, his difficult past, his long-windedness. He owns up to it all, often good-naturedly. There are those who continue to sully his name, to insist that he and his codefendant, John Artis, were guilty in 1966 of the infamous triple murder at a bar in Paterson, New Jersey. Those who still attack his reputation do not know, nor did they ever know, the real Rubin Carter. He is still an image in their minds, in the words of Bob Dylan's immortal song, "Hurricane," the "crazy nigga." Other black boxers have also been demonized by the American public—Jack Johnson, a heavyweight portrayed as chasing white women, and Sonny Liston, always depicted as a big man with a malevolent scowl, just to name two.

Carter, despite his nickname, was not a furious, angry fighter but a methodical and intelligent one. Watching tapes of his past matches, I could see why he was never knocked out: he believed as much in defending himself, fighting in close, as he did in taking out the other guy. Angry fighters leave themselves open to long-range well-timed counterpunches. To Rubin "Hurricane" Carter, boxing was a business, albeit an enjoyable one. His business was to get his opponent out of there as soon as possible while never playing to the fickle crowd.

Carter, born in Clifton, New Jersey, in 1937, is a paradoxical mixture of youthful idealism, impracticality, and hard-earned wisdom. It is hard to conceive that a man so straightforward and direct, who even fought that way, could go into a bar, shoot three innocent people to death while wounding a fourth, and run off into the night. Nor did he commit such a crime.

David McCallum III, the prisoner we were visiting, had written to me and Rubin in February 2004 after reading an interview I did with Carter in *The Sun* magazine. McCallum, in 1985 at the age of sixteen, had been arrested along with another African American male, Willie Stuckey, for a terrible crime, the abduction and cold-blooded murder of a twenty-year-old white male. Not a single piece of forensic, ballistic, or eyewitness evidence incriminated either boy, but the two, under what they claimed was physical coercion, had falsely confessed to the crime. Both boys were convicted and sentenced to twenty-five years to life. Stuckey died in prison in 2001 of unknown causes. It might just as well have been that he died of a broken heart.

In his letter, McCallum said:

I have been incarcerated for nearly nineteen years for a crime that I did not commit, and it has been a passion to prove my innocence or at least bring some awareness to my case by establishing a letter-writing campaign, but no one seems to want to take my letters serious enough.... Fortunately, that has not discouraged me at all....

My question to you is would it be alright for me to share my story with you in a future letter? I am confident that you would be intrigued and interested by my plight. Like your interview with Mr. Carter, my story would be able to inspire and motivate

people to get more involved in advocate work because there are
thousands of innocent people languishing in prison with what
appears to be no hope at all.

David McCallum's letter to us was one of dozens this indefatigable man had sent out. We were on a list that included Bob Herbert of the *New York Times*, Richard Leo of the criminology department at the University of California, Medilex and Medical Legal Case Review, both crime laboratories, ABC News's *Primetime*, forensic science experts, numerous law firms, a polygraph expert, private investigators, ten or so innocence projects, and literally anyone anywhere who might respond to a cry for help. Each of his letters had been similarly crafted to capture the attention of the recipient. Some of the recipients responded with transparent excuses. Others were interested at first but backed out for various reasons, including the absence of DNA evidence and McCallum's inability to pay for forensic tests. Carter's reputation would bring to David the assistance of a brilliant pro bono attorney, Oscar Michelen, of Sandback and Michelen, and Professor Steven Drizin from Northwestern University's Bluhm Legal Clinic, an expert in the field of false confessions.

By the summer, I was able to inform him that he was to be the first case for Carter's new organization. The following reply came from him on September 20, 2004.

Dear Mr. Klonsky,
After receiving the great news, I am finding it extremely difficult
to contain my enthusiasm. I have taken your advice and I am
enjoying this news because for the first time in years, I genuinely

believe that I am on the right path. I am really looking forward to receiving the help of Innocence International.

Mr. Carter's words, "Tell him we are going to come get him," were profound and encouraging. They elicited tears of hope and belief from me. My spirits have been uplifted considerably, and I have no intention of allowing doubt to seep into my thoughts. . . .

I sent a copy of your letter to my mom and dad because I like to keep them abreast of what is going on with me. I am sure they are going to be overwhelmed with happiness.

I am not disappointed about [having to wait until] November 3rd. If I have learned nothing else, I have learned to suppress impatience. It will not be a problem for me waiting on you and Mr. Carter's arrival. . . . I can imagine what it will mean for other men when you and Mr. Carter visit them. What better individual for them to draw inspiration from than Mr. Carter himself in terms of enduring hardships at such a young age. I know that I have.

As we walked through the prison parking lot, Carter speculated that the grapevine would have heard that we were coming—he was later proved correct. The visitors' entrance and the visitors' waiting room were full of signs, some logical, some absurd. These rules, as Carter says, are designed to keep the prisoner and his family confused and submissive. "No weapons or metal objects" makes obvious sense, but why was I forbidden to carry a notebook? I was reduced to taking notes on business cards. One could only wonder at the mind responsible for the following rule: "Physical contact is limited to an embrace and a kiss at the beginning and end of the visit. Brief kisses and embraces are also permitted during the course of the visit. However, prolonged kissing, commonly referred to as 'necking' or 'petting,' is not allowed or permitted."

After a long time of emptying pockets, stashing items in lockers, filling out forms, going through metal detectors, and enduring personal searches, we were finally given access to the visitors' room—that is, the prison cafeteria. The small square tables and hardback chairs appeared to have been donated by a local elementary school.

McCallum, a muscular man with a thick neck and rounded shoulders, stood back near a table as we entered, suppressing a smile. Each of us gave him a hug, his body under the dark green prison garb feeling like an iron ball. He sat between Carter and me, across from Starling. Carter stared at him, beamed at him, for perhaps three minutes. We were suspended in silence. The prisoner gulped down emotion after emotion—fearful, as he later revealed, that he would be unable to control himself. This was the first time anyone who was dedicated to freeing the innocent had ever visited him. Nineteen years he had been there, roughly the same time that Rubin Carter had spent incarcerated at Rahway (now East New Jersey State Prison) and Trenton State (now New Jersey State Prison) for the triple murder. Carter left prison in 1985, on almost the same day that David entered it.

In clear violation of the rules, a couple across from us engaged in some heavy lap dancing that, as Carter informed me later, I should not have been observing. Prisons have written rules, and the prisoners have unwritten ones. The guard on duty, an easygoing, youngish woman, blithely ignored the prisoner's breach of conduct, and, luckily for me, the presence of Rubin Carter saved me from a harsh warning or a confrontation with the inmate. Of course, they had been watching Carter, too.

Under Carter's gaze, McCallum slowly came to life. He had been waiting in his cell since nine o'clock, not going to his daily workout for fear of missing his visitors. We did not get there until eleven-twenty. All that time, he had paced back and forth, reminding himself that visiting hours were from nine to three and that almost four hours remained, but McCallum, by dint of continued disappointments, has an understandable tendency to pessimism.

"It's not optimism or pessimism," Carter told him later. "Optimism built the airplane. Pessimism built the parachute. You need both, my brother."

During the interview, which lasted more than two hours, any doubts I had about McCallum were dispelled. His features, especially his lips and mouth, appeared distorted. His body was off-center, as if the prison walls and the years of waiting had fallen on top of him. He'd been bent, but he hadn't broken.

Carter asked him if he could gather the materials that might prove his innocence or cast doubt upon his conviction. McCallum proved to be just as well organized in person as he had sounded in his letters. Intelligent and articulate, as well.

Carter touched him repeatedly, to make him understand that we were really there. He assured him that we were going to get him out, that the process might take some time, but that we would eventually find a way. And he promised the prisoner that we would be standing right outside that door when it happened. McCallum told us that since his incarceration he had been out of the prison on one single occasion, when he needed to get specialized treatment at a hospital. Shackled on a small bus, through the window he saw trees, sky, people walking: everyday life. He had wept. "Little things you take for granted mean so much," he said.

The final advice that Rubin Carter had for David McCallum was something he had been told by Judge H. Lee Sarokin upon his release from prison. It's the advice Carter gives all wrongly convicted prisoners upon first meeting, when he decides if his innocence project will represent them. "Rubin," the judge had said. "You have to live a pristine life, not for yourself but for all the other wrongly convicted prisoners in the world." Carter asked McCallum if he was able to do it. McCallum did not answer right away but admitted that he had thought about it, about whether the prison had rubbed off on him. Then he gave Carter his solemn assurance along with a promise that he would dedicate his life to helping others in his circumstances. Getting out of prison, as Carter says, is the day your sentence begins, when you commence the hard work of reconstructing your life. Carter's release date, November 8, 1985, he still considers to be the day of his second birth.

After a final hug, as McCallum walked back slowly toward the prison proper, we could see the burden he carried. He looked back one last time, his face a mixture of joy, pain, and, now, hope.

———

The year 2004 had been a challenging one for Carter. He resigned from the Association in Defense of the Wrongly Convicted, the premier Canadian innocence project where he had been executive director for thirteen years, over an ethical dispute with the board of directors. While on a holiday in Jamaica, the house he lived in for more than a decade was gutted by a fire. Much of what he owned, aside from what he had with him in Jamaica, was destroyed: priceless memorabilia, photographs, clothing, furniture. Lacking insurance, he was broke. He had spent the previous year doing nothing but pro bono work.

Rubin "Hurricane" Carter, now Dr. Rubin Carter (after receiving an honorary doctorate from Griffith University in Australia), was being tested again. Yet he didn't cry out against ill luck or injustice. His response to the fire had been, "It's only stuff." He also felt great joy that his big loving cat, aptly named Phoenix, rose from the ashes and survived. He rented a basement apartment, pointing out that with his life's experience he could live in a matchbox and be happy.

The day after visiting McCallum, we drove to Jamesburg. Carter had been asked by the New Jersey Training School for Boys, the juvenile detention facility from which he had escaped to join the army paratroops fifty years ago, to speak to the young offenders. Since his release from prison, Carter has come to see his experiences at the school in a somewhat positive light. He is, however, disturbed by some of the changes that have taken place since his departure. While the school is now blessed with a caring and well-trained staff, unlike the staff he had to deal with during his stay, it has morphed from a self-contained farm and military school into a fenced-in prison. From the same school stage where as a child he had performed in an *Amos and Andy* play, Carter gave the young men a message of hope, that they, like him, like Malcolm X, like Nelson Mandela, could rise from their present circumstances and realize their unlimited potentials, their hopes and aspirations. Plainly, he was revered by everyone there, even one of his former prison guards at Trenton State, who now worked at Jamesburg in drug rehab. That man, Eugene Livingston, referred to him as a "monarch," verifying the reports that Carter's prison cell had been filled with books and that he had been universally respected. To those young inmates, Carter gave the same message that he gives to all people, regardless of their circumstances: *Dare to dream*. It was the message the high school students I taught in Toronto heard from him years ago. On this afternoon at the youth facility, just as on that afternoon at a public high school, he validated the lives of young people. That was to be his payment.

———

Rubin Carter's life embodies transformation: from a troubled, violent, stammering youth, to army paratrooper, to famous boxer, to prisoner, to advocate for the wrongly convicted, to honorary doctorate (he was to receive another doctorate in 2005 from York University in Toronto), to the CEO of Innocence International, where he shines as a beacon for prisoners around the world. Ironically, were it not for his unjust incarceration at Trenton State Prison, he could never have saved himself from hate and bitterness. The introspection and reflections in the pages of this book show that he made the most of his time.

This is the second book by Rubin Carter. *The Sixteenth Round*, a remarkable autobiographical achievement, was written from behind bars and is the only other book in his voice. Amazingly, it was the first extended writing he had ever done. It displays his passion, intensity, and integrity.

Rubin Carter entered prison in 1966; Nelson Mandela was sent to Robben Island in 1964. Both men began life as rebellious children: Carter a violent youth in the streets of Paterson, New

Jersey; Mandela in the countryside of tribal South Africa. Both men were refined by the fire of injustice, and both men would have gladly accepted death rather than be subjugated. They both refused to wear the clothes of the prison. Both achieved a level of integrity that made their jailers understand that they were free despite being behind prison bars—freer, in fact, than their jailers. Liberation was to be the work of their lives. For Mandela, his own liberation became a symbol for the cause of freedom throughout South Africa and, ultimately, for Africans of any country who yearned to escape the remnants of colonial oppression. For Carter, his release from prison gave him a new raison d'être: the liberation of the wrongly convicted from prisons the world over. Both men are motivated by compassion for humanity. Neither has sought revenge for his own sufferings.

In the year 2000, at the first World Reconciliation Day in Australia, Carter spoke on the same stage with Mandela. "Once Nelson and I saw each other," Carter says, "we just cracked up. We laughed. He said, 'We're here, man. We're here. We made it.'" It was, however, just another stop along the road, a brief moment of respite to look back with pride on what both had accomplished. The journey continues.

INTRODUCTION

A Prisoner of Ignorance:
Living in Darkness

If thine eye be single, thy whole body shall be full of light.

—LUKE 11:34

You may have heard of me, Rubin "Hurricane" Carter, as having been a professional prizefighter. That, along with having been a wrongly convicted person who had to spend nearly twenty years behind bars for a crime he did not commit, is a fact. But my journey to self-discovery revealed to me that I was a different type of prisoner even before the wrongful conviction. I was foremost a prisoner of ignorance.

First, I did not have an appreciation for what it means to be a human being. Second, because I lacked self-knowledge, I behaved mechanically, without the conscious purpose that gives life its meaning. I believed what was told to me or what most other people are taught to believe without examining the truth or falsehood of those beliefs.

1

Now, every day I am more certain of the words in the New Testament: "Ye shall know the Truth, and the Truth shall make you free" (John 8:32).

This book is about finding the Truth and acting upon it. It's as simple as that, and yet this simplicity encompasses all of morality and ethics. If I know the Truth I must act upon it, even if, when I do so, others think me a fool.

My personal odyssey and commitment to Truth led me—on Friday, August 13, 2004, nineteen years after my own release from prison—to leave my position as CEO at the Association in Defense of the Wrongly Convicted, the organization I helped found and the organization that became the foremost innocence project in Canada. Commentators and acquaintances asked me how I could do such a foolish thing. How could I resist the siren song of prestige and security?

I had only one answer: knowledge of the Truth gave me no option. I could not be a conscious, moral person if I ignored the Truth. I could not pretend to be ignorant.

Of course, ignorance of any kind can be dangerous. Unlike a disturbingly large percentage of people on this earth, I believe that science and rational thought have an important role to play in the world. I believe that the universe and the earth are billions of years old. I believe that the universe consists of a series of levels, and everything is what it is based upon where it is in this series of levels. I believe that we miraculous human beings have evolved into what we are. I also believe that human beings must continue to evolve if we are to survive, although the world of nature shows numerous examples of creatures failing to adapt. I also believe that the earth is not the center of all things in the universe, and that we can try, even if we fail, to understand the forces of creation and where we fit into the grand scheme of things. To attempt to know who we are and why we are here on the earth, we must become conscious beings again. As we look around at the state of things on this great planet, we might be forced to conclude, despite the many, many people who attempt to make the world a better place, that the majority of mankind is unconscious and deeply troubled—although they know not why or from whence this feeling comes.

For me, and I know this must seem ironic, prison was the one environment that forced me to wake up and regain Consciousness. Prison allowed me to recapture the pure joy of being alive moment to moment. My survival depended upon it. Otherwise, I would have perished of despair. Prison, and the physical and mental discipline I was able to forge, gave me the ability to weather hardships, a burnt down home, the loss of capital. You would think from the way most people think, act, and speak, that life is nothing larger than houses and money. In fact, most people think that life is just one great big shit sandwich—the more "bread" you have the less "shit" you have to eat! Poverty, as long as I have a roof over my head and a little something to eat, need not bring me unhappiness. Years from now, my body will give way to illness or pain, but my Spirit, conscious and ecstatic, is and will always be awake. Even if I could, I would not change a single thing in my life, including my wrongful conviction.

Human beings have it within themselves to live in ecstasy, the feeling that arises from Consciousness. *Consciousness, then, is not a dialogue with the self but an actual state of being in which we love the world.* Very young children, at least those who have not yet been damaged by their environments and before they are taught by others how to look, what to believe, and before every aspect of their lives is analyzed, organized, homogenized, and computerized, live in this state of joy. Unlike many teenagers, they are not prey to boredom, restlessness, and thrill seeking but experience life with immediacy and a rapturous sense of wonder.

Teenagers, through no fault of their own, lose that sense of wonder and much else besides. In the ten years between 1990 and 2000, more North American children killed themselves and one another than all the U.S. soldiers killed in Vietnam.

Speaking of war itself, CBS News reported that at least 6,256 U.S. veterans, many of them young returnees from Iraq and Afghanistan, committed suicide in 2005, an average of 17 per day, with veterans more than twice as likely to take their own lives as the rest of the population. That rate of self slaughter has remained unchanged until this very day.

Suicide is the same side of the coin as despair; despair is born of hopelessness; hopelessness is the loss of appreciation for what it means to be alive. It is possible for these young people, and for us, to become children again, to rediscover and apply the Consciousness of childhood to the lives we now live. Then we can love again, love life, love the Truth, love ourselves.

––––––––

During my years of study in the unlikely environment of a prison, I read a parable that informs my life every day, a small story that attempts to explain why human beings lose their way. I discovered it in my readings on G. I. Gurdjieff, the great Armenian metaphysical philosopher, and P. D. Ouspensky, his interpreter to the Western world, both of whom were concerned with finding "the way" to Consciousness, since one cannot become conscious unconsciously. This story goes against the grain of traditional Christian teaching, which sees humanity as a flock of sheep gone astray.

In the Judeo-Christian parable, the sheep are in need of a shepherd or a messiah to save them from their wicked and foolish ways. In the more ancient story, we meet a rich magician who happens also to have a large herd of sheep. Part of the explanation for this magician's wealth is that he avoids spending money whenever possible. He simply refuses to hire shepherds or build fences to keep his sheep penned in. The sheep know that the magician only wants their flesh to eat and their wool to get rich, so they do what is natural: whenever they see him coming, they run away and hide in the forest. They are smart!

The magician, always on the lookout for an economic remedy and being a skillful illusionist himself, decides to hypnotize his sheep. Once asleep, the first thing he suggests to them is that they are immortal. He also makes them believe that he is a good and kind master willing to do anything for their benefit. He tells them as well that if anything bad is to befall them, it will not happen at that moment but at some unspecified time in the future. Finally, he makes them believe that they are not sheep at all. Some he hypnotizes into believing that they are lions, some bears, some tigers, some even magicians themselves, until all the sheep are convinced that they are lords of the forest, kings of the jungle, masters of the universe. The sheep are now being controlled by the force that Gurdjieff called the power of Kundalini—the power of hypnosis. No longer do the sheep run away. They just wait passively to be shorn and eaten.

If these sheep are compared to humanity, their state of hypnosis reflects our own state of ignorance. Put to sleep, hypnotized by religions, countries, schools, parents, siblings, and friends, we forget we are mortal, and we forget that this ecstatic moment in which we live is all we really have, that the past is forever gone and the future is yet to be. We learn to trust others over ourselves, believing that those others have our best interests at heart and are wiser than we could ever hope to be. We were born perfect, which means complete, with all our potentials intact. We were awake as small children, but now we are asleep. We human beings, like those sheep, could still run away if we wanted to, but the tragedy is that we have stopped wanting to be free. We buy into the program. We build our own fences inside our minds.

Intuitively, we know who we are but have learned to reject our true natures for fear of scorn, disapproval, or ridicule. Fear is the primary motivator of sheep or slaves, or at least those slaves who have never attempted to regain their freedom. If, because of fear, we go against what we feel deep down to be real, right, good, and true, then we go against ourselves. Our sleeping, mechanical state is responsible for much of the needless grief, suffering, and illness we see in the world today. If we look around us, we can see how sleeping people rob, rape, and exploit one another, how we murder indiscriminately, how we abuse ourselves and destroy the earth's ecosystems. We are unconscious of the causes and consequences of our actions. This unconsciousness is foisted upon us and encouraged, through advertising and shallow political debate, by a corrupt and corrupting society that builds its false prosperity upon our ignorance.

On a less lethal scale but no less important, mechanical or sleeping people act with passivity rather than stand up for Truth, choosing expediency over principle. Thus the values we learn and practice are in every sense a mockery of genuine values. Compromise is all; we are taught to accept untruth and injustice. We are told that we need to work sixty hours a week, and we accept it. We are told that our air and water cannot be clean, and we accept it. We are aware of great disparities of wealth in the world, and we accept it. The so-called free press goes to bed with the military in an illegal war, and the protest soon dies out. The barrier between church and state is crossed, and we accept it. Rights are taken away from innocent citizens, and we accept it. Our privacy is invaded by the police, snoops, and advertisers, and we accept it. We get used to these injustices, yet, simultaneously, we know them to be wrong. Is there any line that cannot be crossed with sleeping people? We might even hear it said that these things are being done "for our own good."

Knowing Truth and reality, not blind obedience or the mentality of the herd, is the first consequence of Consciousness, and Consciousness is humanity's only path to salvation. We are not sheep. When we rely on others to tell us what is true, what is real, who we are, what to believe, or that we need to be "saved," then we treat the gift of Consciousness like some vestigial or functionless organ. I believe that Consciousness is not a cosmic accident, just as I believe that life itself is miraculous and meaningful. Along with Consciousness comes a deliberate, purposeful change in our behavior. It cannot be otherwise.

Principled action, rising above the law—not the law itself—released me from my own prison sentence. Practicing principles and acting on Truth, which are dependent upon my staying awake, keep me strong. I might need to compromise in a social environment for the sake of harmony or even survival, but, make no mistake, there are some things that must never be compromised: Truth—yes, there is such a thing as Truth—integrity, dignity, freedom, and good. To compromise these things drains meaning from life and transforms us from human beings into machines.

As long as I have my life and my health and I am free to act on Truth, then nothing can get in my way. Truth is invincible. And it's not enough to only love the Truth; you must be the Truth, speak the Truth, and act upon the Truth. As you will read in the pages of this book, I learned the hard way the cost of allowing my mechanical nature to get in the way of Consciousness. Most people do not have to pay the same price for their unconscious behavior that I did. There is a difference between being alive, good as that is, and being conscious, which is truly miraculous.

———

The house that I leased for over a decade, 155 Delaware Avenue in Toronto, burned down in October 2004 in an electrical fire. I then lived for a year in a two-and-a-half-room basement flat. Six feet under the ground will always be familiar territory to me. But unlike prison, a place of extreme temperatures, the apartment was cozy and warm in the winter and cool in the summer. I liked the place, so don't tell the landlady that it was me who cut away the screen above the couch to give my cat, Phoenix, easy access to the outside world. He was a downtown city cat, a big tabby. The uptown cats kept their distance, but they soon warmed up when they learned that Phoenix was as beautiful on the inside as he was on the outside. If everyone was as happy as Phoenix and I in our basement apartment, I'm sure the world would be a better place.

Don't get me wrong, I loved my old house on Delaware Avenue, all three floors and a finished basement. It was more than just a house—it was magical, full of friendly spirits, and a piece of myself. I had experienced profound realizations within its walls. It was where I had the experience of being picked up bodily from my office chair by a tremendous force and transplanted to a different part of the room.

The house was where, in my second life, I first found the love of another human being, Theresa, whom I had met at a convention in Nevada. Theresa, who lived and worked in South Carolina, came to Toronto and taught me that I could love. I had never known what love was; I had never felt the need to attach myself to another human being before I met her. She lived with me in 2001, and I was never so happy. I expected her to move to Canada with her children; she expected me to move back to the United States. We never found a middle ground.

As you approached my house in the summertime, a beautiful flower garden out front would greet you, and when you entered the house the garden continued. The first thing you saw was a large vase of flowers, a vase that I called Truth, because all Truth should lead to good. Good was represented by an even larger vase of flowers. Because I had been given so many gifts from people around the world whose lives I had touched, I devoted rooms inside the house to displaying those gifts. My living room was my Black Room, where African people and artifacts were displayed along with my trophies and awards and a lithograph of two of my boxer friends in combat, Carmen Basilio and Sugar Ray Robinson. My dining room was for the children of the world, joyful photographs and tributes. There were closets containing other treasured items such as a headdress from the great Sioux chief Red Cloud.

As you walked upstairs, you passed by photographs of people like Muhammad Ali, Tony Bennett, and Bob Dylan, who had stood by me in difficult times. On the second floor was my jungle room painted with thick foliage. Behind a beautiful Japanese sliding door was the guest bedroom. Then there was my office where the Association in Defense of the Wrongly Convicted spent its infancy, was swaddled, nurtured, and spoon-fed its love of Truth. On the third floor was a spacious bathroom with a Jacuzzi and sauna and the master bedroom with my bed raised up off the floor, surrounded by curtains, like a king's perch. Through the bedroom was a balcony that overlooked the garden in the back, a secluded place I called Heaven, with a multitude of flowers, trees, a winding path leading to a pagoda, and a marble table, my quiet place for meditation. You might have noticed in the rear of the bedroom my private barbershop with an old-fashioned barber's chair where my barber from Brampton would come to cut my hair.

While I intended to move back in when the renovations were completed, I found that the owners had erased me from the premises entirely. They collected their insurance, did a thrifty renovation, and were going to sell it in the hot housing market at a huge profit. But first they asked me if I wanted to buy the place. They annihilated me, and then they wanted to sell me the coffin. All that was left of what I put into that house were the speakers behind the walls. Even the friendly spirits had fled.

I took the burning of the house as a wake-up call. I must never forget that things are transitory. Everything can be taken away in an instant. How lucky that I was away! How lucky that Phoenix ran into the basement and survived! I did have to scold that cat, however, when I returned home. I told him that he had been selfish, that he could have at the very least carried one or two of my suits downstairs with him. How fortunate the year had really been, forcing me to live out my understanding, "to walk the walk." I had become too comfortable.

The punch that knocks you down is the one you don't see coming. It's a shock to the whole system. Losing my house and all of my personal possessions was a knockdown for sure, and, unlike the owners, I didn't have a cent of insurance. But that punch also did me a world of good. What happens to us in life is less important than what we do with what happens to us. It was time to shake out the cobwebs and to remember myself for who and what I really am.

Who or what we human beings really are is the first question we must try to answer. I believe that humanity is the only link between the creative forces of the universe, the source of all existence, and organic life on earth. On an individual basis, the question of identity is one that can only be answered by an awakened spirit and not by a human being living under the spell of Kundalini.

———

When I was a child, my father told me a story about a little boy who was walking through his father's fields and found an eagle's egg that had fallen from its nest. The boy picked up the egg, brought it home with him, and placed it in a nest among the numerous eggs of his prairie chickens. The baby eaglet soon hatched amid the brood of prairie chickens and grew up with them. Thinking that it, too, was a prairie chicken, the little eaglet did as they did. It scratched in the dirt for seeds and insects to eat. It learned how to cluck and how to cackle. It flew only in a brief thrashing of wings and a flurry of feathers, never attempting to fly more than a few feet off the ground, before it would come crashing back to earth. That's what all prairie chickens do.

As time passed, the eagle grew old, tough, and thin. It was beginning to get tired as well. Scratching in the dirt for seeds and insects to eat was very fatiguing work for one so big, one built to do much larger things. One day, while scratching for its dinner, its eye was caught by a movement overhead. The old eagle looked up toward the heavens and saw a magnificent bird soaring effortlessly in the sparkling blue, cloudless sky. With scarcely a beat of its strong, golden wings, the bird hung with graceful majesty on the powerful wind currents.

"Oh, what a beautiful creature!" said the astonished and deluded eagle to its prairie chicken stepbrother who was also scratching in the dirt. "What is it? What is that big beautiful animal?"

"Oh, that's an eagle," his stepbrother clucked and cackled, "the King of the Birds. But don't you give it another thought. You could never be like that."

So the once curious eagle never did give it another thought. It went back to sleep and died thinking of itself as a prairie chicken.

This story, like the tale of the magician, illustrates for me the human condition. We are convinced that our limitations are what we truly are; we deny the gifts with which we were born. It points out also how blameless we are in the process. The eagle was put to sleep by the prairie chickens. How could it behave otherwise? And yet there is a paradox: we can awaken. We know just enough to realize that we are not prairie chickens, maybe not eagles, either, but that we must rely upon myth and metaphor to understand this Truth.

We are flowers from the sun—seeds planted in organic life on earth, with the capacity and the ability to grow stronger, wiser, more intelligent, and more beautiful than anyone can imagine. We must try to become what we can be, and not just settle for what we are at the moment. That is the path for humanity if humanity is to evolve. If we fail to evolve and continue down the destructive path we are now headed, then we will simply disappear from this earth.

What most prevents us from awakening to this reality is not our ignorance of our potential, but ignorance of our ignorance. Mark Twain once said, "It ain't what you don't know that gets you into trouble. It's what you know for sure that just ain't so." We "think" we know who and what we really are, and we think we are conscious beings because we have been hypnotized into believing that our illusions are real.

My purpose in life is not only to become what I can be, however difficult that may prove, but also to transcend prisons—the physical, the metaphorical, and the universal prison of sleep. In trying to escape the physical prison of steel, bricks, and mortar and the mental prison of pain, violence, and humiliation, I stumbled upon the idea that most of my so-called waking life had been no more conscious than the sleepwalking I have described here. It is only because I was later condemned on a wrongful conviction to spend three lifetimes in prison as a racist triple murderer, condemned to rot in the despair of a maximum-security dungeon, that I wound up in the one environment that would finally force me to awaken. The only other option would have been to die.

Prison, consisting of bricks, steel, and mortar, is a depraved home, a factory of brutality for people who have been convicted, justly or unjustly, of criminal behavior. Prison is also a state of mind. In my two lifetimes, I have experienced enough of prison to become knowledgeable in this area. In 2003, I received an honorary doctorate of laws from Griffith University in Brisbane, Australia, and in October 2005, I was similarly honored by York University in Toronto, Canada. Those two doctorates could just as easily have been doctorates of prisons. I write this book to those both inside and outside the prison walls to help you see how I got to where I am today and so that you might learn something from my experience. I want you to rise up off the ground and soar with me like that eagle never did.

———

Looking back, it appears as if one of the themes of my life has been escaping or leaving situations where I had been trapped or incarcerated. It is never easy to escape from prison. On your own, it may appear impossible. The place to start, however, is in your desire to escape. Because people have been hypnotized, you cannot take it for granted that everyone behind bars wants to be on the outside. But if you do wish to escape—and I am talking here about the metaphorical as well as the actual prisons—you've got to be very quiet lest you alarm the guards. The guards are standing on a tower, armed with telescopic rifles, or they are inside of you, keeping you fenced in despite the fact that you are physically free. You also need to find other people, guides, who have escaped before you and who know the way out.

My own experience with prison is that I was in one or another kind of prison for the first forty-five years of my life. You may already know that my first prison was a severe speech impediment; for the first eighteen years of my life I could barely talk. My voice was imprisoned inside my body. I had thousands of words running through my mind, but I couldn't get a single one to smoothly pass my lips. I would stomp my foot and sputter, do all kinds of gyrations trying to get a word out. People laughed at me. I didn't know that my problem was hereditary. No one had told me that my father and his father had stammered.

My second prison was my own ignorance and the ignorance of the people around me. My grandfather used to hit my father over the head with raw beef liver in order to stop his stammering. Country folks say that if you stammer when you try to talk then you are lying. Well, I guess I must have been the world's biggest liar.

I tried to compensate for not being able to speak by nodding for yes or shaking my head for no. Being so different from other children took a big toll on my self-esteem. When people laughed at me because they thought my gyrations were funny, the only sound they heard in reply was the sound of my fist whistling through the air. My fists did my talking!

So I was trapped, imprisoned in a world of silence and ignorance, expressing myself with violence, until I was serving in the American paratroops in Germany. At that time, in 1954, I met a Sudanese Muslim who was trying to get his American citizenship by serving in the military. His name was Ali Hasson Muhammad, a wise and dignified man who was to become my mentor. He literally stumbled upon me as we were getting ready to jump from an airplane. Ali Hasson was the first person who ever made a con-centrated effort to talk to me. As a result, he was the first person I ever trusted.

I remember him as being slender and powerful, a panther-like man. He stood ramrod straight and had snapping white almond-shaped eyes that stared out at you from a complexion as dark as night. His skin was dusty dark, not shiny black like mine. He wore his long hair in braids around his head so that his army cap would fit. When he smiled, his eyes danced; he had a way of switching in a millisecond from stone seriousness to childish delight.

He could see that I was quick with my fists and that I lacked self-esteem, so the first thing he did was to connect me with the boxing corps. This was a group of twenty-five amateur fighters who represented the U.S. Army overseas. I had always been a tough guy with a short fuse, but my love for boxing was as much about con-trolling myself, learning the discipline of a sport, as it was about expressing violence.

Because I had been in a state home for boys for years and had enlisted in the army illegally, I was already an oddity. The other guys, the boxers included, would complain about army regulations and army food, but the food was manna to me, and you could eat as much as you wanted. To me, the army was just a more sophis-ticated Jamesburg. I found some stability in the paratroops; all I needed now was to start making some friends. But at eighteen, I was too immature, my tongue would betray me, and I hated to look stupid in front of others.

Ali Hasson, like any good friend and mentor, told me that my stammering would always keep me in trouble. He said, "If you want to do something about it, I know a school that can help you.

If you're too embarrassed to go by yourself, I'll go with you." And he did.

Fearful as a little boy walking to a new school with his dad, I walked into a Dale Carnegie course given at the State College for Economics in Mannheim, Germany. The classroom had a bank of windows; when you looked out, you could see the road down below and a statue of Bismarck on an iron horse at the center of the square. Ali Hasson sat with me through the first part of every class while I learned how to talk. After fifteen minutes, he would go off to his U.S. citizenship class in the same facility. The instructors were mostly Germans, but their English was a whole lot better than mine.

What I learned is that those who had major speech impediments like stammering (people who, I would later discover, included Winston Churchill, James Earl Jones, Marilyn Monroe, Mel Tillis, and John Updike) had to control the many things going on at once in their minds. What they lacked as children, myself included, was a directed purpose. I had to learn to think first about what I was going to say, then say what I was thinking. I also learned to stop talking if words did not come out right—to stop and begin again. Of course knowing what you want to say without blurting out the first thing that comes to mind is good for anyone, not just people who stammer. I found that getting control over stammering is a gradual process; even now, when I get overly excited about anything, I stammer to some degree.

Ali Hasson also taught me about Islam, and to this very day stammering and Islam are linked together in my mind. I listened intently to what he had to say, hoping that at some point I too would have the confidence to communicate these ideas to others. Ali Hasson gave me a new name, Saladin Abdul Muhammad. Saladin was a great Muslim general, a warrior, so for a time I was proud to have the name and would try to be worthy of it. He tried to convince me that my slave name, Carter, was something to be rejected.

In fact, I did not really understand the history of slavery or the concepts of racism and segregation until I joined the military. While in basic training, they sent me to Fort Jackson, South Carolina, with the 101st Airborne Division. When we reached the South, the black recruits had to ride crammed in and standing up while the white troops rode in relative luxury. Throughout basic training, our conditions were very different from the whites, and yet we were all in the same army. The attitude of the Southern soldiers was also an eye-opener. They didn't think we were less than human; they knew it. Ali Hasson helped me understand that what you were born into is what you need to overcome; those attitudes and lies aren't you. Your family beliefs, passed down from generation to generation, are also accidents. Before you can stop being those things and believing that those things are important, you have to learn what you are in reality and what makes us all one.

Islam was important to me at the time because it was a system of beliefs that had not been handed down by white America. Christianity, for many Africans in America, appeared to be a historical contradiction. On the one hand, some churches opposed slavery and took an active part in the Underground Railroad. On the other hand, Christianity was used to justify slavery or to counsel patience until such time as the slave died and would go to heaven. Ali Hasson taught me that slavery should not make me feel ashamed, that I am as much a human being as any other human being on this planet. What he taught me about Islam were the spiritual Truths that form the core of all the great religious traditions, particularly that everything is as it is because that's the way it was meant to be. That everything under the sun is as it should be or it would not be. I learned not to fear death, and to accept my own mortality. I learned to trust in myself and my inner voice, that a piece of the divine, a piece of Allah, rested in me.

As important as these ideas were to my spiritual development, the friendship of Ali Hasson meant more to me than the religion itself. I have since rejected all forms of organized religion because, whatever they might preach and whatever good they might do, they have become agents of separation, even agents of violence and hatred.

Religions themselves are less important than the stories that inform them. Parables, myth (an older form of religion), even fairy tales all originate from the same source that underlies wisdom. The language of the higher mind is not literal but symbolic. The Truth beneath those stories, be they Greek, Christian, Jewish, Muslim, Buddhist, Hindu, or Native, is the Truth that has no name and that is shared by all of humanity. These mythical stories and legends are usually about the same subject: the possibility of individual transformation. Typically, a hero goes forth in search of something or someone, conquers the obstacles in his path, and, in so doing, finds himself.

My early introduction to Islam was my first uncertain step in the direction of self-discovery. At that time, the Nation of Islam, led by Elijah Muhammad, was the most popular form of Islam in the United States. The Nation of Islam did a lot of good, especially among poor black people (in prison and on the street), helping them clean up their acts, kick their narcotic habits, and make new lives for themselves. I had little regard, however, for Elijah Muhammad, his cult of personality, or his strange beliefs that the white man was the devil or that Wallace Fard Muhammad (the movement's founder) was the messiah; all of that had little or nothing to do with the Islam I had learned about. This peculiar American form of Islam sounded to me not only like a religion of hate but also a religion I might well have adopted had I not met Ali Hasson.

I remember on one occasion, at a time when I was still caught up in the race issue, telling Ali Hasson about how the black race was going to rise up one day and take back what was ours from colonial oppressors. I got up a good head of steam, stammering out a whole bunch of shit. He asked me, "You think black people are gonna rise up?" Then he took me on a tour of the local army bases. He showed me the tanks and asked me, "Are any of these in your neighborhood, Saladin?" He showed me the planes and asked me, "Any of these in your neighborhood, Saladin?" I could only say "no," of course. To which he replied, "How the hell do you think you are going to rise up and defeat them? Not by force, brother. You must defeat them with knowledge."

———

Late in 1956, when I came back from the army, I went home to Paterson, New Jersey, wearing a military uniform. I was proud of what I had accomplished, especially my exploits in the boxing ring. For me, going home was like attending a high school reunion and showing off that I had made it somewhere. I went to see my boyhood friend and neighbor, Hezekiah Gray, who had become involved with Elijah Muhammad and the Nation of Islam. While he spoke, I could barely wait to tell him about the ideas I had learned from Ali Hasson. Some of the stuff he was telling me sounded like a fantasy: "Yakub put the sun in the sky. Yakub was a mad scientist who created white people and the devil." The Islam I learned from Ali Hasson, the Islam from the holy Qur'an, was the same Islam that Malcolm X discovered years later in Mecca when he tried to break away from Elijah Muhammad and the Nation of Islam. Of course he was killed in the attempt, murdered by the very Nation of Islam that had saved him from a life of crime.

That day with my old friend Hezekiah (or Zeke, as we called him) was the first time in my life I was able to talk about something coherently. It was a breakthrough in my stammering, a turning point, but I didn't realize it until after I had finished speaking. Zeke stared at me open-mouthed. This was not the same stumbling, bumbling Rubin Carter he remembered from nine years before. Many years later, the year 2000 to be exact, Zeke would sit behind me as I addressed the United Nations General Assembly on the abolition of the death penalty and the preservation of the writ of habeas corpus.

Unfortunately, my being in Paterson resulted in my arrest one month later for having escaped from Jamesburg, the State Home for Boys. Here I had come home with fifty-six hundred dollars that I won in a ten-day card game on the boat from Germany. Twenty years old, able to put the down payment on a 1956 Lincoln, new girlfriend in the front seat, army uniform, maybe a boxing career on the horizon, the world at my feet, and *boom*! I was plunked into Annandale Reformatory for nine months. All of the soul work that I had done with Ali Hasson was compromised, not to be retrieved for another twenty years.

But I no longer stammered! I had gained a small measure of realization that individual transformation was possible.

When the army found out that I had been an escapee from a state home for boys, I lost my entitlement to benefits, including the free education provided for veterans under the GI Bill. Because of my arrest, my father refused to keep up the payments on my car. Regina, my new girlfriend, dumped me. I was devastated.

What I should have understood on this mechanical level of life, on this level of unconscious human insanity, was the truth behind the old saying "What goes around, comes around." I owed that jail time, and nothing I had done in or out of uniform would change that.

Of course, I did not have that depth of observation at that young age. Instead, my reaction was purely automatic. I was furious. I saw myself as a victim. Anger and the feeling of being victimized are conditioned responses we learn by watching and listening to the sleeping people around us.

———

I am not angry or bitter about my past or present circumstances. I do not worry about money or about not being able to pay my bills. I know that they will be paid. It's not faith in God that gives me the strength to endure. For me, religious faith and unquestioning belief are part of our slavery, part of the spell cast over us by the magician. Although I do prefer my creature comforts (I am a Taurus, after all!), they do not have a place of importance in my thinking; the loss of possessions that others hold valuable cannot faze me. My house is brick, my body flesh and blood; neither will be here forever. The house is a shell, the body a vehicle, a wonderful machine that I use to traverse this life. My duty is to remember myself, always and everywhere, and that although I live in this world, I am not of this world. I *know* that I will be all right because I am connected to that source from which all life arises.

Whatever you may lose by being conscious and principled in this world, whatever is taken from you by those who abandon principle, you will ultimately win back through your priceless understanding that life has meaning. You will understand that nothing is more valuable than the love of the Spirit, and that each individual possesses that Spirit. This spiritual Consciousness is easily at hand, it is right there inside of you, but it requires courage to access, because, as I demonstrate in these pages, almost every aspect of the life we live militates against our ever waking up. Sleeping is, after all, a very comfortable state.

I

Boys' Prison:
Light Where the Sun Don't Shine

As a man who has lived in many prisons, I can say that prison is a dehumanizing, soul-destroying environment. Nevertheless, I thrived in the structure of prison, although my "success" in those places rested solely upon my ability to defend myself.

In admitting even this, I do not mean to give comfort to the apologists for an American judicial system that is more racially biased today than ever. An astounding one-third of all African American males between the ages of twelve and thirty-seven are either living in prison or under the direct supervision of the judicial system. Because we are made to fear crime to an irrational extent, we learn to accept adolescents sitting in prisons until they grow gray beards. A system weighted so heavily toward retribution and one so rife with error and injustice is a perversion of the natural brilliance of the human spirit.

But I know enough not to rail, and I know that no amount of tinkering with the system will change the imbalances. The system will still be run by sleeping people, solemn-faced, civilized *savages* in dark suits, savages in wigs and black robes. Fear is the primary emotion of these savages. Of course, savagery is not exclusive to the jungle, even though we have been conditioned to associate the word with the imaginary spear-throwing Africans of Hollywood movie sets. In the end, the justice system, like the government itself, reflects the beliefs and exerts the power of the savages who run it. When push comes to shove, we are all savages! The reactive violence of the criminal is mirrored by the retribution of the judge. That is how it must be on this level of unconscious human insanity.

The ultimate manifestation of unconscious behavior is the death penalty. You might say that the death penalty is a perfect punishment: an eye for an eye. But knowing what I do about the imperfections and prejudices of the people who run the system and the overwhelming numbers of poor people who face execution, I see clearly that too many wrongly convicted people die today and will die in the future. Between 1977 and 2010, 1,217 people were executed in the United States, but more than 138 prisoners (as of 2009) were removed from death rows because of trial errors, recantations of testimony, or DNA evidence. One out of every nine people sentenced to death are innocent of the crime for which they would have died. How many other innocent people who lacked DNA evidence or competent legal representation died unnecessarily? We'll never know. How many is too many? I say one.

The death penalty is supported and maintained because of its savage simplicity. Think about what took place at the high school in Columbine or on the Indian reservation in Red Lake, Minnesota, or at Dawson College and École Polytechnique in Montreal or, worst of all, in April 2007 at Virginia Tech. At Columbine, Eric Harris and

Dylan Klebold, two young people who had been hurt and excluded by others, exacted the death penalty on their innocent classmates. At Red Lake, Jeffrey Weise shot his grandparents and, afterwards, his fellow students. In Montreal, Marc Lepine, violently opposed to women's participation in male-dominated professions, came in to exact revenge for past wrongs. At Virginia Tech, Cho Seung-Hui, the perpetrator, was full of rage for imagined and real hurts from his classmates. Some say the perpetrators just "snapped," but in my view they were heavily influenced by the reactive message that permeates our society, our governments, and so much of the media: *You hurt me. I'll hurt you back.* At both Red Lake and Columbine, the inspiration for the mass killings was Nazi Germany, one of the countries that showed the world an easy method for eliminating problems.

Newspapers and reality television programs present us with violent images of mostly black crime, of car chases, of young men and women being wrestled to the ground and placed in handcuffs. We think that crime has gotten out of control. We feel threatened. We begin to think that stiff prison sentences for young offenders are justified as long as those children are not our own children. Children tried in adult courts become less the exception and more the rule.

And then we have training schools, which used to be known as reform schools. These are places where we put angry children who are living by the same reactive behaviors that they were taught by society. Training schools and boot camps only perpetuate the cycle of violence. We might think we are going to browbeat someone into behaving properly, but that is clearly not possible. The law of the street is the law of the jungle is the law of the courtroom is the law of the penal institution. It is not the children we have to deal with but ourselves.

———

The State Home for Boys in Jamesburg, New Jersey, did not look like an actual prison as it does now. When I first wrote about Jamesburg in my book *The Sixteenth Round*, I saw it through the jaundiced eyes of a wrongly convicted man. I wrote about the retributive violence among the young prisoners. I wrote about the sexual predators who ran the cottages and the depravity of the older prisoners who took advantage of the younger ones. My book was a polemic against the whole system, and Jamesburg was just another part of that system. Because of the inexcusable behavior of some of the adults in that institution, I lost all respect for so-called authority.

In retrospect, it seems ironic that I was sent to Jamesburg, an institution that was full of adult pedophiles, for attacking an adult pedophile. I have sometimes wondered if the sentence against me would have been half so harsh or harsh at all if our skin colors were reversed. Who would have been called a criminal then? This pedophile, and it was commonly known among the white community that he was a pedophile, was also an important man in the community. He had attempted to "interfere" with a friend of mine. Even at a young age, my instinct was to defend others.

There's a saying that's been around for a long time: *If life gives you lemons, make lemonade.* The hell that is prison was a learning place for me even if it may not have appeared to be at the time. Being thrown into a boys' training school (I was identified as number 18,577) was definitely a whole lot of lemons. But within this den of iniquity were opportunities and decent individuals who gave me an education that I may not have appreciated at the time.

Mr. Hart, for example, ran the dairy at Jamesburg. In those days, the training school was a self-contained world where we raised our own food on a truck farm, mainly grain, corn, vegetables, and livestock. The farm was a good setting for me because I had not grown up solely in the streets of Paterson, New Jersey. Part of my extended family still lived on farms in the South, where, as a very young boy, I would work during summer vacations to earn enough money for my fall school clothing. Although part of my family came north in the Great Migration—the twentieth-century exodus of blacks from the agricultural South to the urban North—my connection to the rural southern United States has always felt more important to me.

Mr. Hart was maybe five feet tall, around fifty, very stern and powerful, a man who whistled all the time, so you always knew when he was there. Through my boyhood eyes, he seemed ancient, but we connected. I always got along with stern people as long as they stayed true to themselves and they didn't put their hands on me in anger. I felt good around him because he was a hard worker and he spoke just a little bit more than I did. He could see that I loved being around animals, so he gave me responsibilities in the dairy, always summoning me from wherever I was to assist in the birth of a calf. Those one hundred or so cows meant everything to him; woe be unto anyone who messed with them! A group of us used to milk them by hand twice a day, at four o'clock in the morning and then at five o'clock in the evening.

That barn was a one-room schoolhouse. One of my cows, number 319, was a real kicker. She slammed more than one person into the barn wall. I had to put her in leg braces and shackles to tie her down. Mr. Hart made sure that I had all the bad cows, not as a punishment but because I was so good at handling them. That was my psychology class.

I also loved pitching hay from the hayloft to feed the cows, because I could always grab a smoke up there, dangerous as that might be. That was my recess.

Mr. Hart came to get me and Lou Van Dyne, another violent young man I grew up with, at about three o'clock in the morning to prepare the hay or, in the wintertime, the corn-and-molasses mixture to feed the cows. Then we went out into the pasture, brought the cows inside the barn, and got them into place for milking. We had to keep an account of how many gallons of milk each cow gave every day. That was my math class.

We were in charge of the fertilization of those cows and the birthing of the calves, clearing out their breathing passages and cleaning them up. That was my biology class.

Then there was Reverend Van Pelt, at that time the only black person working in the system. I wish the Baptist preacher had affected me more. Looking back, I think it's funny that they foisted Catholicism on us (we had to say Hail Marys and Our Fathers in the cottages every night before going to bed) but we had a Baptist preacher on Sundays. I guess they thought that one or the other would rub off on us. Reverend Van Pelt was also a short man, but he, unlike Mr. Hart, always dressed impeccably in dark suits and ties. He had graying hair, and his skin color fell somewhere between redbone, like Malcolm X, and a shade darker.

Let me digress for a moment about skin color. Africans in America—or black people, as we came to call ourselves—are keenly aware of the differences in shades of skin. Cross-cultural identification, wherein one tribe cannot discern the features of another tribe, is one of the scourges of the criminal justice system. The idea that we are all black skinned is ridiculous, even though I continue to use the term "black" as I do here. The so-called science behind the slave system decreed that the lighter a person's skin, the more intelligent and, therefore, the more expensive the slave. The mulattos, quadroons (one-quarter white), and octoroons (one-eighth) were usually destined for the manor house, while the dark-skinned folks like me were turned into field hands. Even now in Haiti and Jamaica, the darker your skin, the lower down the mountain you live. As a young boy, I fantasized about marrying a woman whose skin had a yellowish hue. When it comes to the measure of a human being, skin color is a meaningless distinction, although one cannot ignore the historical significance of race. I believe that we are all of one race, the human race.

Reverend Van Pelt used to tell us that because he was chaplain at both Jamesburg and Trenton State Prison, he would meet those of us he had known here at Jamesburg on our way to the electric chair in Trenton State. You could chart our "progress" through the institutes of lower learning, what I call a step up the criminal justice ladder going down: Jamesburg, Annandale, Bordentown, Yardville, Rahway, and Trenton State. Looking back, it was a powerful message about recidivism, but we were much too hip then to hear it.

"You ain't talkin' to us, old man," someone would always say.

I took part in a lot of violence at Jamesburg. It was expected. Young people at the time saw Jamesburg as a place where you could learn how to fight and where your reputation would follow you when you got out. No question, I eventually became one of the toughest boys in the place, what they called a "Duke of State." I didn't see myself as a bully but would set certain people up to fight me. Those certain people would be the ones who took advantage of vulnerable or physically weak people. If you wanted to hurt those people, then you would have to fight me. You might say that it showed my early sense of injustice.

The ends may have been praiseworthy, but the means were wrong. Looking at my present life, how much different is it to spring an innocent man from prison than to defend a vulnerable person from victimization? I would say not a great deal different.

The best example of defending a vulnerable person that I can remember goes back to a time when I worked on laundry detail at Jamesburg. The boys in cottage 6, where I lived at the time, did the laundry for everyone in the institution. My particular job was ironing shirts for the staff. Each cottage had three floors: a basement where the inmates lived, a main floor that consisted of a recreation room with television and a laundry closet, and a top floor where the cottage mother and father lived. Once a week, as a ritual, the cottage mother would hand out the clean laundry. The cottage mother and father could see the whole dorm from the landing outside their apartment. At night, if the cottage father gave us permission to use the recreation room, a strong boy might force a weaker boy to stay downstairs in the darkened basement while the others went up to watch television. The adults would look the other way at this behavior, and for good reason. The cottage mother and father were just as likely to abuse their power for sexual favors with the prisoners, especially with the five house boys who stayed behind during the day to clean the cottages.

The assistant superintendent at Jamesburg, as I remember him, was a heavy breather, a big lump of a man with thick, purplish lips. His size, his position, and his loud voice gave him total control over the prisoners. One day, as I was delivering shirts to cottage 7, where they housed children from six to eleven years old, I heard a boy crying in the basement. I went down to check and saw the assistant superintendent fucking the boy. This cruel, sadistic act so infuriated me that I attacked the man with all the power I had at my disposal. It may be difficult for you to imagine that a wiry sixteen-year-old could beat up such a large man, but I was to have a career as a professional boxer, a middleweight who could fight heavyweights and was considered one of the hardest punchers in the business. I cocked a Sunday on him, getting in the first punch! That man was a bloody mess when I got through with him. They put me in solitary for what I did, but I never regretted it for a moment.

———

Some of the violence at Jamesburg was random and insane. A young man who didn't want to go on a work detail to the manure pile asked me to accompany him behind the cottage. I wondered why he had a baseball bat in his hands, but since we were friends I didn't expect any harm coming from him.

"Break my knee," he told me. "I don't want to go to work."

I wouldn't do it at first. Then I asked him, "Are you sure?"

He told me to go ahead, just pleaded with me to do it.

I swung that bat like Jackie Robinson and hit his knee. He didn't have to work that day or for some long time after that. When I saw him in Paterson fifteen years later, he was still limping.

———

Jamesburg was also a military school where we learned self-discipline and how to march. I had always known that I could control my tongue, as many people who stammer can, by speaking rhythmically or singing. As young kids in Paterson we used to go around to people's houses and sing. I also sang in the church choir. At Jamesburg training school, I was a line sergeant for my cottage because I was so good at counting cadences, and of course it was easy for me to do that later on in the military. I brought in my own rhymes, like an early version of hip-hop, except we didn't wear baggy clothes. Six days a week we were dressed in khaki uniforms, and we held our heads high. A line sergeant stands outside the lines; that was me, always wanting to stand out from the crowd.

We had a duty officer named Mr. Unger who drove a shiny film-noir black Ford around the campus, license plate 649, always on the lookout for stragglers and smokers. He was a stumpy, pigeon-toed, bowlegged man whose belly had grown out and married his barrel chest. He'd pop out of that car like a jack-in-the-box if he suspected anything was going down. If you talked too loud during mess, he might make you stand out in the center aisle for the whole meal with your arms spread like Jesus on the cross. He made sure we marched back and forth from work. Wherever we went, we had to have a pass with the time stamped on it, and you had to account for any time gaps between point of departure and point of arrival.

Jamesburg used to have a close relationship with the surrounding rural community and the greater community as well. We used to go out and caddy at Forsgate Golf Course. We also went out frequently and performed. I was in a gospel quartet that sang for the Lions Club. There was a group of four boys at Jamesburg called the Ham-boners who appeared on Ted Mack's *Original Amateur Hour*, a popular TV show, and won the top prize. The Ham-boners performed their routine to a military cadence.

> *Hambone, Hambone, where you been?*
> *'Round the corner and back again.*
> *Hambone, Hambone, where's your wife?*
> *Round the corner shootin' dice.*
> *She shot seven, I shot four,*
> *Come on, baby, let's shoot some more.*

Because of their success on *The Original Amateur Hour*, every cottage at Jamesburg was given its first television set.

We also had a drum-and-bugle corps in which the two toughest prisoners would play the tom-toms. I'd be in my blue-and-yellow silk monkey suit beating on those drums and feeling like a million bucks. That experience with military drill and my knowledge about how to shoot and handle guns, which I got from my father and uncles, made me dare to dream of enlisting in the paratroops when I escaped from Jamesburg.

———

To every human being in prison, guilty or innocent, I would say that everything depends upon attitude. The physical body is the vehicle in which we traverse life, but our attitude is our steering wheel. In prison, people find themselves at the bottom of human existence. What a prisoner must say is, *OK, whatever I've done in life has led me to where I am today. Therefore, if I want to get out of prison and stay out, I've got to turn around and go back the other way.* Prisoners must use this time to learn how to read if they don't know how, to learn to write, to learn a skill if they never had one. Use this time to better themselves. Maybe on the outside they didn't have time for any of these things. Now they do. This time has been imposed upon them. Use it to look at themselves, to make themselves indispensable, to awaken.

Just as a flower in my garden reaches perfection in its full growth, so a person's purpose must be to seek perfection in whatever soil he finds himself. If an individual wants to be what he could be, he first has to stop being what he thinks he is. That eagle was no prairie chicken, but he could never see himself in the mirror. We are mirrored in life by our actions and our deeds. The power and the glory are in the individual's ability to transcend his conditioning. If people like Malcolm X, Nelson Mandela, Jomo Kenyatta, Patrice Lumumba, Anwar Sadat, and even Rubin "Hurricane" Carter can come out of their prisons as better people, awakened people, able to shape their countries and the world itself, then you can too. What a message that sends about the inherent worth of every individual human being!

———

The Jamesburg I returned to in 2004 was different from the one I remembered. The faces were now 85 percent black, closely reflecting the situation in prisons across America. The kids wear purple jumpsuits, slouching and ambling from one place to another. The whole campus is enclosed by prison fences, sealing off the institution from the surrounding subdivisions that have taken the place of woods and farms. That double fence has a huge psychological impact upon everyone inside it; it is no longer possible to imagine yourself at a military school in the country. There are no barns or animals; food is brought in on trucks. The young people now work for slave wages at corporate enterprises such as eyeglass manufacture and graphic design. Admittedly, these are also learning opportunities, but in a state where large groups of African American males are desperately seeking employment, when enterprises such as these are turned over to the prisons, the non-prison population is denied the possibility of a job. Since people without jobs are more likely to wind up in prison, it's a vicious cycle. I was number 18,577 at the training school, and they are well past 80,000 now.

If I had to add the pluses and the minuses of my time at Jamesburg, I have to say they are about even. No matter how many good experiences you had, the place would not let you go right. Those who obeyed the rules were considered weak. You were also expected to participate in the culture of violence and to keep quiet about the sexual exploitation. One generation was being conditioned to act in the same way as the generation before it—big fish swallowing small ones. As long as people are asleep, it cannot be any different.

Now don't get me wrong. There are good sleeping people. There are bad sleeping people. But the collective efforts of sleeping people, good or bad, sometimes work out, but more often they lead to chaos.

Intentions have little to do with results at penal institutions. At this time, the recidivism rate at Jamesburg is 82 percent, even though fine, caring people work within its fences. If merely 18

37

percent of the young people within the facility's jurisdiction are able to avoid future incarceration, clearly the system neither trains nor reforms. The purpose of the training school system cannot be rehabilitation, or the system would have been abandoned long ago. Instead, the true purpose of the system is what it actually accomplishes: keeping "dangerous" young people locked up. That is why Reverend Van Pelt, and future Reverend Van Pelts, would continue to see most of us as we worked our way through the system.

―――――

A lot of boys ran away from the place but would almost always be caught. When they escaped, a loud whistle would blow from the water tower. The older boys in cottages 3 and 6 would be sent out "on pursuit." The farmers in the area would also be placed on alert. I was in cottage 6 during my last year and had been out on pursuit a couple of times. Many small roads led away from Jamesburg; all but one circled right back to the front gate. We knew where the escapees would return, and we also knew the one road that led to freedom. That was knowledge I could not resist using to my own advantage.

In 1954, I ran away from the State Home for Boys in the dead of night with two other prisoners. Those two eventually got caught, but I walked all the way to Newark, some thirty or forty miles through woods, past farms with big barking dogs, and on to back roads. A relative in Newark gave me the bus fare to Paterson. I stayed outside my house to make sure the police were not inside waiting for me. When I came inside, my mother, notified by authorities, said, "I've been expecting you." She gave me a hot meal, and then I took a bath and got dressed. Luckily my father was not at home or he would have turned me in. My sister drove me to New York City where I caught a train to Philadelphia and stayed with a cousin. Shortly thereafter, I enlisted at the recruitment center by telling the lie that I was Rubin Carter from Philadelphia. I had escaped from Jamesburg, but my time in the prison system had only just begun. Even though I knew the right road out—the long, dark New Jersey road—I carried the prison out with me.

2

The Prison of Family:
What My Father Didn't Tell Me

One of the more profound illusions that people are born into is the illusion of family. No institution receives more lip service than the family. *Blood is thicker than water,* we are told, and my family lived up to that old adage. My father used to beat me, drawing blood with belts and an ironing cord, what today would be called child abuse. My mother said he did it because he saw himself in me. My father was a proud, strong, independent black man. My mother was the only person who could get him to stop hurting me.

"Stop beating that boy, Lloyd," she would say.

It might have worked for the moment, but I continued to get into trouble, sometimes of my own making, and the beatings continued.

During the late thirties and early forties when we lived in Passaic, New Jersey, we were on the second floor of a building with three other families. Each family had a bin in the basement to keep its coal. During the winter, our responsibility as children was to go down, pick up the big lumps of coal, and keep the fire burning in the cast-iron stove in the kitchen.

One day I came home and saw my older brother, Jimmy, crying on the stairway. A poor family from Alabama had moved in with their eight-year-old son, Bully. Jimmy had caught him stealing the Carter coal and confronted him, and Bully had beaten up my brother. As I look back on the incident, I realize those people from the Deep South must have been freezing, but in those times you had to protect what was yours.

I went downstairs to the basement, attacked Bully, and came back up all proud with our coal. When my father came home that night, he was confronted by Bully's mother about what I had done to her son. My father asked no questions, just barged into our room with accusations in his mouth and anger in his eyes. I tried to explain to him why I had done it, but only a stammer came to my lips. Out came the belt. He beat me terribly, and I was left in blood, tears, and confusion.

I did what I had done with the best of intentions and in the unspoken belief that family loyalty was of great value, just as family values have always been said to be important. Even now, a day does not go by when we don't hear politicians and religious leaders talk about family values. What are family values? Words. That's all, nothing but words, especially for those politicians who do little to support actual families.

No question that there are good families. Some of us happen to be born into stable, loving, and loyal families. To them I say, *How lucky you are!*

But luck and fortune are rolls of the dice, pure accident. Whom you were born to, your social status, where you were born, your religion, the color of your skin—all are accidental, all part of what can be called the law of accident. This level of life in which we live and breathe and exercise our beings is controlled by the law of accident.

To explain the law of accident, I would liken humanity to six and a half billion unconscious machines, like automobiles traveling on a twenty-four-lane highway going in different directions at different rates of speed. The front windshield, our future, is partially opaque; we have only a dim idea of where we are headed. The back windshield, our past, is seen only through mirrors. In effect, we are surrounded by illusions, continually bumping into one another and careening off the soft shoulder of the road. These accidents are what some call blind fate; the very idea of fate is a reflection of our own blindness to the forces that drive and shape us.

Family is our first line of conditioning. We take upon ourselves the social status, customs, religion, politics, likes, and dislikes of our parents and siblings. Our personalities, on the other hand, are our first line of defense against this conditioning. We take on false personas to protect our essences from outside intrusions, like the shell that protects the yolk of an egg, useful for only a short time. Unlike the eggshell, which is soon discarded, personality remains as an artificial construct that we come to believe in. Even revere. We might blindly imitate our parents or, as I did, oppose them, but neither stance represents what we truly are. In fact, it is considered good to sacrifice our actual selves for the family, the first in a whole line of sacrifices that will benefit everyone but us.

Family identification is another illusion foisted upon us. Family may in fact put us to sleep, not just when we are tired babies but for the remainder of our lives. The propaganda we are subjected to around family values and family ties causes us to expect too much from the institution or from ourselves. When our families fail to live up to false expectations, we think that either we or they must be at fault. Through no fault of their own, my nuclear family, my wife Mae Thelma, my daughter, Theodora, and my son, Raheem, are no longer a part of my life.

I see family as an anchor. An anchor provides stability, but it can also be a weight around your neck, holding you down, keeping you from realizing your dreams. When the youthful hero of legend sets off on his journey, you don't see his family tagging along.

―――――

A well-known story tells of two monks on their travels in the springtime, a young monk and an old one, both belonging to a sect that practiced celibacy. As they were walking through the woods, they came upon a river at the side of which stood a young woman. By her body language, they could tell that she was afraid to enter the water. So the old monk bent down, the woman climbed on his back, and the party of three waded across the rough waters. When they reached the other side, the old monk bent down, the woman climbed off, and the two monks continued on their journey.

The young monk seethed with indignation for the rest of the day. He could not believe what he had seen. Finally, he burst forth: "Tell me, old man, how does it feel to break your vows of celibacy after all these years? How does it feel to have a woman's soft thighs wrapped around your waist? Her succulent breasts pressing against your back? Her smooth, sweet arms wrapped around your neck? Tell me, old man, how does it feel to carry a beautiful woman?"

The old monk looked amusedly at the young one and said, "Perhaps it is you who should tell me how it feels to carry a beautiful woman. I put the woman down back there by the river, but you are obviously still carrying her."

I tell this story to illustrate a slightly different point. Most people carry families on their backs long after the family has served its purpose. Psychiatrists make their millions based upon our past obsessions with family slights, with abuses, with insufficiencies. You might say that modern psychiatry and psychology have created a third science called "psycho-ceramics," the study of crackpots. That's what we are: cracked pots.

What is so tragic about this is that our dysfunctional families can separate us not only from ourselves but also from other human beings. If there is love in your immediate family, by all means cherish it, but family love is in no way superior to any other kind of love in the *human* family.

———

Segregation of the human family used to be the law of the land in the United States of America, and its evil effects reached far beyond the South. I was born in New Jersey in 1937 into a society that restricted use of buses, washrooms, drinking fountains, restaurants, hotels, and the like for people of my skin color. There were few people in the forefront talking about segregation when I was a child. I did not realize how dangerous it was for a black person to break the rules or to openly challenge the separation of blacks from whites. I learned the false reality that the adults in my life presented to me.

If my father had explained to me how deadly it was to openly oppose this white-ruled system, I might have understood. Our neighborhood, after all, had all kinds of people in it, more mixed than you generally find nowadays. One of the ways we made a little money was from Jewish people on Friday nights. They were not allowed to turn off their lights on the Sabbath, so we, the *Shabbas goyim,* would come and do it for them.

A family legend that I learned much later tells of the time my grandfather moved his family from Georgia because one of his sons, Marshall Carter, was involved with a white woman. The Ku Klux Klan had served notice that they were going to lynch him. My grandfather had a huge family, thirteen sons and three daughters. He sent two of the sons, including Marshall, to Philadelphia to buy shotguns for every member of the family. That was a well-armed household. The Klan, knowing full well about the guns, didn't come, but my grandfather decided soon after to move his entire family to South Jersey. That was the real world I lived in. No one ever spoke to me about races or racism.

———

I have some fond memories of family. I always liked being with my uncles, many of whom were preachers. Those were the only times I remember my father joking around, even being joyful. The clan of brothers would go on frequent hunting trips, and I always wanted to go along. I knew when my father was going hunting because his boots would be sitting in the front hallway in the evening. Not wanting to be left behind, I would take his boots into bed with me.

I could hear my father come in at night and ask my mother, "Bert, where's my boots?"

And she would say, "Lloyd, you know who's got your boots."

So my father would come into the room before dawn, wake me up, and take me with them.

There were no big parkways, interstates, or turnpikes at the time, so we drove in caravans on the local highways. We never stopped at the restaurants to buy anything or use the bathrooms at the gas stations. We would go out into the woods to do our business. I never knew that we couldn't eat at the restaurants or use the gas stations, that there were laws preventing us from entering those places.

Once, as we were driving through Newark, we went up a ramp onto the McCarter Highway, which was the old Route 1. Two of my uncles were with us and, according to the custom of the time, had placed their shotguns in plain view in the rear window of the car. As soon as we got near the highway, a great big truck cut us off. My father tried to get around him, but the driver kept blocking our way. No question about it, this truck was messing with us. My father pulled off to the side of the road. The truck stopped, too. The truck driver got out of his cab carrying a jack handle. My father stepped from the car, and one of his brothers took out the shotguns, of which the driver had apparently taken no notice. When the truck driver saw those shotguns, he turned tail, scampered off, and left his truck sitting by the side of the road. I was never more proud of my family than at that moment. I thought, *The Carters ain't taking no shit from nobody*. Of course the truck driver was white, but at the time the color of his skin was not a part of my thinking.

———

Somewhere inside the institution of segregation was the secret of my father's violent behavior toward me. Fundamentally, Lloyd Carter was a decent person. Despite the beatings, I loved the man. His father's family had always gone to church on Sunday, as did we, and we were seen as important members of the congregation. My father and his brothers were either deacons or preachers. My father even helped build the local Baptist church. In retrospect, I think the religiosity of my grandfather's family was a little less devout than they let on. Outside of church, they drank and womanized like everyone else.

My father was slim, wiry, and muscular, strong as dirt and six feet tall, just like his brothers, of whom my uncle King was the tallest. My grandfather Thomas named his sons in such a way that nobody could think of them as "niggers." What a sad commentary on that society. The brothers were named King, Prince, Marshall, and Martin Luther; my father Lloyd's original name was Lord. He was hardworking and fiercely independent. As I said, he used to joke and carouse with his brothers, but otherwise, at least to me, he was stern, humorless, and unforgiving of my trespasses.

He loved fishing and was a great sportsman. In the wintertime, he hunted raccoon, rabbit, squirrel, and pheasant on or near our two farms in South Jersey. Those were rough times. This was at the tail end of the Depression, but we fared better than most. My father would bring us his hunting bag and lay out all the animals. We would skin them down, my mother would cook them up, and there'd be some good eating.

When the United States entered the Second World War, my father was given a victory garden at the Manhattan Rubber Company where he worked. Victory gardens were plots of land where employees were able to grow their own vegetables. Because of rationing, large families had to find different ways to put food on the table. There never came a time when my father was not able to feed his large family, which consisted of my mother, three younger sisters, one older sister, and my two older brothers, seven kids in all with me, Rubin the renegade, smack dab in the middle.

When we lived on Twelfth Avenue in Paterson, there was a pool hall called Posey's right around the corner where I used to hang out and try to look tough. One day, years later, on a visit home during my prizefighting career, I told my father I was going to go shoot pool around the corner. I always thought of myself as a good pool player but never wanted my father to know about it. Pool halls in those days were considered to be dens of iniquity. He said, "Boy, you can't shoot no pool. Come on, I'll walk around the corner with you." No son looks at his father as just another human being. This was my father. I lived with him for years. I saw this man in church every Sunday. People loved to hear this man pray. Tears would be rolling down his cheeks. What could this devout Christian, this pillar of the community, know about shooting pool? So we walked around the corner to Posey's and went to the rear of the smoke-filled joint. It's no exaggeration to say that I was probably the most famous person living in Paterson at that time. A silent crowd gathered around to watch the game, and my father just tore my ass up! I don't think I got three shots in the whole time, while he cleared the balls off that table like a vacuum cleaner. I hadn't felt so small in a long time, but at least no one had the nerve to laugh in my face about it. My father looked at me and said, "Boy, how you think I supported our family through all those lean years?"

The truth is, he was a hustler in every way. Along with working three jobs, running two businesses, shooting pool, hunting, and fishing, he was even able to buy property while other people scrambled for food.

———

In this context, I would like to recognize that while segregation is, was, and will always be an evil, some of its side effects were actually beneficial. During the years when black and white people were separated, de facto or by law, black businesses serviced the needs of the black community. Of course, many of these establishments were small, and their wares were expensive, but they allowed for a certain amount of prosperity. Far fewer black folk by percentage are today involved in small businesses, because the integrated department stores and, later, the big box stores were impossible to compete with. Don't forget either that there were black nightclubs, Negro baseball leagues, and a whole lot of other successful enterprises. Even now, the so-called revival that's going on in Harlem and some other boroughs of New York is a way of spreading gentrification to the former ghettos while forcing poor black people to move to other areas. So it's also true that whatever appeared to be a benefit to Africans in America usually had a major downside connected with it.

My father and his brothers talked about family and how important it was to protect one another. No lesson I learned in elementary school, where I went with all my siblings, had as powerful an effect on me as the lesson of family loyalty. One hot day, my classroom door was left open and I heard footsteps running down the hall. I looked out the classroom door only to see my sister Rosalie flying by with a male teacher chasing her close behind. I shot out into the hall after them and tackled him. I was ten years old, but I fought like a wild animal in the woods, beating him about the head with my fists. That night at home, my father whooped me bad. How could I have attacked a teacher? I couldn't understand how I could be doing right and be so wrong at the same time. After all, Rosalie

was family, wasn't she, and I was supposed to protect her, wasn't I?
I never did find out why that teacher was chasing her, and it really
made no difference to me.

It wasn't until I was much older that I stood up to my father.
When I left the military in 1956, I had a huge altercation with him
over my brother, Jimmy. Jimmy was going to Harvard, where he
had gone on scholarship, and was home on vacation. I heard that he
was hanging out with homosexuals he had known from childhood.
As kids, all of them used to dress up like women on Halloween, and
they looked better than most women on the street. At the time we
understood that they were children, perhaps one or two years older
than I was, but still of the age where those things were acceptable.
Now they were grown up, and they were doing the same stuff. So I
confronted my brother about it. Jimmy and I started fighting, and,
of course, I beat him up. I had been in a reformatory and had my
own ideas about homosexuality. Inside a penal institution, it meant
that you were weak and unable to protect yourself. No brother of
mine was going to act like that.

That's when my father got involved. He jumped me in an
attempt to protect my older brother. I pushed him away, told him
not to touch me, and made it clear that no one, especially him, was
ever going to touch me in anger again. He ran into his bedroom
and got his shotgun, and I ran and got mine. We met again in the
living room with our shotguns pointed at each other. People of my
mother and father's generation felt that if you put your hands on
your parents or even threatened them, then they had the right to
take you off the face of this earth. *We brought you into this world—
we'll take your ass out of it.* That's what happened between Marvin
Gaye and his father.

51

Luckily, my mother got between us and said, "Rubin, get out of the house," in her usual strong and quiet way. I left and came back three days later when things had cooled off.

I look back upon this incident and see the absurd contradiction of what I did. Why would I have any more right to attack my brother than my father would have to attack me? I see it now as stupid, arrogant, immature, and even egotistical, but at the time, and for years after that, violence was a part of who I was. I was acting mechanically, doing everything that I had been conditioned by my peers to do.

Later that month, the police came to pick me up for having skipped out of Jamesburg. That had to be a terrible embarrassment to my father with the neighbors looking on. I could see in his eyes what he didn't say: *Here we go again. The cops are in my house. Rubin's in more trouble.* When I was taken to Annandale Reformatory, he wouldn't speak to me. I think the incident with Jimmy played an even larger role in his rejection of me than the embarrassment in front of the neighbors. The fact that Jimmy was a hugely successful academic—later he was to become one of the youngest Ph.D.'s in the history of Harvard University—made me appear to my father as nothing more than a thug.

When I became a well-known boxer, I asked my father to become my fight manager as a way of reestablishing our relationship. I knew he was worldly-wise and would not allow people to take advantage of me. He agreed to do it. Soon after, he asked me to buy a boat for him, because he wanted to take his brothers and other deacon friends on fishing trips.

What did I know about boats? But I went ahead and bought a boat, a thirty-six-foot yacht, and docked it in Seabright, New Jersey.

I wanted to share my success with my family, particularly my father. He also asked me to buy a business for two of my sisters, Rosalie and Doris, so that they would not have to work all their lives in a dye factory. I thought those few years in the early sixties were the best years I ever had with my family, but that was all an illusion. If family is with you for the good times, they have to be with you for the bad as well.

When my father stopped being my manager in 1965, I was stunned. He refused to tell me why until more than ten years later. At the time, I was facing a bail hearing in Jersey City before my second trial on the wrongful murder conviction. He came up to me in the bullpen and told me that the "wise guys" had wanted me to throw a fight, to lose deliberately so that they could make some money on a bet. He told them that his son would never do that. They said in so many words, *If you don't do as we ask, we'll get even.*

My father thought that they were going to do something to *him.* He had no idea that they were going to do something to *me.* That something played a big part in my wrongful conviction. The police were told by the Mafia that I had killed those people at the Lafayette Bar and Grill.

When I went to Trenton State Prison in 1967 on the wrongful murder conviction, my father refused to come see me at all. I phoned him up and asked for his support. Before he hung up, I heard him say, "All your life I've been going to prisons, and I won't come anymore." I felt like I was hearing an echo. When I had gone to Jamesburg State Home for Boys, my father came and said, "I'm not coming back here anymore." So I had lost him and my whole family, and this time it was for good. The yacht and everything else had to be sold to pay my legal expenses. While it may have hurt him to lose the boat, it hurt me more to think that my family would believe that I had committed so heinous a crime as the cold-blooded murder of innocent people.

In 1983, when I heard in prison that my father was on his deathbed, I went to see him. There were only two reasons for which you would be allowed out of prison, and you could choose one: a funeral or a deathbed visit to a parent or sibling. Because they said that my father had requested to see me, I chose the deathbed visit. Family values are also played up in prison, although my family had to cough up five hundred dollars to pay the guards overtime to escort me. I was bound and shackled, thrown like a piece of meat into an armored prison van, and driven to a hospital in Glassboro, New Jersey. One day before, I had been totally unaware that my father was even sick. When I emerged from the prison van, I could see that we had been accompanied by a caravan of police cars and heavily armed guards.

They brought me chained and shackled into his room, and I could see tubes running in and out of him. He was catheterized and completely immobile. I will never get the picture out of my head. He couldn't talk, but I could see in his half-dead eyes that he recognized me, his son, once again in chains, surrounded by the law. Was my presence a rebuke to him? Did he remember that he'd called the cops on me as a young boy, that he hoped they would scare me into behaving myself, that he had already beaten me with his belt and one of my eyes was swollen shut, and that he gave the green light to a police officer to beat the hell out of me in front of him? Why didn't he just talk to me? I would have done anything for him. I loved the man.

Then I had an insight that would have been impossible for me to have years before, an insight that went far beyond such narrow thinking. My father knew that in segregated America I would be killed if I continued to show "attitude" toward white authority. My problem was that I had no fear of white people or anyone else and would show no deference, while my father did. All of the beatings were his way of protecting me from the society of white faces that surrounded us. That was the secret I had never before understood. He thought that if I didn't learn to back down, I would never be able to survive. He was wrong about that, because I did survive, and I never compromised myself. But how could I ever hate someone who was trying to save me from destruction? Someone who saw in me his own rebellious self that he had successfully repressed? Mafia, police, schools, prisons—they were all the same to him: parts of the white man's system against which he knew no remedy. I grew up ignorant, believing I was equal to all of them, but the law of the land and everything else said otherwise.

I stayed in his hospital room for about half an hour. By this time, I had been studying Plato, Gurdjieff, Viktor Frankl, Jiddu Krishnamurti, and all of the world's wisdom, trying to find my spiritual path to freedom. I was convinced that if I had been able to touch this man, my father, he would rise up out of bed and walk again. I was positive that I had that power. But I wasn't able to touch him. Both sides of his bed were barred, and my hands were shackled to a chain around my waist. And what could I say with the armed guards standing there? What could I say that meant anything? "Get up, old man. I'm here." That was all that came out.

Back in my cell that night at Trenton State Prison, I had a dream. A blue and white horse-dog, whatever that is or means, came to me in that dream and asked me, *Rubin, where is your father?*

I said, *In Paterson.*

I bolted awake. I had just told a lie! I knew he was in Glassboro. So I questioned myself, *Why did you say Paterson, Rubin?* The lie struck me as either a betrayal of myself or a mystery that needed to be unraveled.

The next morning, I got up and used the prison telephone to call my family for the first time in seven years.

I asked my mother, "Where's my father?"

She said, "Rubin, your father's in Bragg's Funeral Home. When you left the hospital yesterday, your father died fifteen minutes later."

Bragg's Funeral Home was a prominent black business in Paterson. We knew the Bragg family quite well. So I hadn't lied to the horse-dog. My father was indeed in Paterson. The dream linked my father to me in death just as we were in life, and in the same silent way.

———

We lived in a violent society, a society that enforced its rules by the use of violence and the threat of violent retribution, lynch parties, dogs, mounted police, hoses, and the like. Rather than making me fear the white man, I lost my fear of my father. He had, without realizing it, passed the violence on to me. Violence only begets violence. It will always create more problems than it solves. If you can see, as I do, that every single human life on this planet is precious, then you will also believe that violence, even violence done in response to violence, is wrong. In fact what is all violence but a conditioned response to violence? There has to be another way. And there is.

We are all born free but immediately fall under the laws of our parents, under the laws of society, and, if we get into trouble, under the laws of the criminal justice system. Then we might go to prison and be under the laws of the prison. Prison is the lowest place we can be on earth without being dead, because in prison we are under more laws than any other place in society. The more laws we are under, the less free we are.

I lived under paternal law, American law, the law of segregation, criminal justice law, military law, and prison law, so I was never any freer than a slave would have been before 1865. No matter who you are, you are born into the universal prison, the world of sleeping people and mechanical laws. Even if you were the "highest born" person, the Queen of England let us say, you might live under the illusion that being the queen is somehow more important than your humanity. The America that controlled my father took control of me. The only escape from the physical, the metaphorical, or the universal prison of sleep is to wake up! As an individual, no matter what the circumstances in which you find yourself, you have this miraculous power.

Early in life, we need our families for our physical and emotional development. Spiritual development, however, can and usually does occur in the absence of family. In prison, where I would eventually learn to let go of useless anger, especially the anger I had toward society and my father, I understood that no one but me could be held responsible for my fate.

The only thing you can change on this planet is yourself. You cannot change another single thing. You can't change your mother, your father, your wife, your husband, or your children. You can't change your ancestors. You cannot change the government in anything but name. But you do have the possibility of changing yourself. The second miracle I discovered in prison is that when you change, the world around you also changes; it is in fact the only way the world can change.

3

Image and Identification:
Two Ways We Keep Ourselves Asleep

In 1961, when New York State legislators were deciding whether to allow professional boxing to continue as a sport in that jurisdiction, they asked Muhammad Ali, then Cassius Clay, and me to testify in front of a Senate committee. Clay, already a popular figure, was testifying as an Olympic gold medalist, and I, a former prisoner with few job prospects, needed boxing to make a living. At the time, Clay projected an image of himself as a brash, arrogant young man exuding superiority. Image is identical to false personality, unreal constructs in which we come to believe. To further this image, Clay carried a shiny black walking stick, something I could not help but see at that time in a negative light, as if he were a rich white dandy with a top hat and tails. We stood together outside the Senate chamber in Albany when a little boy walked up and asked him for his autograph. Clay took the walking stick and knocked the paper right out of that adoring child's hand.

I told him, "You're a big punk. Nothing but a punk." He did not like hearing himself referred to in that manner.

After that incident, Clay, who was in Angelo Dundee's "stable" in Florida, would try to get his stablemates to whoop me. One was Florentino Fernandez; I knocked him through the ropes and out cold in the first round. Another was Gomeo Brennan, the champion of Bimini, whom I defeated at Madison Square Garden. Then there was Jimmy Ellis, a future heavyweight champion, whom I also beat. On the other hand, I lost a ten-round decision to Luis Rodriguez.

Clay would always show up at the fight, walking stick in hand, and get introduced before the main event by Johnnie Addie, the great ring announcer. Who could fail to notice that Clay always received greater acclaim than anyone else in the ring, including me and my opponent?

At some point I'd had enough. I went and told him, "Clay, you get in there. You can't whoop me." Since I was then Sonny Liston's sparring partner, fighting top heavyweights was no big deal to me. At that time, he didn't take me up on my invitation, although in 1975 (before the Rumble in the Jungle with George Foreman), we agreed to an exhibition at Rahway State Prison that was called off by the authorities. In truth, the whole dispute between us boiled down to nothing but machismo, one false image or personality against another.

———

Later on, Muhammad Ali and I, on the surface so different, became very, very good friends. Our friendship represents the triumph of inner essence over outer personality, of Truth over imagery. He went out of his way to help me while I was in prison, becoming one of my greatest supporters in overturning my wrongful conviction. Anything I asked him to do, he would do immediately. He attended rallies on my behalf. He even did things for me I would never have had the audacity to ask for. In 1976, I was given a second trial on the triple-murder conviction. The judge granted bail, very high in those days at thirty-five thousand dollars, to me and to John Artis, the young man convicted with me. Neither of my two defense committees could come up with the money, but Ali did. When I left the courtroom, I rode with him in his limousine to New York City where I was reunited with my wife and daughter. As we got to the city, Ali asked if I had any money on me, and we both laughed out loud knowing full well that I was broke. He took my big hand in his bigger ones and closed my fist around fifteen one-hundred-dollar bills.

Some people wake up because of a shock, an event, or a series of events that challenges their whole system of beliefs. Ali may have been shocked by the reaction of the American government to his stand against the Vietnam War, his five-year prison sentence for refusing to serve in the army, and the government's subsequent refusal to let him make a living in the ring. Or maybe the shock was his awareness of his mortality as his magical boxing skills slowly eroded.

———

Ali's eventual transformation and my own are signs that anyone can wake up. As the most identifiable and identified-with athlete in the world, he could have thumbed his nose at everybody. Instead, he opted for the Truth. Muhammad Ali had, and still has, the heart of a champion both in the ring and in the world.

The world of spectator sports is designed to lure both the athlete and the fan away from their true selves. The principal means by which this feat is accomplished, as it is with family, is imagery, illusions that tie the body and the mind to the business of sport. From an early age we are conditioned to identify with these images; the branding in the brain can last a lifetime. Both the athlete and the fan inhabit a fantasy world, and the Truth, walking among them as a beggar, can no longer afford a ticket to the game.

If you strive to be a prominent boxer, a marquee athlete, a movie star, or anyone in the public eye, you have to develop an image. Since you are a product to be displayed and sold by the media machine, your image is your advertising. Early in my boxing career, I decided to follow in the footsteps of Jack Johnson, the first black heavyweight champion, and shave my head. While I did not make a point of chasing after white women like he did, I would do and say whatever I pleased. In my hooded robe, I looked like a black crystal ball with violent intentions. I also grew a heavy beard and a Fu Manchu mustache, in those days images of defiance.

My life experience, my time in prison, and my interpretation of the political situation at the time made my negative persona nearly inevitable. I looked around and saw black people rising up, demanding what was theirs. In those days, I identified with the ideas of Malcolm X, his philosophy of "by any means necessary," rather than what I misinterpreted as the passivity of Dr. Martin Luther King.

Journalist Jack Newfield, in his book *Somebody's Gotta Tell It*, states, "Some of the fighters I've gotten to know have been the nicest of people." He then places an asterisk in the text, and if you read the footnote it says, "My exceptions to this generalization have included Jake LaMotta, Don Jordan, and Rubin 'Hurricane' Carter. They were not nice and not pleasant to be around. Sonny Liston was also a criminal thug." Newfield, a fine writer, is certainly right about me and Liston as far as press interviews and public appearances were concerned. But people should not mistake the persona for the person, nor should they forget that the "nice humble guy" might be just as much a persona as the evil or arrogant one. Look at professional wrestlers who take on roles and throw them off like bathrobes.

What I did was to cultivate my image in the public eye, although I was always careful to show the utmost respect for my opponents in the ring. Living under the law of accident, I had no idea where this role-playing was going to take me. Like many controversial athletes, I thought of myself as superior to the press, but those guys just let you hang yourself. You stare into the cameras, your face filling the screen, while they just sit there smiling, knowing they've got a great story about how Rubin "Hurricane" Carter said he would go out and shoot some policemen. Think of Tiger Woods, Barry Bonds, Terrell Owens, Pete Rose, O. J. Simpson. Famous or infamous. Controversy sells, and the bigger the controversy, the better.

When you take on an image, you willingly become a stereotype. Stereotyping can also be imposed upon you by others if you, as I did, allow the stereotype to take root. In the seventy-plus years I have been upon this earth, people have stereotyped me, and I have stereotyped myself. They've called me a vicious murderer, a racist, a nigger, and there were times, especially as a boxer, when I promoted and made use of the stereotypes. Just like the young Cassius Clay, I lost myself in the process. Now I have even stopped identifying myself as a black person. It doesn't mean that I am ignorant of my history or what I look like, but I am a human being first. I know the color of my skin, but, in the end, I am not a word.

———

You may, without even being aware of it, live in a state of identification just as I did. What that means is that you identify yourself with an image of something that is not you: family, religion, country, school, career, car, house, wealth, an athlete, sports teams, whatever. Human beings tend to identify, and corporate advertisers with their clever logos know this about you. Politicians and those who run politicians behind the scenes also know this about you. Once you enter into a state of identification, you no longer exist as an independent rational being. The "thing," the institution, label, or object with which you identify, eclipses you. Belief in one's own image or identification with an image is pledging allegiance to that which is not real.

Some young people identify with being black, as did I. By wearing baggy prison-style clothing and calling themselves "niggas," they are taking on fearful personalities that amount to nothing more than a white person's stereotype. Because of bias in language, blackness itself can already be a negative identification. On the other hand, people will smile at me and tell me that they are Christians. They wish to identify in that way, and it seems to make them happy. All I can say to them is "How sad. I'm sorry. That's really sad that you see yourself that way."

People are not a label or a word. It's unimportant to me that people think of themselves as Jews, Christians, Muslims, Americans, Canadians, Republicans, liberals, or Democrats.

Political preference is especially prone to a state of identification. Listen to what people of opposing parties say about how different their ideas are from one another's, but then watch what they do. Their day-to-day lives, their houses, their comforts, their cars are virtually interchangeable. By observing their lifestyles, you would not know liberals from conservatives.

The politicians themselves are all about imagery, packaging, and messages. Until the day they might be unmasked by some outrageous scandal, the public has virtually no idea who these politicians really are. But how could we, since we are all conditioned to buy into the image? In the aftermath of Hurricane Katrina, when George W. Bush was accused of callous insensitivity toward the poor, his handlers made sure that he was photographed with his arm around the shoulders of a little black child. In case we missed the message, former president George H. W. Bush and his wife, Barbara, went on CNN to tell the world that their son was a compassionate man.

Things like religion, nationality, and politics are all accidents of birth or signs of conditioning, but they do not define a person. Neither does a job or profession. If people ask what you do for a living, the emphasis should be on what you *do*. You are not a judge, a lawyer, a doctor, a schoolteacher, a plumber, a corporate vice-president. Those are just words, and words are the simplest of images. To identify with a word is to deny your essence and stifle your potential for growth; instead of continuing your life's journey, you have arrived prematurely at the terminal. However comforted you may feel by these false distinctions or however good or important they make you feel, they are not you.

Many of these identities—Jewish, Native, Armenian, African American, Muslim, Christian—are based upon suffering and victimization. But we are born into these things; they do not belong to us. It is foolish to deny that attempts were made to exterminate some of these groups of people, nor can one just wish away the history of slavery and discrimination. But if that suffering and victimization form the core of your identity, where do you go from there? How is it possible to evolve and to transcend those chains that bind us to this earth?

Where we identify, we apply our intensity. Misusing our energies—intellectual, emotional, sexual—in this way is always a fruitless endeavor. Your house, as the saying goes, will be out of order. Identification, like fear, is free floating; it can be placed onto anything or anyone. Put two well-known people or teams in competition against each other, and the crowd will decide, based on imagery, habit, or place, who should be loved (rooted for) and who should be hated (rooted against).

But that so-called love is especially fickle. I learned early on in my boxing career to have no illusions about the fans. Fans love anyone who shows awesome, destructive power, and they hate him if he fails to come through. They might love you when you walk into the ring, but when you leave, they might very well hit you over the head with a chair. I wouldn't even look at the audience or allow them to touch me in any way. That fit with the image I was cultivating, and gave me the reputation of being mean, surly, and elusive.

Of course, the crowd pays your bills, so in that one very important way you must rely on the fans. But it's an illusion for any professional athlete to believe that he is in full control of his career or the adoring crowd. They are not there for you as a person but for who they think you are. They have identified with your image, but such identification is transitory.

Everything on this level of life passes away. No one should know this better than the athlete whose career is a living example of the birth, growth, and death of all human beings. Athletes move from raw rookie to powerful youth to prime (a combination of power, skill, and guile) to past prime (when skill and guile have to be enough) to over-the-hill in a brief span of years. The crowd might pity you when you're over-the-hill, but usually the love is gone. Nobody wants to attach himself or herself to a loser.

Even in the midst of all the death, destruction, disease, famine, and war in the world, even in the face of environmental catastrophe and dire poverty, people still spend hundreds, even thousands, of dollars to attend sporting events. Sporting events are a banquet of illusions; fans line up at the trough and mistake the slop they feed on for filet mignon. One widespread illusion is that sports provide a significant bonding ritual for fathers and sons. It used to be that a father would pass on a skill or a trade to his son, and a few still do. But all the son learns in becoming a fan is to identify with a team and to waste many hours at expensive sporting events, talking about sports, or watching sports on television.

In addition, the army usually shows up at the big games, especially football games, flying jet planes over the field. They are there to recruit, but if you don't happen to be at the game, don't worry. They will advertise right into your home. Praise is heaped upon the young men who sacrifice their bodies on the field or who have sacrificed their lives for "freedom." The son is being conditioned to devalue his own being, to accept being a casualty, to feel that the needs of his team or his country come before his own.

A second illusion of the sports fan is that he and the team on the field have something in common. When people with team caps, painted faces, or team jerseys are gathered in coliseums and arenas, they don't think about what they really are; in fact, they are not thinking at all. That's why mobs are so dangerous. Only the individual creates; the mob destroys. That mob will trample you dead if something happens that they don't like. What's worse is that they feel no responsibility for mob behavior. They have been taught that winning is the only thing that matters, winning at any cost, an ideology that seeps into other walks of life, especially legal and financial. Some of these fans feel diminished when their team loses, just as they think their lives are somehow enriched when their team wins. They become enraged or even depressed when the people on the field or in the ring fail to perform for them.

Living vicariously through identification never brings satisfaction. There will always be the next bout or the next game or the next pennant race. Of course, identification with images serves to fill the coffers of the corporate owners of the team and their sponsors. When teams are introduced, they are referred to as "your" team, despite the obvious reality that those people on the field have nothing to do with you, don't even live in your city, and would likely leave you flat if they were offered more money to play elsewhere.

———

Ali Hasson once told me a Sudanese story about a man, a very fat man, who fell asleep while shelling peas one night in the cramped quarters of his hovel. The hut mysteriously caught fire, and the village people rushed to the scene trying to save the sleeping man. They couldn't do it. The house was too small and the man too big to move. The wise man of the village happened upon the scene and saw the struggling mass trying to save the sleeping man. He called out, "Wake him up! Just wake him up and he will save himself!"

Of course, waking up is not so easy to do in reality, because nobody believes that he is asleep. A sleeping person defines who he is by his relationship to others; his identity is determined by the needs of others. The point of Hasson's story is that the fat man is so larded up with false identities that his inner essence is buried.

To remember yourself, to reacquaint yourself with your essence, is to recognize who you are and what you are and to be awake to your possibilities. Knowing who you are, understanding that singular reality, you soon learn what is you and what is not you. Being true to yourself releases you from dependence on others to take the risks for you.

You might have been taught that your impulses are evil or that in some significant way you don't measure up. Because you have been conditioned to think that you are incomplete, you latch on to something that you believe will make you whole. This sense of incompleteness is the main reason we take on false personalities or project false images to the world. The truth is that you, from the day you were born, lack for nothing. You have a genius inside you.

Nationalities do not exist on a higher level. Neither does politics. There are no religions. No names. No time, even. There is only now. The eternal now. No races, only the human race. We are bound to one another by our common needs as if there were but one gigantic bloodstream coursing through all the life on earth. One spirit, dividing itself up, gave birth to all the souls that struggle in the universe. One spirit. One mind. One self. On a higher level, we cannot be separated. We do not exist by ourselves or for ourselves. Our narrow preoccupations and identifications can and must be transcended.

Having met Ali Hasson as a young recruit, I had some familiarity with ideas such as these, but back in New Jersey there was no soil for me in which conscious thought could be sustained. When I was arrested at my father's house in 1956 and sent to Annandale Reformatory, I thought the only saving grace was that Annandale was full of young men who wanted to become boxers. I had been trained as a boxer in the army, had fought more than fifty amateur fights, and was the army light-welterweight champion. These men in prison did not have my training or experience, so I was easily able to go through the competition. It was there that I honed a reputation for meanness, an image designed to keep people at a distance, and it was also there that I began to drink.

I was released after nine months, but Annandale stayed inside me for many years: all the meanness, the violence, the hatred, the isolation, and the early stages of alcoholism. Undisciplined and depressed, I gave up on boxing and began work in a plastics factory.

It didn't take long for the violence to reassert itself. I had a cousin, Adolph Mincy, an out-of-wedlock son of my uncle Prince. He was a beautiful young man with chiseled features, a real Adonis. Like a lot of us at the time, he had a fancy car, a black-and-white Oldsmobile, like a big saddle shoe. He lived just up the street from us and was going out with a nurse who had access to narcotics and was able to trade hospital drugs like morphine for street drugs like heroin. Mincy became a part of the growing drug scene and finally overdosed. He was found dead in his Oldsmobile on a back street in Paterson.

Enraged and drunk, when I heard of his death I became a ticking time bomb. I went out on the street, attacking people for no reason, and mugged an older woman, taking her purse in the process. I was arrested for these assaults and served more than five years at Trenton State Prison, from 1956 to 1961.

I'm not making excuses here for my actions. I did what I did. People lose people they love all the time and commit no violence. Mincy's death was simply a catalyst for my rage. I know that now.

What was most dangerous is that I did not feel connected to what I did. Somehow, it wasn't my rage. This rage existed before I was born. Rage is not natural to one kind of people, as is often averred, but a learned behavior employed to frighten other people. I had taken it upon myself like a ratty old coat. Prisons are equipped to deal with rage, but the street is not. Having expressed this rage in the way I did, I can understand why others leave prison and quickly commit another offense.

———

When I emerged from Trenton State Prison in 1961, I used boxing to make an honest living, but I also tried to use it to channel and control rage. I did not wish to drift blindly into another brush with the law, but, as a fighting machine and a soon-to-be public figure, I had little chance of awakening to a different reality. You see, no sport better replicates the law of accident than boxing. The fighter, blindly parading around like he owns the world, may not be a sheep, but he's sure to be a sacrificial lamb. No athlete is more exploited than the boxer who could be killed or disabled every time he steps into the ring. No athlete is more subject to the whims of promoters and agencies. None is more desperate to get work even if he may be headed into a mismatch. Boxers not only get knocked unconscious but also do their best to keep themselves unconscious of the mental and physical price they must pay to pursue such a barbaric career.

Carmine Tedeschi, who would become my boxing manager, was a pretty good con man. Late in 1961, after my release from Trenton State, my uncle Martin, without my knowing it, told Tedeschi about my potential as a boxer. Bucky Leggatt, my trainer, brought me up to Paterson from Trenton in the early stages of my career to spar with a heavyweight, Attilio Tondo, who was scheduled to fight that Friday night in Madison Square Garden. When I arrived at the Market Street Gym in Paterson, I saw a large crowd of people, so I knew something was going down.

It felt like a dream where you find yourself on a stage but aren't quite sure of the role you're supposed to play. Tondo and I began sparring, but unlike most unequal-weight sparring sessions, he was winging lefts and rights from every angle, really trying to do me in.

After the first round, I went over to his corner and told him to cool it. "I'm no heavyweight. I'm not even getting paid. You need the work. I'll give you some work. Don't be trying to knock my head off."

His corner ignored me, pretending not to understand English. When the second round began, he started winging again, but this time I was winging right back. Next thing you know, I knocked him out cold, and they had to run and get a doctor. The doctor gave him a needle to revive him. I didn't know who was pulling the strings, but I could see someone jumping up and down, real excited about what had taken place.

Later that afternoon, Leggatt introduced me to Tedeschi, the same man I had seen jumping up and down, as my new manager. Without my knowledge or consent, I had been sold like a slave on the auction block, and I slipped right into the image tailor-made just for me: *the mean, vicious brawler with deadly punching power.*

As you might guess, Leggatt was somewhat of a con artist himself. Con artists are attracted to boxers like flies to syrup. After my first fight with Pike Reed, a four-rounder in which I almost died from exhaustion, Leggatt signed for me to go ten rounds with the great Holly Mims. Managers or trainers will sometimes put fighters in the ring in a total mismatch. They themselves might need the money at the time to support their own families and pay down their debts. They might also have minimal faith in their own boxer and figure that this one payday is about the best they can ever hope for. Leggatt was a poor man, so the immediate money tempted him to make a foolish and potentially dangerous decision. He never bothered to tell me whom I was fighting; had I fought Mims in 1961, he would no doubt have killed me. Nor did my trainer tell me that he had been given a three-hundred-dollar advance of which I saw not a single cent. When I learned about that money from a misdirected letter, I confronted Leggatt and cursed him out. But what was I to him, after all, other than an ex-con?

If you think that I was being manipulated, and I was, pity my poor sparring partner, a seventeen-year-old kid named Winnie. A boxer in training for an important fight needs sparring partners. Winnie was all that Leggatt could afford. He had heart, I can tell you that. I was straight from prison, training and fighting almost constantly, and this kid would stay right in there with me trading punches day after day. When I heard from his sister one evening that he had gone into convulsions, I was afraid I had killed him. Luckily, he survived.

Throughout my career, it was always hard for me to get sparring partners. I demanded that my partners be in perfect condition, just as I was. They had to get up for roadwork at five in the morning. By 1964, I would have five of them fighting me one or two rounds each so they would always be fresh. I had a special pair of boxing gloves made up, twenty-three-ounce gloves that would supposedly limit the damage to my sparring partner. Normally, gloves are sixteen ounces for sparring and eight ounces for the actual fight. Sonny Liston and I were the only fighters who used twenty-three-ounce gloves in training. When you put on those eight-ounce gloves, you feel as though you're wearing no gloves on at all.

Liston and I became sparring partners in Philadelphia. He was, by then, the number one contender for the heavyweight championship. We used to have wars down there, Liston keeping me at bay with his left jab while I tried to crowd him. He was at least fifty pounds heavier than I was, and that left jab of his was explosive, one of the great left jabs in boxing history. I took my headgear off on the final day we sparred and was shocked to see a bowl full of blood. The blood pouring from my ears told us both that Liston needed a new sparring partner.

Clay Thomas, a light heavyweight from Paterson who fought for Lou Duva, was another sparring partner of mine. Many years later, at the International Boxing Hall of Fame in Canastota, New York, I met Duva again, and we talked about those times. I used to mess up his fighters in sparring sessions. In my view, Duva for a time was a one-man wrecking crew for boxers. He fed those guys to the gristmill with little concern for their future well-being. If you needed fighters up in, say, New Haven, Connecticut, it seemed as if Duva would pick them up off the street, give them a few days of training, and send them up there to cement the reputation of some up-and-coming young phenom. They would get paid forty dollars, a meal, and bus fare to get their brains beat out.

Thomas was one of Duva's "clay pigeons"; boxing left him mentally unstable. He was in prison with me—Big Bad Tom, we called him—and he instigated the Rahway riot in 1971, two months after the Attica Prison massacre in Buffalo, New York, that killed more than thirty people, inmates and guards. Completely drunk on prison hooch, he tossed a chair through a movie screen while a film was playing.

Like Thomas, who stayed with Duva, like so many fighters, desperation forced me to stay with Leggatt through all of 1961. During that time I was able to beat Joey Cooper, Frankie Nelson, and Herschel Jacobs, a light-heavyweight. When Tedeschi stepped in, he, my father, and my uncle Martin, both of whom he had carefully enlisted, asked me to fight the light-hitting Jacobs again instead of Mims. Tedeschi was no fool; he did not want to spoil his new investment.

After the second Jacobs fight, which I lost on points, Tedeschi brought in Tommy Parks to be my trainer until I started to fight on television. The closer I got to being ranked and pulling in big paydays, the more Parks and all of the other black people I knew were pushed away. If you look at tapes of my old television fights, my whole corner is white. The perception that some people got from this imagery was that the white folks "made" the black guy. *We made you*, they would say, as if black people were incapable of understanding the strategy of the boxing ring. Of course, that was another illusion fostered by the media and accepted unquestioningly by the public. It didn't seem to matter that whenever the bell rang, my manager, my trainer, and my cut man would grab their stools and leave the ring. Like any fighter, I carried out my strategy alone, but whenever I threatened to leave Tedeschi, the media would point out how ungrateful I was.

In 1962, I became a part of the Madison Square Garden farm program run by Freddie "Duke" Stefano. Even in those terms, *farms* and *stables*, boxers are seen as animals. The popularity of boxing at that time produced farm programs and fight clubs. On Monday, there were fights at St. Nicholas Arena on Sixty-sixth Street in New York, fights on Wednesday in Chicago, and on Friday in Madison Square Garden.

The ultimate reward for any fighter, aside from a championship, was to fight the televised main event Friday night at Madison Square Garden. On my way to that goal, my next three fights were promoted by Jimmy Colotto of Jersey City. After I knocked out Tommy Settles and Felix Santiago, each in one round, and Jimmy McMillan in three, Colotto dubbed me "the Hurricane," a name I did not like but one that has stuck with me to this day. To me, "Hurricane" represented a force out of control, something like mindless rage. I would have preferred something cooler like "the Black Panther," the image stenciled on my robe, but history had other designs on that moniker.

When I continued my string of knockouts in Madison Square Garden, it was just a matter of time before I started pulling in large purses. I was assured that all of the taxes were being taken off the top, but in reality tax hadn't been paid for the first year and a half I was boxing.

Tedeschi kept the purses, giving me whatever money I needed, but he could not control his own expenditures. I knew that something was up when Tommy Parks told me that a twenty-five-dollar check he had been given by Tedeschi had bounced. I had to fight eighteen times from 1962 to 1963 to pay off debts and accumulate some capital. Compare that with the big-time fighters today who need only two or three bouts a year to make millions. It's a good thing, too, because the fighters' risk of serious injury is reduced.

In December 1962, I was scheduled to fight Gomeo Brennan, the champion of Bimini. I was told he had come down with the flu, and they had to find a last-minute substitute. They showed me a list of fighters to "choose from," and one of them was Holly Mims. I had seen Mims in the lobby of my hotel and gone over to him to say hello. I wondered why they whisked him away before we could exchange a greeting. The choice of opponents was merely an illusion they were trying to foster. Mims was to be my opponent right after Brennan's cancellation. If I mentioned another fighter on the list, they would start to explain that he was a dangerous unknown or a deadly puncher. Not knowing I had seen him in the hotel, the promoters pretended that Mims was down in Washington, D.C., and that I needed to make the decision by one o'clock for them to retrieve him. I just had to play along with the whole charade, but this time I was lucky. We went the distance, and I won the fight. That fight, more than any other, established me as a true championship contender.

———

I first became a boxer because I could not speak and found boxing to be a means of expression. To be paid for doing what I loved to do was a bonus. And what I loved about boxing was the training, the action of the boxing ring, the assertion of my will, and the drug of the screaming crowd. At first, I had no aim beyond that, although I also loved the accolades on the street and the pictures in the paper. There were times I would have agreed to fight for nothing.

While now there are boxing councils, associations, and organizations and a whole slew of in-between weights, the undisputed middleweight championship used to be the second-biggest prize in boxing. The focus now is no longer on weight class and championships but on the viciousness and the bloodletting, on gory bouts repeated dozens of times on sports stations at odd times of the day and night. In this context, I will only mention here the disgusting and decadent madness of "ultimate fighting," a so-called sport that deliberately puts athletes at risk of serious and permanent injury. We are now drifting ever closer to the Roman gladiators, because death, virtual or otherwise, sells as much as sex.

I signed on in 1964 to fight Joey Giardello, the middleweight champion, in Las Vegas. The bout was to take place on October 14. Joey was a crafty boxer who had been a professional since 1948, a veteran of nearly 150 fights. When we got to Vegas, Giardello stayed on the Strip with the big hotels and casinos, while I had to stay at the El Cortez in East Vegas. At the time, black people who performed on the Strip, even Sammy Davis Jr., Eartha Kitt, and Dorothy Dandridge, could not stay there. Equality in the United States was just another illusion we lived with (and still do), but we won't get into that now. Giardello began as a 7–5 favorite. During training, the odds went to 5–1 for me, an almost unheard of variation. The pundits could see that I was stronger and sharper than I had ever been. I was ready to take that title. Giardello's lawyers got promotional rights to my next three fights in case I won, hardly a vote of confidence for their man.

The day of the fight, Giardello refused to enter the ring because he was owed a hundred thousand dollars in advance. I offered to give Giardello my share of the purse (twelve thousand dollars) and to fight for nothing if he would agree to step in the ring with me. The promoters were offering him eighty thousand dollars. He refused my offer because the total still came up short.

New promoters were found, and they set up the championship fight for December in Philadelphia, Giardello's hometown. I had only fought eleven rounds that whole year; I beat Jimmy Ellis in ten and knocked out Clarence James in the first round. I hadn't fought for six months, and I didn't fight my fight in Philadelphia. Giardello was a champion, and though I tried to get him early on, I couldn't knock him out. Although he may have looked a lot worse at the end of the fight than I did, he punched effectively enough to keep me at bay and retain the championship.

Driving home after the fight, I was pulled over by a cop for running a stop sign. In retelling this, I am reminded of how my life was circumscribed. The message to me was that I was being watched and followed, but I'd be damned if I was going to change the way I acted.

The political situation surrounding race in the United States was exploding all around me while I—with my bald head, my Fu Manchu, and my beard—kept telling Africans in America that we must protect ourselves against police brutality. It pays to be a villain in show business, but you're also running around with a target painted on both sides.

I had fallen completely in love with my image. I even forgot it was an image. I was the "Hurricane": tough, mean, brutal, and remorseless. The media kept trying to get me to say or do something controversial. I had the FBI on my tail. They were following all possible "subversives," including Dr. King and Malcolm X. The police made me sign on as an ex-con every place I went. When I protested this treatment, I was accused of being paranoid.

Sonny Liston and I had an informal contest about who would appear most in the papers—"the big bear," Liston, or "the little bear," me. He was having run-ins with the Philadelphia police because he was complaining about police brutality, and I was becoming public enemy number one in New Jersey. I got locked up for bar fights and disorderly conduct. I chased women, even though I was married. In my judgment, Liston was one of the nicest, gentlest people you'd ever want to meet, but people were frightened of him because of his portrayal in the media. Both of us got sucked into it; when the media came around, we became more and more ornery, easier to stereotype. We were laughing at them, but the laugh was really on us.

For Liston and me, there was no news in being good. Publicity feeds the media, and bad publicity is the biggest meal of all, the meat and potatoes. Here I thought I was a big-time famous fighter with a fancy car, hangers-on, the world at my command, but I was nothing but a puppet. That's how the system gets to you and then makes you intoxicated with the re-creation of yourself. It's not always the money that lures retired fighters back to the ring. The public lie is just as addicting.

———

I carried my reputation for brutality to training camps because I knew that reporters hung around these places looking for stories. In my training camp out in the country, I would bring my guns along for target practice. Even though I had grown up around guns, I used them at camp purely for the sake of image. I also wanted to build up the take for the upcoming fight, and the reporters wanted to see their bylines in the paper. My camp had to be newsworthy.

One day after training, I conspicuously took a couple of rifles out back where a hill provided a good backdrop for target shooting. The reporters followed me just as I expected they would. After a few minutes of pinging rocks and bottles, I was asked by one of them if I could see a robin sitting way up on a scraggy tree branch near the top of the hill. Of course I saw it—red breast against a deep blue sky. Couldn't miss it, especially back then when I had two good eyes working in my head.

He asked if I could hit it.

"Sure," I said, thinking how attractive that reporter's story would look.

Without another thought, I squeezed the trigger, and that bird fell over dead. Suddenly, I felt just terrible. Whatever was good and decent inside of me, whatever had not yet been lost, came to the surface for a moment. I walked up that hill, picked up the small bird, and brought it back down to bury it. To this very day, aside from fishing, I have never taken another life.

———

Only a small minority of prizefighters have ever made a decent living. We might hear today about multimillion-dollar purses and think that boxers are well off, but there are no revenue-sharing agreements in boxing. If you make the top ten, train hard and regularly, sacrifice your social life and your family, then you can earn enough money to take you through a decade. But what then? What can a fighter do? Most of us do not even have small pensions until we qualify for social security. Many fighters need to take other jobs while they are in training, and these might prevent them from reaching their full potentials. The damage to their bodies and minds that they tried to ignore for years doesn't just go away. After a fighting career, people expect you to act normally, as if a soldier coming from the battlefield can all of a sudden adapt himself to civilian life. You've been running twenty miles a day, eating raw meat, sucking up raw eggs, drinking quarts of milk, all with mayhem on your mind. You might even have a vicious nickname that you're stuck with, making it difficult to start a normal life.

A couple of decades ago, great boxers like Tommy "the Hit Man" Hearns, Marvin Hagler, Muhammad Ali, and "Sugar" Ray Leonard began to pick and choose their opponents. They ran themselves like businesses, made millions of dollars, and retired to enjoy their money. No boxer should ever forget that Don King, the wild-haired promoter with the image and attitude problem, made all of this possible. He and Bob Arum made sure that the boxers would keep a large share of the purses. When I was fighting, the promoters and the managers made more money than we did, and we didn't know where our money went. Still, I'm not complaining. It was fun for me while it lasted.

My record shows clearly when my boxing abilities began to fade. I became more image than fighter. Life was spiraling out of control. Boxing seemed irrelevant, as any sport does when real life intrudes. Television showed Dr. King fighting segregation on the front lines and a lot of violence being done to people who looked like me. In America, any time a bill came through the legislature to protect Africans in America, a whole lot of us would die in the streets. In March 1965, Dr. King asked me, along with many others, to accompany him to Selma, Alabama. I refused to join those brave people. If the "Hurricane" was attacked by dogs, batons, mounted police, or hoses, he would have to fight back and kill someone or, even more likely, be killed.

In September of the same year, I received my political education in South Africa where I had gone to fight Joe "Axe Killer" Ngidi. The violence of apartheid was no different to me than the violence of segregation, except that the black South Africans were fighting back. I went back to South Africa in 1966 to fight Ernie Burford for the third time. I have admitted before that my real purpose in going back was to support the African National Congress. To that end, I brought along four duffel bags filled with guns. Those bags, labeled BOXING EQUIPMENT, were placed out on the tarmac. Only luck saved me from being discovered. I was only living up to my image, but in the act itself you can see my stupid, careless, and unconscious behavior. Not that the ANC was a bad cause—just the opposite, in fact—but the way I tried to help amounted to nothing more than a death wish. Or maybe I thought that Rubin "Hurricane" Carter was invincible.

Whenever I spoke out against the oppression I was seeing, people were always saying to me: *Rubin, leave those people alone. You're not in the ghetto anymore.* But I could not and would not separate myself from what was going on, no matter what that cost me. That is one part of my past I am truly glad about. Nowadays, black celebrities learn the opposite lesson. Just entertain, be funny, or play your sport. We'll let you make plenty of money, and we'll allow you to live in palatial homes. Just stay away from politics. A role model, something I never claim to have been, should be someone who puts himself or herself on the line for other people, someone who understands oppression but who can also lift people up. Most every media darling in the United States—black, Hispanic, or white—knows that he or she has to keep away from political controversy to continue raking in the cash. The system allows athletes of African descent to become corporate icons and multimillionaires but keeps many millions more hidden in dire poverty or behind bars. These systemic injustices facing poor Africans in America will not change any time soon, even though the country has chosen a black president.

When was the last time you remember a radical political statement from any athlete, white or black, like John Carlos or Tommie Smith and their Black Power salute at the 1968 Olympics in Mexico City? How dared they mix sport and politics? They are still the most reviled American athletes in Olympic history, and they didn't take performance-enhancing drugs! But who challenges the right of the armed forces to show their wares at the Super Bowl? It's not sport and politics that don't mix, but sport and the wrong kind of politics. The biggest sporting controversy of the last several years was Janet Jackson's bare breast during the Super Bowl's halftime show, hardly a statement of any sort. Change the channel and you'd see something really pornographic: pornographic crime shows, pornographic advertising, pornographic violence. But Janet Jackson's breast? Now that really got the sleeping people worked up into a frenzy. It was said to have been an attack against family values. Since when is a breast against family values? Instead of hearing the sound of reasoned debate and even laughter, the whole reactive nature of the system was brought into play.

If you—like me, like Muhammad Ali, or like Justin Timberlake, Janet Jackson, or the Dixie Chicks—pretend that the system does not exist, say anything that comes to your mind, or do something outrageous or politically unpopular, eventually you will feel its full weight come crashing down on top of you. I thought I was "free," but that kind of freedom is nothing more than ignorance. For unconscious souls, for sleeping people, freedom comes only at the pleasure of others.

When I was arrested with John Artis in 1966, I was thinking, *Here we go again, just another attempt by the police to show me who's boss.* I found myself accused of walking into a bar and shooting four people, killing three, although I was wearing a cream-colored sports jacket and was the best-known and most recognizable person in Paterson. I wanted to laugh, but the faces around me looked serious. It seemed like a game, a dream, the same as when I had fought Attilio Tondo at the Market Street Gym. Just as I felt at that time, I had no idea of the role I was supposed to play, but then all the plans were being made for me behind my back. My only thoughts were, *How dare they mess with Rubin Hurricane Carter! Don't they know who I am?*

My problem was that I couldn't answer my own question. My everlasting regret is that the image I cultivated, the image in which I was trapped, brought John Artis down with me as well.

———

Image and identification, along with displays of power, grace, and superhuman effort, are integral to the allure of sport. What's true for the fan is also true for the athlete. While the fan is trapped into identifying, the athlete can also be a prisoner of his image. Being a fan is a mechanical act, a habit; there is nothing conscious about it. Anything that keeps you from the knowledge of self is designed to keep you asleep. You thought you were free, but now you see the prison bars that are holding you in place. If you wake up, you will want to stop this automatic behavior, and you will have to stop believing in these illusions. You will no longer allow yourself to be manipulated for others' purposes. You will discover your own purpose.

Self-discovery is at the core of all religions, yet religious practices in churches, synagogues, mosques, and temples have little to do with self-discovery. I call the Creator the Absolute: the Absolute is alpha and omega, the beginning and the end and everything in between. Athletes who invoke God or the Absolute or religion in sports are my idea of true blasphemers. As if God cares about who wins a football game or a boxing match! When the athlete points up to the sky after making a great play, it's money they want to start raining down on them.

Nor should anyone be fooled by those prayer groups after the games. That's all imagery. These athletes are in many cases young people without much education who have had fortunes plunked into their laps. They buy cars, wristwatches, and palatial homes. Like King Midas, everything they touch turns to gold.

Millions of children, some of whom live in appalling conditions, who may be lucky to eat one decent meal a day, and who can barely read or write, look up to these young stars. *If I practice enough,* they tell themselves, *I'll be rich and famous, too.* These young boys really do number in the millions, but the places for rich basketball, baseball, and football stars number in the hundreds.

What those young people must come to understand is that they too are stars, fragments of the sun, and that the hardwood floor or the boxing ring or the baseball diamond or the ice rink or the soccer pitch may not be where their genius lies.

4

Surviving Prison:
Awakening to Myself

A little child once said to her father,
"Tell me, sir," asked she,
"What is the meaning of freedom
And what is liberty?"
"Oh, they are one and the same, my child,
Only two ways to say one word,
But for a better answer
Go out and catch yourself a bird."
The child did as she was instructed;
Successfully and full of pride
She brought a sparrow into the house
And sadly watched it die.
The child then turned to her father
With teardrops on her face,
"Why did my sparrow die, sir,
Didn't he like this place?"
"That's not the point,"

Said the father to his child,
"And I say to you in these few words,
No one knows what freedom is
But the lack of it killed that bird."

I wrote this poem one night after a prison visit from my wife, Mae Thelma, and daughter, Theodora, who might have been seven years old at the time. Each month when she came to visit with me at the prison, she would ask, "Daddy, why can't you come home with us?" I would try to explain to her what I was doing inside those walls but could never find the right words. This poem came to me instead. It is the only poem I have ever written, as I'm sure is obvious to anyone who reads it. I realize that the poem neither answered her question nor applied any salve to her wound, but it did make me understand the degree of my own suffering and the suffering of other wrongly convicted people inside the walls of a prison from the arbitrary loss of freedom.

Dostoyevsky once said that to measure the degree of civilization in any society, just enter into its prisons. By this standard, the United States and Canada join a long list of uncivilized societies. You cannot find too many good prisons throughout the world because the model for prisons has become more and more reactive, demonstrating the outrage that self-righteous citizens feel about the criminal behavior of others. Crime, it is thought, must be followed by severe punishment—the worse the punishment, the better, or kill 'em altogether.

Part of the punishment of a prison is geographical isolation; federal, state, and provincial prisons are often located in out-of-the-way places, making it almost impossible for poor families to visit with any frequency. Although there were times when rehabilitation of human lives was the stated ideal of politicians and prison designers, what prison actually does is to destroy families and destroy human dignity, mental health, and self-respect. Can a person who hates himself ever be rehabilitated? Can a person exposed to hostility, viciousness, and calculated disregard for human decency become anything but hostile, vicious, and indecent? A prisoner's life is worth two cartons of cigarettes if he happens to be good looking, somewhat less if he's not. And if he is not strong enough to defend himself, and few people are, he may be raped and pillaged. Let any part of that prison touch him, and it will spread its ugliness like poison ivy; let any part inside of him, and he will have consumed a poison with no antidote. Penal institutions are themselves the cause of recidivism. The only worthwhile lesson they teach anyone is how to survive inside a prison.

As an innocent but reviled man in prison—a black man convicted of the racist killing of three white people and just narrowly escaping the electric chair—you could have bet your family inheritance that I would never again be free to see the sunrise. And because of my attitude, and because of my absolute, unwavering conviction that I was innocent, and my supposed lack of contrition, my chances of living long enough to get my case back into court were very poor at best. But I could not give in to the threat of violence or isolation. Being found guilty by a jury of twelve misinformed people, a jury fed on lies, perjury, and manufactured evidence, did not make me guilty. So I refused to act the part of a guilty man. I refused to become a good prisoner. Resistance was my defense. I would not speak to the guards nor would I acknowledge their existences. I refused to move to the rhythm of the prison or obey its arbitrary rules. I refused to wear its stripes. I refused to eat its food. I refused to work its jobs. I would have refused to breathe the prison air if I could have done so and yet remained alive.

What I had that could never be compromised was my innocence. I wasn't even aware at that time that I had a Spirit, but that inner voice, that resistance, shows me as I write this today that my Spirit was very much alive and kicking.

My belief in my innocence and my stubbornness earned me many trips to solitary confinement, the black hole of silence. Trenton State Prison was built in 1849—it was a dungeon—and solitary there was six feet under the ground. I spent close to ten of my twenty years in darkness with no sanitary conditions, no toothbrush, no running water, five slices of stale bread to eat, and a cup of warm water to drink. I ate the bread because I was determined to survive. Morning, noon, or night did not exist for me, just different shades of darkness. There was a smell down there, down under the ground, of body rot and filthy waste buckets not emptied for three or four days. It really was a hole. Every fifteen days we were allowed to take a shower, and every thirty days we were given a medical examination.

Since they viewed me as a triple-racist-murderer, they tried to break my resistance by taking me down to the lowest level they possibly could. They would rather have broken my Spirit than killed me, but if I died in the process nobody would have cared, and they would have found an easy explanation for my death.

Just as television presents a false picture of the courts, the public is also shielded from the reality of its prisons. Prison is raw, naked violence, hatred, and bitterness. Every day in that prison, my life was threatened. I was trapped at the bottom level of human society, the lowest point at which a person can exist without being dead; solitary confinement mimicked a coffin. Aside from my innocence, I had nothing else to hold on to but my life.

When Nelson Mandela was imprisoned on Robben Island, he said that solitary confinement was the hardest part of his experience. He looked forward to the cockroaches walking across his cell floor and climbing the walls so that he would have someone or something to talk to. We used to say that solitary confinement at Trenton State Prison was so bad that even the cockroaches kept their distance. These subhuman conditions take a terrible toll on those who are actually guilty of crimes, but for those who are there in place of the guilty person, for those who have been wrongly convicted, every waking moment is pure torture and agony. *Why me?* the prisoner keeps asking himself over and over, like a cancer patient.

———

Prison is a society within society that is under the most laws on this earth. Universal laws govern the earth, and laws of civilization begin with constitutions and charters that devolve all the way down to mechanical laws: survival of the fittest, the law of the jungle. Prison is the easiest place to hurt others and to be hurt. Behind those walls, prisoners are always engaged in life-and-death struggles. Any altercation or show of disrespect can be fatal, particularly in the morning. Someone may have gotten a letter from his wife's lawyer suing him for divorce, from his girlfriend saying she's found another man, or from his lawyer informing him that his latest appeal has been denied. When those cell doors open, the place becomes a pit of poisonous vipers. Prisoners may have been mouthing off to one another during the night. Now they have to pay the piper.

Oh, I was angry, too—angry for a very long time. I was eating hatred and victimization as though they were succulent morsels of buttered steak. I was angry at everything that moved. I was angry at the two state witnesses who lied. I was angry at the police who put them up to it. I was angry at the prosecutor who sanctioned it. I was angry at the judge for allowing their testimony. I was angry at the jury who accepted it. I was angry at my own lawyer for not being able to defeat it. I was angry at my family because they wanted me to quit, to give up, to be ordinary like the other prisoners so they could come and visit me once a month for ninety minutes. They wanted me to give up my protestation of innocence, the dream of freedom that meant everything to me. They wanted me to die virtually and wait to be buried.

Being sentenced to three lifetimes in prison was, as far as the duration of my life was concerned, forever. I had no way out. Even if the system became compassionate in the future, after twenty-five years I could only be paroled to my second life sentence. I was twenty-nine when I went in; after fifty years, I could only be paroled to my third life term. I would then have to serve another twenty-five years before becoming eligible for actual parole.

On my way from solitary confinement to one of those physical checkups in what they called the prison hospital, I happened to pass a mirror hanging on the wall and stopped dead. The grotesque image that glared out at me from that glass shocked me. I saw the face of hatred in that mirror. I thought, *That cannot be me!*

I saw a monster. Bulging out of its head were two big, glassy eyes. The skin was stretched so tightly over its face that it was shining. Its lips were thin and drawn back, revealing big yellow teeth, rotted gums, and a perpetual grimace of pure sadistic delight.

Hatred and bitterness had taken me over. I wanted revenge. In the words of Bob Dylan, "If my thought-dreams could be seen, they'd put my head in a guillotine." Such a terrible deed had been done to me that I imagined killing millions of people in revenge. I was then capable of even that.

Solitary confinement wasn't exactly the end of the line, but I could certainly see the end of the line from where I was. Yet somehow I was able to maintain the irrational expectation that I would soon be released. With that expectation came the dream of resuming my boxing career and even receiving a hero's welcome back into the ring.

Then something unspeakable happened. Boxing, the prison doctor told me, had left me with the beginnings of a detached retina. An operation was necessary. He was a doctor. Who was I to argue with him? But because I was deemed a triple-racist-murderer, the authorities, no matter how much I protested, would not let me leave the prison to go to a proper hospital.

Compared with the treatments now available, retinal surgery forty-three years ago was in its infancy. The prison hospital did not have the expertise, the equipment, or the sanitary conditions to perform such surgery, but so great was my desperation to get back into the ring that I ignored my natural instincts.

The surgery was botched. When the bandages were removed, I was blind in my right eye with no hope of recovery. Like Samson, I wanted to flail out and bring the whole prison structure down upon everyone.

In prison, you have no immediate outlet for your anger beyond hating your jailers and fellow prisoners. That hate, as I learned, only consumes the vessel that contains it. It doesn't really hurt another soul. There are prisons within prisons just as there are worlds within worlds. Within Trenton, there was solitary confinement, and then there was my own private prison—the conglomerate of personalities that made up what people used to call Rubin "Hurricane" Carter. These personalities existed separately from one another, ignorant of one another, and reacted to external stimuli just like machines. If I was going to survive that prison, I had to change. I had to rise above the level of that prison. I had to become something different, someone whose behavior was not at the mercy of external forces. The prison itself sure was not going to change.

The first step in that process of change was to rule out open defiance and to resist expressing any negative emotions. Resisting the expression of one's negative emotions even on a good day outside a prison is difficult. What I did to survive the prison was to find a space—not an actual physical space, but a moral and ethical one—where I would not compromise myself and yet stay alive. I eased around things. I already said that I ate the bread in solitary. The white pajamas I had worn in the prison hospital became my prison uniform at Trenton State, just as I later wore a barber's smock at Rahway. I would never confront the guards, just ignore them. While I would not go to the mess hall to eat the food destined for the general population, I willingly ate the food made for the guards that the kitchen workers were sometimes able to sneak down to me. Thom Kidrin, my great friend on the outside, brought me cans of Campbell's soup that I ate once every three days. I broke rules, but many of the rules I broke—for example, the wearing of beards, mustaches, watches, rings, and one's own personal clothing—I was eventually able to have legalized so that the other prisoners were also able to have these things.

I refused to shave my beard. The authorities deemed that a breach of regulations, so I took my case to court. To shave my beard, I argued, would constitute "tampering with and destroying evidence," since the actual perpetrators of the crime at the Lafayette Bar and Grill had been described as having only thin mustaches. My beard, therefore, became a testimony to and a symbol of my innocence. My argument was successful, establishing to the prison administration and the guards that I could use the law to protect my interests.

To deal with the constant hunger, I had to control my many cravings, which meant controlling both body and mind. I had to overcome all of those things that advertise your hunger: the growling of your stomach or a headache or visions of your favorite foods. I became a fakir. Hunger and pain, to a fakir, can be controlled by the mind. The physical body knows nothing about pain, heat, cold, time, or hunger, but the mind does. The mind then imposes its conditions upon the physical body, while our capacity to endure is far greater than we realize. Of course my career as a professional boxer, having the stamina and endurance to go the distance many times, came in handy in this regard. The cartoon version of the fakir shows him lying on a bed of nails; there is more than a little Truth in this caricature.

Another form of self-discipline for me was commitment to a project, a goal to work toward, even if it seemed impossible to attain. I decided upon two projects with one goal: freedom. First, I became an expert in the field of criminal law. Second, I decided to write a book about my life. Actually, my first inkling about writing *The Sixteenth Round* occurred even before I went to trial in 1967. Arthur Dexter Bradley, one of the state's key witnesses, who was paid to testify falsely against me, was being held on the third floor of the Passaic County Jail while I was down on the first floor. He and Hector Martinez, "The Motel Bandits," had a history of armed robberies up and down the coast of New Jersey. Bradley was brought into the jail from Bordentown Reformatory because the prosecutors were formulating their deals to convict me. He was in the path of danger from two sides. First, the courts were planning to send him away for ninety years for his crimes if he refused to cooperate. But he was also in danger in the prison system, because everyone knew that my arrest was based on his lies. To ingratiate himself with me and the other prisoners, Bradley sent me notes that I was able to receive through the prison grapevine. From him I learned how the prosecution was going to proceed against me. I sent his notes to my lawyer, Raymond Brown. Had Bradley not sent me that information, we would have walked into the courtroom totally blind. The knowledge we gained saved Artis and me from being electrocuted. Those notes made me decide that if we were convicted, I would have to find a way to make our story known to the world outside the courtroom and the press. I said to Artis, "OK, I got you in here, but I'm going to get us out. I'm going to write a book and continue to work the law, and somehow I'll find a way to free us."

From that day on, I kept a journal. I wrote down my thoughts, my feelings, and my experiences, whatever details my memory could come up with. I figured that if I could train my body to become an elite professional prizefighter, then I could also train my mind to study law and write a book.

Writing *The Sixteenth Round* was one of the most difficult tasks of my life. To begin with, prison was a rough place run by rough people I had known from previous brushes with the law. And they knew me. I was in solitary half the time, writing on anything I could find, envelopes or little pieces of toilet paper, with the small nub of a pencil. I developed my own shorthand. Writing books had previously proved to be a risky business for people that the system earmarked as dangerous. George Jackson wrote *Soledad Brother* in 1970 and was killed in prison by the guards ten months after the book was published. In the movie, *The Hurricane,* you see Denzel Washington (playing me) in his cell with a typewriter. The film does not indicate, however, that typewriters at the time were only permitted for matters of the law. The only item of communication you were allowed in prison was a set of headphones for which you paid twenty-five dollars that were hooked up to the prison's radio with three stations. To get around the typewriter rule, I never let anyone read what I was writing. The guards, who were both intimidated by my presence and respectful of me, were happy enough to believe that it was just another legal brief. I would peck away on that big, old, black Underwood, transferring and adding to all the details from those ragged pieces of paper. If you've ever written anything in the dark, you know how bad the handwriting can appear when you are trying to make sense out of it. Add to that the problem of the constant cell searches by the guards and having only one working eye, and you can get some idea how arduous the process was. Even so, I was able to recapture my entire life in words, an accomplishment that provided the groundwork for the spiritual awakening I was to have after my second conviction.

Richard Solomon, an old acquaintance, was able to get the manuscript to Linda Yablonsky at Viking Press, and I was given a ten-thousand-dollar advance to complete the project. I still send copies of the book around the world, although it never ceases to amaze me that I really wrote it. Or that my name could be mentioned alongside the James Baldwins, the Claude Browns, the Eldridge Cleavers, and the other good, angry black writers of that time.

Not to say that I didn't have a little help in writing it. I only had an eighth-grade education. Trenton State Prison and Rahway had other aspiring writers, there being an underground book industry growing in American prisons at the time, and we would help one another. Tommy Trantino, reputed to be a cop killer, wrote a group of short stories called *Lock the Lock* that was published four years after *The Sixteenth Round*. Frank Andrews, Al Dickens, I, and a few others wrote a prison short-story anthology, *Voices from the Big House*, that we published ourselves with help from David Rothenberg of the Fortune Society. Andrews was also writing his own book. Most of these guys had gone the same matriculation route from Jamesburg that I had, so we were basically self-taught. If I had writer's block, I would send the pages down to Andrews, and he would get me straightened out. He also sent things to me, and I would provide him with a fresh perspective on his material. It also helped that I had read a lot as a child. Cowboy writers such as Louis L'Amour impressed me by the way they could keep a story fresh and interesting through powerful metaphor. I tried to imitate his writing style. I found out recently that he was also a former boxer.

I used the book as a lifeline. After the fallout from the killing of George Jackson in California and as an indirect result of Watergate, prisons were less likely to kill you or hurt you if they knew that outsiders were paying attention. I had the book sent to influential people, hoping they might read it and respond with an offer of help. Once I got that treasured response, I grabbed on to that person, gently but firmly. That became the means by which I slowly pulled myself up. When I got to the top of the walls, I saw in my mind's eye other wrongly convicted or persecuted people who were able to look out over their prison walls, Nelson Mandela, the Chicago Seven, Bobby Seale, all of us who would one day successfully transcend the confines and the culture of the prison.

The book was sent to Bob Dylan, Dyan Cannon, Muhammad Ali, Ellen Burstyn, Stevie Wonder, Aretha Franklin, Harry Belafonte—anyone who could publicize the case, anyone who might be in a position to help me. When Dylan came home from England, he spent three days with me at Trenton State. I was naïve enough to feel confident that with all this high-profile assistance, there was no way they could possibly keep me in jail.

Alternatively, the book was meant to be a "letter in a bottle" that I threw out over the thirty-six-foot-high walls into the ocean of life, hoping that somebody, anybody, perhaps a stranger, would find the bottle, read the message, and come to help Artis and me.

Imagine what it means for a wrongly convicted prisoner to know that people on the outside have faith in him! Then imagine that those people are some of the best-known people in the world. The state authorities and those at the prison know that you cannot just be made to fall off the map and disappear, that they must face the pressure of all those outside eyes on the inside. Then the judicial authorities know that they cannot bury you beneath a mountain of bureaucratic procedures and that they have to, at some point, deal with your case. Then imagine what it means to have Muhammad Ali walk into a courtroom and plunk down the bail money for you and your codefendant. All those opportunities were made possible only by the discipline of writing a book.

Another discipline I learned in prison was abstinence. In 1972, when the U.S. Supreme Court temporarily abolished the death penalty, Trenton State Prison still had a death house, twenty-eight isolated cells that had now been vacated. Because those who work the prison system are conduits of top-down information and rumormongers, prisoners know and feel what is going on in society even before those living out in society know. Prisoners can feel those ebbs and flows. When society becomes oppressive, prisoners are returned to stripes, chains, and shackles, isolation and violence. When society became liberal, and those were liberal times, the former death house was turned into a contact-visiting hall. The bars were removed, and the prisoners went inside with their visitors. A lot of babies were conceived in that death house, which to me had become nothing more than a brothel. There were written rules against sexual intercourse as there always have been, but the authorities did not enforce them. Maybe they figured that a prisoner who was able to have sex would be more pliable than a frustrated one. I found the whole practice completely disrespectful and would not allow my wife and child to visit me there. How degrading to pretend that a former death house where 160 tortured souls were put to death was a Shangri-La. Add to that the fact that you had to strip naked and have someone look up your butt before you were allowed the visit, and you can understand why I, as an innocent man, would find the whole charade repugnant.

Under the circumstances, I made a conscious decision to be celibate. The wonderful energy of sex is the most powerful energy to which a human being has access. That fact should come as no surprise, since sex is the act through which life itself is sustained. Abstinence and celibacy, however, if practiced with a directed purpose, can gather up this energy that we normally expend so nonchalantly. I wouldn't even indulge in the prisoner's solace, masturbation. Whatever the prison allowed or encouraged, I did not want, since it would all be under their auspices and control. Human sexuality must take place in freedom unless you enjoy feeling like an animal in captivity. And love, how can one talk about love in such a place? Love is free, and it must remain free—or it is not love.

The monk and the priest are supposed to be celibate, but this celibacy should not be seen, as it is by so many people, as an unnecessary punishment. There is nothing innately wrong with celibacy just as there is nothing innately wrong with sex. We are made to think that some priests are lecherous or prey upon children because their natural desires are suppressed, but I would say that if a priest is a womanizer or a pedophile, then that's the way he was before he became a priest. The real purpose of religious celibacy is to create the inner fire of Spiritual liberation and crystallize one's many "I's" into one "I." The fire arises from the friction that comes from the struggle between celibacy and desire; between abstinence and the habitual behaviors that enslave us; between essence, which is real, and personality, which is not real. Ultimately, when the inner fire, the Spiritual fire, burns hot enough, what emerges from the ashes is the positive energy of the higher mind.

———

All of these actions were connected—training my body through the discipline of denial, training my intellect through writing a book and studying the law, training my Spirit through the struggle with desire, through daily meditation, and through studying the works of the world's great minds. These actions or disciplines were steps along the way toward an idea of freedom that I could then just begin to imagine. It was a process in which I eventually learned that even while inside a prison there was no barrier in my life too great to ascend, too wide to get around, and that we live in a universe of unlimited possibilities.

In a very real sense, going to prison was the best thing that ever happened to me. Without it, I might never have stopped long enough on my journey to find out who I was. I would have been a bald-headed, mean-looking ex-prizefighter talking through a screen of conditioning, spewing forth anger and bitterness. Nevertheless, prison is not an experience I would recommend to anyone else. Sacrificing your physical freedom is not a necessary step on the road to self-discovery. Far better that you start the process of finding yourself today while still outside those brick walls. Far better that you understand the universal prison of sleep into which we are born. Start to find yourself by learning to control the habits that enslave you or the habits that may force additional prison time upon you.

You certainly don't want be another number in the prison population. That's because keeping folks who look like me locked away inside those iron cages has become big business. I'm old enough to remember when the prison system of the United States reflected its general population. If Italians, for example, were a certain percentage of the general population, that is roughly the percentage of Italians you would find in the prison population. So, needless to say, the prisoners were mostly white. They were served pasta fazool on Monday, shepherd's pie on Tuesday, Irish stew on Wednesday, and so on. The black folk caught hell from all sides, pure hell!

In the 1950s, when segregation began to be challenged openly, the United States assimilated a lot of its white prison population back into society, and began to fill the prisons with people of color, mainly blacks, because blacks were telling society with more than just words, *We want to be able to eat in this restaurant; we want to drink out of this water fountain; we want to ride on the front of this bus; we want equal education; we want to make a decent living.* The net was cast far and wide. Many young black men were arrested on petty or trumped-up charges or crimes of the poor, such as drug possession, prostitution, or vagrancy. More than 25 percent of the prison population is incarcerated because of drug convictions, but if you would add property crimes and violent behavior resulting from drug addiction it would be closer to 50 percent

For me, the drug problem in the United States mirrors the Opium Wars and the attempt by Great Britain to take over and subjugate China through the proliferation and trade of opium. The War on Drugs was and is a fantasy; the War on Drugs is just another war on the poor. Drugs destroy the body along with one's personal ambitions. Addiction creates numerous opportunities for exploitation. The society that is riddled with drugs usually imprisons the small growers, the users, and the street peddlers, not the big importers or the drug companies who fatten the coffers of political parties. Where money is everything, big money is God. All of these wars, the War on Poverty, the War on Drugs, the War on Crime, and even the War on Terror, stem from a society hooked on war. Wherever war is declared, Truth, as it is said, is always the first casualty.

On this level of life, the holy trinity is property, privacy, and material success. Six and a half million mostly poor American people are under the jurisdiction of the criminal justice system today. The cost of prison construction per year in the United States is more than 2.5 billion dollars for state-of-the-art penitentiaries, with almost 70 billion dollars spent annually on prison operations. Who can resist the smell of all that money?

That's why much of the system has been privatized. American justice is an oxymoron. It's big business. Behold, Lady Justice isn't blind! The dirty bitch has got dollar signs for eyeballs. It takes three billion dollars a year to house the 132,000 lifers alone. One-third of those serving life sentences are there for burglary and drug offenses but are doomed by the "three strikes" laws, which, after three convictions of any sort, can land a burglar or a drug addict in jail for life. This money might be better spent on programs to alleviate the conditions that breed crime, but then you would harm the profitable people-warehousing industry and its numerous employees.

Since 1970, there has been an actual decline in the crime rate, but the prison population has swelled to six times the number. Cemeteries inside prisons are growing faster than ever because parole is harder and harder to obtain and the writ of habeas corpus almost impossible. Politicians throw around prison building contracts like candy on Halloween.

Were it not for the out-of-the-way prisons on the back roads of America, many rural economies that used to depend on small-scale farming would be hard-pressed to keep their populations. In fact, urban criminals in these institutions are included in the rural census, giving these communities a disproportionate amount of political power. Of course, prisoners are not allowed to vote.

Now, I know there are those who want to believe in the justice system or may believe that the system is working to bring about a more just society or that nothing is perfect and so on. They may continue to believe, in the face of all evidence to the contrary, that Africans in America are a criminal class of people and that crime is a genetic trait of some sort. In response to these illusions, I'd like to point to another statistic that shows that the United States is not the only place where such things as racial profiling occur. In France, 10 percent of the total population is Muslim, but 50 percent of its prison population is Muslim, similar to the percentage of black people in the U.S. prison system based upon the overall population. The prison representation of Native populations in Canada and Australia is also largely disproportionate.

What I am saying here is that justice systems tend to function as a means of population control against a particular group; abstract notions of justice are a convenient fiction to hide behind. There may be good people within the system, but they are in no position to decide which acts constitute crimes and which crimes will send a person to jail. Up until recently, possession of more than five grams of crack cocaine was a felony that drew a mandatory sentence of five years, while possession of a hundred times more powdered cocaine, a drug that has worked its way into corporate offices, is a misdemeanor. In July 2010, Congress changed the ratio of powdered cocaine to crack from a hundred to one to eighteen to one and restricted the five-year sentence to dealers. Despite more or less equal drug use between blacks and whites, African Americans are still thirteen times more likely to wind up in jail on drug charges. In New York, according to the New York Civil Liberties Union, more than 90 percent of the people in prison under the Rockefeller drug laws are African American and Hispanic. Those laws, enacted in 1973, remove judicial discretion in sentencing.

As to dangerous drugs, cocaine and heroin are not as dangerous as Vioxx, an anti-inflammatory medication that may have been responsible for heart attacks in an estimated fifty to one hundred thousand cases. Now that's a real crime! Until recently, an outright pardon or community service was given to those about whom judges and lawyers said, "A jail term would serve no purpose." I always laughed when I heard that. There are only two purposes of incarceration: to hold you or to kill you. I defy anyone to prove otherwise. Any purpose that prisoners find in prison does not arise from the creators and administrators of the prison but from themselves.

What we need to understand more than anything is that brutal or unnecessarily lengthy punishment in a hostile environment does nothing to alleviate the problem of crime. Execution does not serve this purpose either. To quote no less a thinker than Albert Einstein: "No problem can be solved from the same level of consciousness that created it." I recognize that certain people need to be off the streets because they are a danger to society, but we must not delude ourselves into believing that we are doing anything more than punishing people in the most reactionary way. If a boys' institution such as Jamesburg, with no holding cells, has an 82 percent recidivism rate, what can be expected of giant prison warehouses? If the prison system worked, then the United States of America would be the world's safest place.

———

September 11 was the punch that America did not see coming, though maybe it should have. Tony Blair said that September 11 briefly awakened the world to the reality of terrorism, but then the world went back to sleep. I agree with him insofar as we should have awakened and stayed awake, but I would argue that we need to learn as much about ourselves as about the vicious nature of terrorism.

The West may have concluded that something is not right in the world and that changes needed to be made. But I would argue that what was needed was a change in our perceptions of the world and in our wasteful, arrogant ways. I think this awakening happened among a large segment of the population. For one brief historical moment, I saw people of every nationality, both victims and outsiders, showing concern for one another and recognizing their common humanity.

But Bush, Blair, and their handmaidens in the media focused on the actors instead of the evil act. We were treated to a Christian morality play and the usual display of false duality. America was good. Bin Laden was evil; the terrorists hated our way of life. "Either you are with us or you are with the terrorists," Bush proclaimed. Another of the "evil ones," Saddam Hussein, was presented as the ultimate villain who, it was falsely alleged, threatened the world with his weapons of mass destruction and whose reign of terror had to be overthrown.

Not only did we, the people, lose sight of the actual enemy, but we also failed to understand what we were fighting against. With the good-versus-evil scenario, it was no longer necessary to look inward, nor was it necessary to analyze the rage that other people felt against the United States. In fact, George W. Bush told Americans to go shopping, to continue to do what they had been doing, and to be only as afraid as he said they ought to be. The reason people went back to sleep, then, is that they were encouraged to do so.

One component of the law of accident mirrors Newton's Third Law of Motion: for every action there is an equal and opposite reaction. The only means of stopping this endless cycle of action/ reaction on this level of life is by waking up, by rising above the mechanical, and by choosing to act from Consciousness. We must not forget that September 11, as awful and spectacular as it was, did not begin the chain of events but was itself a reaction to a long heritage of colonial policies in North Africa and the Middle East. We cannot do nothing (how can one do nothing in the face of slaughter and destruction?), but what we do must be aimed at alleviating the problem, not adding to it.

What I mean by adding to the problem is reflected in how the Bush administration dealt with September 11. The so-called war on terrorism began with the UN-sponsored invasion of Afghanistan to root out the Taliban and the illegal invasion and occupation of Iraq, even while most of the terrorists originated from Egypt and Saudi Arabia. Inside both the United States and Canada, we witnessed the abandonment of due process, further restrictions on granting writs of habeas corpus, and permission to use torture by proxy. It is hard for me to see how any of these reactions were justified. Only a sleeping population could allow itself, for some false notion of security, to be manipulated into believing that we must remove the very legal protections through which our society gains the respect of our own people and of others around the world. How could the United States have imprisoned people for years without letting them know the crimes they had been charged with?

The Supreme Court struck back in 2006 and told Bush that these detentions without charges were illegal, so the Bush administration and Congress changed the law itself. The Military Commissions Act of 2006 denied the right of habeas corpus to non-citizens the president "deems to have provided material support to anti-

American hostilities." In June 2008, the Supreme Court, in a land-mark 5–4 decision, restored *limited* habeas corpus rights to those at Guantanamo Bay. The wonder for me is that the decision was so close while the right is so fundamental to any democracy. Writing for the majority, Justice Anthony Kennedy did not mince words: "The laws and Constitution are designed to survive and remain in force in extraordinary times."

The United States was established by visionary, awakened, and conscious people, slaveholders though many may have been; the religious zeal, the outright blindness, and the avarice of the Bush administration have compromised the Constitution, thereby weakening the country's very foundation. These measures, according to American security sources especially requested to look into the matter, have served to increase the numbers of angry, fanatical people blowing themselves up and killing innocent bystanders. In fact, our exclusively warlike reactions, because they are mechanical, have been predictable, whereas the terrorists have maintained the advantage of surprise.

On that day, September 11, I was in an airplane at Toronto's Pearson Airport, taxiing down the runway. I had been scheduled for a speaking engagement in Rhode Island and was thinking about what a beautiful day it was. Suddenly the engines cut off. We were not going anywhere. So we sat there and sat there until finally the pilot announced that we were going back to the terminal. The televisions were playing in the terminal, so we were soon made aware of what had happened. The authorities had closed America down, completely and utterly. Nobody was going in or coming out.

The totality of that act frightened me and reminded me of a nightmare scenario I've had in the back of my mind for quite some time. I may have first heard these ideas from Malcolm X. He would say that if another holocaust were to occur in this world, it could only occur in the United States of America. In this nightmare scenario, I hear someone of authority ask the question: *What are we going to do with this mass of undeveloped black humanity that has invaded our inner cities and lives in ghettos? Who are the consumers of everything and the producers of nothing? Why don't we take back our cities and get these people out of the way?* During the aftermath of Hurricane Katrina in New Orleans, a general whose soldiers had just shot and killed four desperate people said much the same thing: "We're going to take back this city."

There was no need to kill anybody. The United States already has a prison population of more than two million people, the largest in the world, many times larger per capita than even China, which has only one and a half million prisoners even though it is a virtual police state with more than a billion people. Yes, China does brutally execute many of its citizens but not enough of them to come anywhere near the incarceration rate of the United States. African American women are being incarcerated at the same rate as white men: eighty-six thousand and counting.

I must repeat that one out of every three Africans in America between the ages of twelve and thirty-seven is already under the control of the criminal justice system, one-in-nine actually behind bars. One out of every four prisoners of any type worldwide is held in the United States. More than 70 percent of the prison population is nonwhite, poor, and largely uneducated.

Is it too farfetched to imagine an even larger number of people of color being rounded up and put into more and more holding cells and prisons...and then, maybe, eliminated? Who would oppose the United States? They have already opted out of the International Court of Justice and the Geneva Conventions. The only thing preventing a holocaust anywhere in the world is respect for the rule of law, but, with the passage of the Military Commissions Act in October 2006, it was shown that American law hangs by a slender thread, the 5–4 Supreme Court vote that restored *limited* rights of habeas corpus to foreign nationals.

The Military Commissions Act was passed because of fear, ignorance, and paranoia. It still shocks me that America, that great shining example of democracy to the world, could have moved in the direction of the totalitarian monster it so much reviled.

Since the beginning of human history, civilizations have risen, prospered, and fallen along two very definite lines of development: the line of construction and the line of destruction. The line of construction consists of the institutions we create: schools, libraries, economic structures, systems of government, the ideas behind them, and the buildings that house them. The moment we begin to place value on the line of construction, we immediately introduce into the picture the line of destruction, because we want to protect that which we see as being valuable.

That is why America's military is run by what is called the Department of Defense. As long as the lines of construction and destruction grow side by side, one helping the other, that society will flourish. If the line of construction gets too far ahead of the line of destruction, that becomes a weak society, a society that cannot defend itself from military conquest. But if the line of destruction, expansion, conquest, and control gets too far ahead of the line of construction, that society also fails.

Those who serve the line of destruction begin to believe that the line of construction was created for them. In the United States of America, the line of destruction—the military, the prison system, the FBI, the CIA, and now Homeland Security—has for decades increasingly consumed more resources than the line of construction. Of course, these institutions have a protective function, but it is alarming that more money is spent on prison operations and prison construction, for example, than on school construction. The bloated military-industrial complex has redundant powers, maintaining more than seven hundred military bases around the world, keeping and selling an arsenal of weapons that could destroy humanity many times over. Science departments and research labs at universities continually prostitute themselves for military contracts.

Where might all of this excessive destructive capacity be leading? During World War II, in Germany's Third Reich, the line of destruction completely obliterated the line of construction. Germany became a state dedicated to the production of death. A large proportion of the general population was either in uniform or serving those in uniform; the factories pumped out weapons and death; the trains delivered death; the concentration camps produced death. Science itself, the greatest of all life-sustaining disciplines, was placed in the service of human experimentation and death, the science of producing mass death as quietly and efficiently as possible. That is the worst extreme to which the line of destruction can lead a "civilized" society.

American prisons also kill. Diseases permeate these places; some are almost impossible to resist. Before my release from prison in 1985, a dangerous epidemic of tuberculosis broke out at Trenton State. Unbeknownst to me, I had contracted the germ, which then lay dormant for seven years. In 1989, that old TB woke up and knocked me flat. I almost died. After I had recovered, the TB germ attached itself to a stitch that had been negligently left in my eye during the botched prison operation. More than two decades after the eye surgery, I had to have the whole eye removed.

If you say I was lucky, that TB is better than AIDS, which has killed thousands of prisoners since 1985, you would be right. Because the prison population has a large percentage of intravenous drug users and persons who engage in homosexual activity, prisons are a high-risk environment for both HIV and hepatitis.

But the conditions in a prison, even for those who abstain from drugs or sexual activity, foster the spread of illness. Prisons are crowded places, especially in the privatized world of the United States, where each prisoner means so many dollars. Individuals live side by side, stacked one on top of the other in five-by-seven-foot cages. The environment is not only enclosed, but there is no ventilation. The prisoner can hear the person next door to him brush his teeth; he can hear and smell him going to the bathroom. When a cold or the flu starts to circulate or a prisoner or food worker has tuberculosis, the entire population is at high risk of contracting it too. Sadly, the only reason that anyone cares about these epidemics is worry for the health of the guards and the prison administration.

I have heard from African American community leaders and others that the reason for the public's disregard for the welfare of people in prisons is racism. I would like to draw a distinction here between racism and tribalism. Tribalism is a better description of our group psychosis.

In our societies, people are conditioned along tribal lines. I use the word *tribalism* because racism presupposes that there is more than one race of people on this planet. That is just another lie we live with. There is only one race of people, the human race. We all belong to it. The drawing of artificial distinctions among people, and skin color is the most artificial of all, is the result of tribal conditioning. Tribes attempt to ensure the survival of people who look like them, act like them, smell like them, talk like them, or believe like them at the cost of any other segment of humanity. A tribal mentality divides people into opposites, black and white, French and English, rich and poor, Muslim and Christian, or any other unconscious way that divisions can be made. Only in the examples of language and religion are the differences more than superficial, although still not meaningful.

One day, I was flying back from the West Coast, and in the seat pocket in front of me was a newspaper folded open to an Ann Landers column. In that column, Landers printed a poem by James Patrick Kinney that fits perfectly with my understanding of tribalism. It is called "The Cold Within":

Six men trapped by happenstance
In dark and bitter cold;
Each one possessed a stick of wood,
Or so the story's told.

Their dying fire in need of logs,
The first man held his back,
For of the faces 'round the fire
He noticed one was black.

The next man looked across the way,
Saw one not of his church,

And couldn't bring himself to give
The fire his stick of birch.

The third man, dressed in tattered clothes,
Then gave his coat a hitch.
Why should his log be given up
To warm the idle rich?

The rich man sat back thinking of
The wealth he had in store,
And how to keep what he had earned
From going to the poor.

The black man's face bespoke revenge,
While fire passed from sight,
Saw only in his stick of wood,
A way to spite the white.

The last man of this forlorn group,
Did nothing but for gain,
Give only unto those who gave
Was how he played the game.

The logs held firm in death-stilled hands
Was proof of human sin.
They died not from the cold without
But from the cold within.

That is the problem of tribalism, and that will be its deadly, destructive consequence as long as people remain asleep. The poison from opposite sides of the fire seeps down into every aspect of human lives all over the world. In the world of wrongful convictions, my own included, injustices do not originate with the law itself but with the tribalism of people who enforce the law and those who must live under it. When tribes are continually at war, a wrongful conviction is nothing more than collateral damage. And don't ask about lethal prison conditions. Don't those people deserve it?

Prisons may not yet be concentration camps, although they do share some of the same practices, virtual slave labor for one. Prison can destroy all that is valuable in a human being, be he innocent or guilty. He becomes an object to be guarded with a maximum of security and a minimum of compassion. He has a number, albeit not branded on the arm, by which he is referred. He is caged, kept, and counted. Cruelty, humiliation, degradation, and constant danger are so destructive to his psyche that the prison system doesn't need to kill him *physically*.

In all ways possible, those behind bars are dehumanized. All the prisoner's decision-making powers are taken away. He is told when to eat and how fast, when to sleep and for how long, when to leave his cell, when to go back in. He might get to decide whether to exercise or whether to stand up or sit down in his cell. But once released, if he is lucky enough, he is expected to act normally, to be self-sufficient, as though he had just nipped out to the corner store for a newspaper and didn't return for twenty years. As if he is not suffering from mental disorders like post-traumatic stress, depression, and disassociation. Do you wonder why released prisoners, offered little counseling and less opportunity, tend to become drug addicts and pushers, if they haven't already become that while behind bars?

Don't forget either the terrible toll imprisonment takes on

families, friends, and relationships. Children—how do they come to terms with the disappearance of fathers and mothers who seem to have abandoned them? And parents—how do they continue to believe in their children when the system says they are criminals?

Young people living on the streets or in desperate circumstances look around them and see poverty, violence, and despair. On television and in film, they have seen the lives of people far better off than themselves. Even on the streets, they see the drug dealers, the hustlers, the supposed success stories in their neighborhoods, driving around in Mercedes and BMWs. The message to them is clear: *It's OK to get anything you want, any way you can.* They arm themselves. They live by codes that are throwbacks to the Wild Wild West. "Disrespect" them and you'll be shot. God help innocent bystanders or anybody who talks to the police. These young people go on to fill up the beds in the emergency wards of our hospitals, the training schools, the penitentiaries, the death rows, and the cemeteries.

Is there some master plan at work here? Could it be that the need to fill the prisons is the cause both of the numerous wrongful convictions and of the lack of opportunity in the black communities? At least that would explain the punitive drug laws and three-strike programs in the United States. In reality, though, I do not think that I am talking here about intended policy. If it were intentional, it would not have "succeeded" to the degree that it has. More likely, these things happen not by design but by the kind of unconscious human insanity that dominates everything on this level of life. Governors, presidents, legislators, and judges believe or have convinced themselves that they are being "tough on crime."

When you get right down to brass tacks, all it really means is hurting others of a different tribe. But those who bring forth and pass such policies have to also live with the consequences of these policies.

Most prisoners will eventually return to society at least once or twice. They will not come back as reformed, gentle souls. Through contact with others in the system, they might even have learned to be better criminals. Once prison has robbed them of their self-respect, they will no longer have any respect for you, your life, or your property, especially if employment is denied, and no counseling awaits them on the outside. If a person is treated as though he were inhuman and he then behaves inhumanly, should you be surprised? Should you be surprised if he fails to respect your rights? Stripped of his humanity, he has no problem taking your valuables or your life. When we make it impossible for people to be anything but criminals, they tend to live down to our beliefs; when we encourage, work with, and believe in them, they tend to rise to our expectations.

The picture I have painted here is somewhat hopeless, but I am an optimist, and the picture also represents the necessary conditions for awakening. The election of Barack Obama to the presidency of the United States is a significant moment in history, a crossroads where people can go in a different direction. His very election is a blow to tribalism, but the potential to subvert this opportunity is immense. Young people, not scarred by the bitter racial divisions of past years, made Obama's election possible. With the many problems he faces, none may be greater than the expectations of black people. Africans in America, who have suffered disproportionately from a flawed justice system, expect to see the system become less punitive and more responsive. He will face enormous opposition.

For many of those wrongly convicted who have tried in vain to tweak the system, hopelessness can only be vanquished by the most intensive efforts. Their numbers are great; various legal organizations in the United States estimate that at any given time, between 0.5 percent to 10 percent of all criminal convictions are in error, or anywhere from 12,500 to 200,000 people. Hope for them is not to be found in the abstractions of the law, since blind justice is a fiction. Although they need to use the law to be released, they must get beyond the law to find true liberation. They must escape the universal prison of sleep before they walk out of the actual prison. Hope comes not from within the system but within the self. Hope comes in the form of one who can see what has not yet come to be and causes that to come into existence. Hope is a hole in the wall.

5

The Hole in the Wall:
Finding the Higher Path

My first conviction in the Lafayette Bar and Grill murders lacked the ring of "Truth" because no motive had ever been established for the crime. When John Artis and I received a new trial in 1976, the state suddenly concocted a story that I was a black racist intent on exacting revenge upon all white people. A black bar owner had been shot and killed by a white man earlier that night in another part of town. Establishing this motive was key for the prosecution. Most of their witnesses were shady and unreliable, jailhouse snitches, people who might have difficulty convincing a jury that they were telling the truth. But if I were to defend myself in court by testifying on my own behalf, the prosecution was going to read into the record, out of context, passages from *The Sixteenth Round* in which I expressed anger toward white people. But if I did not testify, the book could not then be entered into the record on rebuttal, because of the Fifth Amendment right against self-incrimination. So I decided not to testify. My silence did not play well with the jury. It never does. And notwithstanding the lack of hard evidence against me, the prosecutors were able to successfully establish their false motive of racial revenge, a motive that rang true to a jury that was living through years of racial rioting and political turmoil in America's inner cities. Once again we were found guilty.

Going back to prison in December 1976 was the lowest point of my life. I felt that I'd let down all the well-intentioned people who had tried to rescue me. All their work had been wasted. All the money from concerts: Dylan's "The Night of the Hurricane" in Madison Square Garden; the benefit concert at the Houston Astro-dome; and all the resources of the Hurricane Trust Fund had been swallowed up by lawyers. Two juries now believed that John Artis and I had murdered three innocent people. I saw friends turning away from me, feeling it was time to cut their losses and close the ledger. And who could blame them?

While I was out on bail before the second trial, my speeches were provocative and violent. In my mind, I was simply telling it like it is, "socking it to them," as they used to say: "Somebody put his hands on you, send him to the cemetery." Osama Bin Laden had nothing on me! I spoke at universities. People even urged me to run for political office, to run for Congress. What a ridiculous idea! I was seething inside. But then, don't we sometimes elect narrow and reactionary people who reflect our own emotional states?

My advocates and supporters also did not understand that when I was granted bail before the second trial began, a long road, legally and spiritually, still stretched out ahead of me. The general feeling seemed to be: *We got you out. That's what you wanted us to do. You got a new trial.* They did not understand that convictions, especially murder convictions, are the fuel and the grease of the criminal jus-tice system. Once a person has been found guilty, it takes a monumental effort to reverse that decision. Careers—political, legal, and otherwise—are built upon criminal convictions. Successful police officers are promoted; successful prosecuting attorneys become judges. A successful judge goes to a higher court, even the Supreme Court. A successful judge in our system of jurisprudence is a careful judge, not necessarily a wise or just one, but one who makes sure he is rarely reversed on appeals.

So I was back in prison in New Jersey. My despair was deep and indescribably wrenching, but, despite all I had learned and all of the legal work I had done, I was not yet ready to leave the prison. I was still angry. I still considered myself a victim. Before my second trial, I was just desperate for the clean air of freedom. I didn't know that prison life had warped me just as I had been warped after leaving Annandale Reformatory; that ten long years of anger and hate and bitterness at Trenton State had warped my very soul. All I knew then was that Rubin "Hurricane" Carter was an innocent victim, and someone would have to pay the price for that!

The first thing I did was to barricade myself in my cell and go back to the beginning of my case. I thought I could find some legal loophole that had been overlooked to bolster another appeal attempt. Even after two bogus trials, I still believed in the power of the law. I was convinced that some wise judge would understand that the power of Truth had not yet entered the courtroom. I did not realize that the law and the Truth were incompatible—they do not exist on the same levels of life—and that a wise judge was an exception to the rule.

Wrongful convictions and the appellate process are like corridors in one of those wide suburban motels: the appellant and his lawyer can be found walking up and down the halls, hoping that the missing information lies behind one of those doors—the recanting witnesses or that piece of DNA evidence that will exonerate the accused. Sometimes the door is slammed in their faces; they hear the chain and the deadbolt. Sometimes they find the door unlocked and the room vacant; they can see from the soiled linen and cigarette butts how others have tried this room and failed. Sometimes they see a gold nugget sitting on the bedspread, a precedent, perhaps, that has worked in other cases, and begin to celebrate, only to have the court reject their arguments because they were out of time; they missed the deadline! The appellant gets only one chance in each room, and then the room is sealed forever.

By 1977, I was running out of doors. To make matters worse, because I was now twice convicted, fewer people believed in me, so there was no longer the same pressure on the state from outside the prison. Soon, I started running low on the one element that had sustained me to date: hope.

The prison itself was unbearable. The heat was suffocating. If it was ninety degrees outside, it was one hundred and five degrees inside. In winter, the cold rattled teeth and bones. Behind those walls, all disguises of civility no longer existed. Everything now was simply raw, naked violence, pain, humiliation, and hatred. All of the normal states of identification—social, religious, and political— were now gone! I felt I was dying to the world, falling out of the picture. *Democracy gone! Constitution gone! Normality gone!* There was precious little I could trust or believe in. I was then in a perfect place and in a perfect state of mind for my Spirit to begin its journey.

———

When you spend a great deal of time in darkness (where I spent ten out of twenty years), you might begin to see things more vividly than you have ever seen them before. It might take days, weeks, months, years, but, if you don't go stark raving mad or kill yourself, you might begin to see yourself as you have never seen yourself before. While you cannot look into darkness from the light and detect forms, from the darkness you can see forms in the light. From the darkness of solitary confinement, where I could not see outwardly, my blind eye found the light by looking inward.

From that very cell, I remembered the biblical story about King Solomon, who had a dream in which God came to him and told him, "Ask me for anything and I will give it to you."

And King Solomon answered, "I am but a little child. I know not how to go out or to come in, but I am a servant of thy people. Give me, therefore, an understanding heart that I may judge thy people wisely and fairly."

And God said, "Because you did not ask for the lives of your enemies, did not ask for longevity, did not ask for riches, because you asked only for this one thing, understanding, I will give you understanding. There will be none wiser than you on this earth."

In remembering this story from my childhood, I was always impressed by King Solomon's wisdom and humility. As a judge, he wanted to be wise and fair, but he also understood how difficult such a task would be. He seemed to care little for the things most other people lived for. Most important, King Solomon made me understand that I can still be a man and yet not seek revenge for the wrongs that have been done to me. This may be a foreign idea to the mythology of imperial countries or in the minds of religious fanatics, but it now took root in me.

I also remembered what my good friend Ali Hasson had said about the divine spark in me and in every other human being. I realized that even the people I hated—those who had put me in jail—must also have this divine spark in them. I also had to admit for the first time that I was not blameless; the acts I had committed, the words I had said, the attitude I had carried resulted in my being in this place and in this cell.

———

One very hot day in the dead of summer, I decided to go out on the yard. Being locked in a five-by-seven cell, I could only take four steps forward and four steps back. The yard at Trenton State Prison is built over a paupers' cemetery. It is rectangular, one-eighth of a mile in circumference, barren of vegetation, stifling hot, and bone dry. Manned gun towers loom above from where the sun beats down.

That day I walked that eighth of a mile, the longest I'd walked in a very long time, and sat down against the wall completely exhausted.

As I leaned against the wall, I looked across the yard at the opposite wall, a thirty-six-foot brick wall. I was just staring at the wall, and something strange began to happen. I rubbed my eyes because I could not believe what I was seeing. A pinprick of light was coming through that solid wall. As I stared at the light, it began to quiver and grow bigger and bigger. Eventually, I could see through the wall! I could see cars passing by in the street. I could see schoolchildren coming back from classes.

Am I hallucinating? I thought. *Can anybody else see this?*

And the moment I began to think about it, as suddenly as the hole appeared, it disappeared.

I was absolutely flabbergasted. I could not shake off the experience. Maybe that hole in the wall was my avenue of escape, just as that one road out of Jamesburg had proven to be. I became determined, right then and there, to find that hole in the wall again. I was prepared to do whatever it took, and this time I was going to walk right through it, even if it deposited me somewhere in infinity, even if it seared the flesh off my bones, even if that hole meant my instant death. I was going to walk right through it. Anything is better than a lifetime in prison.

When I returned to my cell that afternoon, I gathered up all of my law books. I had been immersed in the law for more than ten years; I knew hundreds of legal precedents and all of the Latin phraseology. My case was and is the longest-litigated case in the history of New Jersey, and most of the legal work had been done by me. In filing many of the legal briefs for myself, I learned how to do the same for other prisoners. But that day I gave all of my law books away.

The other prisoners could not believe it. They thought I had gone crazy, and from one point of view, I had. But I knew then that the law was not my way out of prison. The law had become for me, at least for the moment, a dead-end corridor. The law, bound in as it is in logic and precedent, was just another prison. My way out of prison was finding that hole in the wall again and crossing over.

I was convinced that if I was able to train and control my physical body to become one of the top fighters in the world, if I was able to train my mind to write books and study the law, then if there is such a thing as the Spirit—something higher than this level of existence—if that hole in the wall really showed me the way to freedom, then I was going to find it again. I would train my Spirit to go the distance.

This was the discipline of all disciplines. I began to understand that if you want the ultimate, you have to be willing to pay the ultimate price. These ideas came to me beyond the normal level of thought—I didn't think them, I felt them. They were irresistible and inevitable just as the Truth is irresistible and inevitable.

When I sat down in my empty cell that night, I cried and cried, not from sorrow but from the exhilarating experience of affirmation. My life now had a purpose and a direction. In fact, all of life has purpose. How difficult could it be for me to transcend the law when I already knew that its prison walls are insubstantial? The law is a product of the mind just as those prison walls are nothing more than mind made visible. Whatever doubts I had about becoming psychotic or unhinged from being institutionalized too long vanished. Doubt can never coexist with affirmation.

I locked myself down, again. This time, it was not from pride, anger, or defiance but from the need to explore, in a concentrated fashion, the furthest reaches of human thought, both scientific and metaphysical. I stopped reading the hate mail and the fan mail. I stopped responding to the autograph seekers, answering endless questions about what foods I liked, about my wife, about Muhammad Ali, Malcolm X, Miles Davis, Martin Luther King Jr., and other famous people I grew up with and had known. These piles of letters were pushed into a corner under the bed. That was all triviality to me now. I would transform my prison cell into a laboratory of the human spirit.

One of my last remaining lifelines to the outside world was Thom Kidrin. Along with cans of soup, he brought me philosophical works, books on history, religion, and metaphysics. These books reaffirmed for me a world I now knew existed, a world of infinite possibility, a world of Consciousness that soared far above the limitations of everyday life. I would study for three days at a time, seventy-two hours straight, eight or nine books laid out on the bed.

I was panning for gold, searching for that hole in the wall. I began to know after reading two or three pages if what I was reading was conscious material or something to be discarded. I read the New Testament and found in all the words of Jesus a call for mankind to awaken. I became familiar with Einstein, Plato, Socrates, Krishnamurti, Frankl, Nietzsche, Zola, Gurdjieff, and Ouspensky. These were my new cellmates.

In man's search for meaning, Frankl helped me understand that even in the most horrific conditions—a concentration camp—a person can still find meaning. I could intensify my inner growth rather than giving in to the squalor and degradation. Well, in my mind, I, too, was in a concentration camp. Like Frankl, I was innocent. My captors hated me as his captors had hated him, and for the same irrational reasons. I saw myself doing what he had done, trying to throw off hatred and thoughts of revenge in the process.

I reread sections of the Old Testament and the Qur'an, immersed myself in the Bhagavad Gita and the Kabbalah. Days at a time, eschewing hunger and other worldly desires, I felt my mind undergoing a literal transformation. The understanding I had been seeking was to be found right there.

Krishnamurti, in *What Has Happened to Mankind*, made me understand that being alone was an opportunity: "When the pain of loneliness comes upon you, confront it, look at it without any thought of running away. If you run away, you will never understand it, and it will always be there waiting for you around the corner." Krishnamurti, however, believed that spiritual freedom could be attained in a single spectacular moment of understanding and awakening. The traditional viewpoint demands a much longer approach. Nevertheless, what captured my interest in his teachings was his belief that inner richness and happiness require the death of the man-made self, the death of our own self-image, which is an obsession for the majority of humankind. This message struck a chord with me, the "Hurricane," bald, black, bearded, and mean!

The moment I picked up P. D. Ouspensky's *In Search of the Miraculous*, a physiological phenomenon began to take place in me each time I went back to its pages. I experienced a tingling sensation in the top of my head, a hint of ecstasy, like a Geiger counter in the presence of radioactivity. While Krishnamurti talked about "how to act" from the level of Consciousness, Ouspensky—through his memorializing of G. I. Gurdjieff—taught humanity how to attain Consciousness because, as they agreed, one cannot become conscious unconsciously.

In studying *In Search of the Miraculous*, I realized I had come into contact with something far different than the faith-based system of Christianity I had known. Gurdjieff broke the universe down into an understandable, scientific plan, a plan that is compatible with quantum mechanics and twenty-first-century physics. Unlike Judeo-Christianity, in which man is said to be given complete dominion over the earth, Gurdjieff taught that man's place in the universe is the evolving portion of organic life on earth. This tendency to see ourselves as different or separate from other life on earth is just another illusion propagated through the power of the magician, the power of Kundalini. Kundalini, then, is not really the life-giving force that some occultists have deemed it to be, but the power of hypnosis that causes us to be satisfied with the imaginary instead of the real.

I also began to understand why I had ended up inside a prison. I was part of a "mechanical world" which my persecutors and I had been born into and then put to sleep. Childhood defiance against my father grew into open defiance against the injustices of America. That made it easy for police and the legal system to collaborate in my wrongful conviction. They needed me to be guilty! We were all trapped in a cycle of savagery, condemnation, retribution, and self-justification.

I also became aware of a merciful Creator. The Creator, the Absolute, had placed me in this depraved place for a reason. I then extended this reality to everybody—both those inside and those outside the prison walls. Without Consciousness, we are all in maximum-security lockdown, doomed by genetics to play out our mechanical roles until the day we die. Darwinian theory, in its most mechanistic interpretations, is applicable on this level of life. As I said before, it's big fish swallowing smaller fish.

I came to understand that mercy itself lies in the fact that as individuals we can escape the confines of this maximum-security prison of sleep, and that we have been given all of the necessary tools to accomplish this task. The level of life on which we find ourselves is real in the sense that physicality, joy, thought, suffering, and death are real, but it is an illusion—driven by the power of Kundalini—for us to "think" that this is the only level available to us. Consciousness is available to us only on a higher level, the place where absolute Truth is not a beggar but a king. A Chinese proverb illustrates this point to perfection: "There are three truths: my truth, your truth, and the Truth."

During my studies, I came to understand that this level of life—this level of unconscious human insanity—unlike the level of absolute Truth, is subject to immutable laws: karma, "what goes around, comes around," "what you sow, so shall you reap," action/

reaction, and the like. These laws describe the mechanical nature of our lives and the inescapable consequences of our actions. I began to understand that everything I had done for as long as I could remember had been driven by my image, or living up to my image, as opposed to my real self.

As I continued to immerse myself in "the work," the tingling sensation in my head that started out as only a seed began to grow and expand until my entire brain was filled with ecstasy. I had never been blessed with anything like that before; the longer I worked, the more the seed grew. And this drove me on. I didn't know the end point, but I was certain that the path was right. And it was!

One night, as I pored through these books, the seed in my head burst, and my entire body was filled with radiance. I became one with everything that existed! I thought I was going to die! No one could feel this way and live. But when the guards roused the prisoners the next morning, somehow, I was still there, weeping and laughing. A heavy part of me seemed to have died. I had never felt so thankful for everything that is.

Had I become the light I had been seeking? No words can describe the ecstasy that I felt. If you were able to make love to the person of your wildest dreams, you may feel an nth of the ecstasy I felt at that moment, and what was most wonderful was the realization that the experience was not just transitory. There were days when I would soar far above the surface of the prison. I actually felt ideas, ideas from every part of the world, blending inside me into one harmonious whole with the universe. I felt love for the world and everything in it. Former prisoners and guards have told me that they could hear my laughter and sometimes my cries of joy in every dark corner of the prison. I had "gone away," about as far off as I could go and still be on the earth. In describing what happened, I can only say that the protective shell of the "Hurricane," that tic of personality, had been breached, and my essence was now revealed.

I looked into the mirror again and began to understand that the bald-headed, mean-looking, ex-prizefighter who hated everybody—who was conditioned to hate everybody including himself—was not the real Rubin Carter. The face I saw was no more real than a Halloween mask. It was a persona I had taken on because people admired and expected it. The more people admired me for it, the more mechanical and reactionary I became. Now, for the first time in my life, I began to love the man I saw in the mirror. I no longer had to wear the mask. A new life for me was possible, but only if I dared to continue down this road to change.

———

Years after my release from prison, I went out to dinner with Denzel Washington. It was my job to find an actor to play the role of Rubin "Hurricane" Carter in an upcoming film directed by Norman Jewison. I had already interviewed quite a number of actors: people like Samuel L. Jackson; Lou Gossett Jr.; Isaac Hayes; Wesley Snipes; Marvin Hagler, the former middleweight boxing champion; and even Spike Lee! And now I was with Denzel Washington. After dinner, I left the table for a washroom break, and when I returned, the actor had also left the table. I wondered for a second or two if he had walked out on me. But then I noticed him at the front of the restaurant making strange gestures while staring into a mirror. When he returned to the table, we continued to talk, and something began to happen that I can only describe as falling in love! I loved his vocabulary. I loved his attitude. I loved his stridency. And

I just loved his laughter. For another brief moment, I wondered if all those years in prison had finally got to me. But then it hit me like a double left hook and a straight right cross. As I had watched him peering into the mirror, he was clearing his canvas, so to speak, in preparation for portraying me. And when he returned to the table, he began giving me back to me. And I was loving what I saw. I loved me! Washington was only an actor doing his utmost to sell himself for a role he wanted. But my feelings for my likeness sitting across that table showed me how far I had come from self-hatred to the love of self.

———

While still locked away in Trenton State Prison, the ecstasy I felt opened other doors. I read incessantly. I grabbed on to ideas any way I could. I swallowed ideas, gorged myself on them, to the point where everything else seemed extraneous. I wouldn't spend time at the parole board where the proceedings had become nothing but a mindless charade. I needed all of my time for my education. Everything about the prison was for the prison, not for me. I would not mop their floors. I would not waste time talking to their psychologist or being tested and evaluated. I did not need to please them. They knew nothing about the Truth. I was looking for Truth—only Truth! Truth was my guide, Consciousness my aim and my purpose. It soon became clear to me that all Truth, if it is Truth, should lead to the level of good—the level of Consciousness. Knowing the Truth, then, was connected to how I was going to act from this moment forward. I learned that morality is behavior; for good to be good, it must be made manifest. So I began practicing principles and acting only upon the Truth. This new practice, which could be called "principled imagination" or foresight, allowed me to know the cause and effect of my actions before I acted.

When prisoners came to me with ideas about escaping or rioting or just raising hell in general, I refused to join in. By rising above that useless, blind, destructive turmoil, I was able to save my own life and the lives of many others.

I learned that there are three stages in "the work" of personal change or transformation. The first stage of enlightenment is the appreciation of the self. In Christianity, we are taught to love God, to love Jesus, to love our families, even to love our country—in short, we are taught to love everything and everyone except ourselves. "Love thy neighbor as thyself" seems to just boil down to love thy neighbor. But loving your neighbor is not possible unless you love yourself. This love is not to be confused with narcissism or self-infatuation but is an acknowledgment of the undivided miracle that you are, the reason it is said we are all made in God's image.

The second stage is giving the work back to someone else. The student must now become the teacher. Teaching another person about these ideas, or "emptying your vessel," helps you comprehend these ideas on an even higher level. Professional teachers know that their greatest learning comes not from books and preparation but through actually teaching their students. During this second stage, I found Ulysses (Sam) Leslie, a tall, shy, reserved person with pale brown freckled skin who was serving thirty years at Trenton State for a crime he did not commit. He came into prison confused and unbalanced. He had no idea where he stood in this community of the living dead. His first and most important task was to find himself, and, since he respected my single-minded seriousness, he turned to me for help.

While I was to become his tutor, Sam brought my attention back to the everyday world. He forced me out of my cell for walks in the yard. A few years later, when I came back to working with the law, I prepared Sam's legal briefs and found flaws in his trial transcripts that eventually resulted in his exoneration and release from prison. Our friendship and understanding have endured to this very day. My goal when I wrote *The Sixteenth Round* was to free John Artis and myself from the actual physical prison; my goal with Sam Leslie was to free Sam and myself from the universal prison of sleep.

When I first met Sam, there were a lot of fish (the term describing new prisoners) coming into the prison. You can tell when a "school of fish" has arrived because of their new inmates' clothing. You see them coming out of quarantine with their false bravado, and you can also see the sharks begin to circle. These new prisoners will have to find their safety in niches. In those days, the niches might have been the gamblers, the weightlifters, the basketball players, the handball crowd, or even the junkies. This group of eight or nine that came in with Sam were all searching for that safety zone.

This new group began to get interested in the ideas I was talking about. I drew sketches in the dirt detailing Gurdjieff's "Ray of Creation," and we sometimes sat in a circle as a discussion group. I would tell them how miraculous it was to be a "human becoming"—rather than simply a human being—by overcoming habits and conditioning that had degraded us and resulted in our being here in prison. As difficult as these ideas were for people with little formal education, none of them had any trouble understanding at least two important facts: we, for whatever reasons, were all in prison together, and we had to transform ourselves permanently if we ever wanted to make our lives any different. Most of the group were recidivist like me and did not wish to walk out the door only to be brought back in again.

We walked around the yard at the same time every day, talking to one another like a group of Greek philosophers. The guards, looking on from above, must have wondered what was going on. *What are those sketches drawn in the dry dirt that Carter's group is looking at? What are they up to?*

Of course, we were plotting our escape—but not like in some Hollywood prison film, and not just from the mentality of the prison—but from the false personalities that we wanted to leave behind. Because we were attempting to escape, we did not wish to alarm the guards, not the ones with the guns above us in the towers or the mechanical guards inside of us who wanted to keep us asleep. We spoke quietly, carefully, kept to ourselves, and caused no trouble.

Later at night in my cell I would type up lessons and make carbon copies for distribution. Unfailingly, just when I began to feel like Socrates himself, one of the group members would lose interest and drop out. Before too long the group was whittled down to three people: Sam, Robert Sigler, and me. When we were separated into different units of the prison, we continued our discussions for two years by in-house correspondence.

Sam had been a drug pusher, and Sigler was an addict. Much of our correspondence focused on our unconscious behavior, behavior that could be sustained only by a serious web of lies and self-deception. Eventually, and after much struggle and backsliding, I saw Sam change while Sigler fell back into narcotics. The changes that Sam made were profound, the kind of changes that happen in people who have discovered something that enables them to exist as more than just breathing, eating, shitting machines. Fear that he was neither smart enough nor good enough had held Sam back from being who and what he truly was. I would always remind him that he had to live up to his real name, Ulysses, the great person that his parents once thought he would be.

————

Over time, Sam and I began to understand that if we were able to escape the universal prison of sleep, if we were able to wake up, this visible stone prison could no longer hold us.

The first message of "the hole in the wall" was that all barriers are products of the mind. Trenton State Prison was no different from the prison of unconsciousness that we were born into. Nor had we understood that human beings are the only creatures on earth with the ability to apprehend the larger picture, and that without our labels, without classes and artificial identifications, we are all fundamentally the same. This sameness was not to be resisted for some false idea of individualism but was actually a miracle to be embraced. Our genetic sameness allows the human race to continue its evolution.

Nor did we need to trample on the lives of others to make our lives meaningful. We could make ourselves secure without making others insecure. For a former boxer, just as it was for a former drug dealer like Sam, this lesson was particularly difficult. My purpose in the boxing ring had been to destroy the other person, but now I had to understand that destroying others—because we are one and the same miracle—could only destroy my own self. I now knew what John Donne meant when he said, "Any man's death diminishes me."

The second message of the hole in the wall was "Dare to dream that life can be better." This message coincides with the third and final stage of the work: taking it out into the world. The ecstasy that I was feeling could spread to some small segment of sleeping humanity. Through teaching, I came to understand that relieving the pain, suffering, and ignorance of another human being is never in vain. It is the good made manifest. It is a person's love of humanity, and not the love of a particular group of people, that will always lead to right action.

Rereading the Bible after all those years away from church brought me back to Moses and his story of personal transformation. After Moses had freed his people from bondage in Egypt, they were forced to wander forty years in the wilderness. A Talmudic legend tells us how the Israelites made camp in the territory of a certain Arabian king who had heard about Moses, respected him as a man of God, and so sent his best portrait painter over to paint his portrait. When the portrait painter brought the portrait back, the king gave it to his wise man, one who was skilled in discerning a person's character by the lines on his face. The wise man told the king, "Sire, this is the portrait of a very mean man, an angry man, and a vain man, one who is full of hedonistic desires, and one who thirsts for power!"

The king couldn't believe what he was hearing. He was flabbergasted. "How could this be? This is Moses, the man of God! I'm going down to see Moses for myself. If my portrait painter has not painted the real Moses, I am going to have the painter's head chopped off!" So the king went down to see Moses. He saw right away that the portrait was an exact likeness and that the painter should be spared.

The king then told Moses, "I'm going to chop off the head of my wise man, because it is obvious that he lied to me."

Moses held out his hand. "No, sire," he said, "you must spare him, too. Both your portrait painter and your wise man are correct. In my lifetime, I have been all of those things. I've been mean. I've been angry. I've been vain and full of hedonistic desires. I've thirsted for power. But my greatest task in life has been to resist those things until that resistance has become second nature to me."

In my twenty years of unjust imprisonment, I had resisted everything about that foul abomination of the human spirit, but I also needed to resist those things about myself that had put me in prison. I was just as capable as anyone else of hurting people, jailing, enslaving, cursing, disrespecting, and raising hell. I was endowed by nature with all of the weaknesses, frailties, and human failings that every other human being possesses. Knowing this allowed me to understand that compassion and forgiveness begin with the self. Before we can forgive anybody for anything, we first have to forgive ourselves for being the very things we hate. If you can forgive yourself for the things that you did while you were asleep, only then can you forgive others who have done or still do those things, "for they know not what they do."

———

This self-remembering, remembering who I am, and subjecting my spirit to the rigors of the wilderness, is an ongoing, difficult, and sometimes exhausting task. The story of Moses made it clear to me that his old self was still recognizable, potentially dominant, just waiting below the surface. That is the reason that the great leader, after being made to wander from place to place for forty years, saw the Promised Land but was denied entrance.

Like anyone else on such a journey, I am constantly being tested to keep the old Rubin "Hurricane" Carter in check. And, like anyone else, I must also partake of the human condition, backsliding in particular. Some years ago, I went to the U.S. Consulate in Toronto to have my lost passport replaced. When I came out it was almost lunchtime, so I walked over to a restaurant I frequent on Queen Street to get a Wiener schnitzel. After placing my order, I went downstairs by elevator to the restroom. On the elevator coming back up, there were four teenagers—two young women and two young men—and one older gentleman, more or less my age. The elevator suddenly reeked of ganja.

Without thinking, I opened my mouth and said, "You young people ought not be smoking that stuff in public. It may save you some trouble down the road."

One of these kids says, "Who the fuck are you? What you talking about, you smokin' the ganja!"

The other fellow on the elevator looked at me, shook his head, and said, "Lord! Lord! Lord!" And this kid just kept running off at the mouth. I turned and really looked at him for the first time. He couldn't have been more than sixteen years old.

Right then it flashed before me. I said to myself, *Rubin, that's you! That's what you did when you were that age. Didn't give a fuck about nobody. Somebody poked you in any kind of way, you just jumped right on him. And here it is coming right back at you. No way will you deal with this boy. You will walk away from here.*

But as we got off the elevator, the boy's voice continued to intrude upon my thoughts. "Who the fuck you think you are, old man?"

Well, the old Rubin "Hurricane" Carter couldn't take it anymore, and his voice came out from way deep down inside me. "I'm your daddy, boy! Didn't your mama tell you that? I'm gonna have to have a talk with that woman."

The other guy from the elevator, who had stuck around for the fireworks, laughed and said, "He's got you there, buddy."

I turned around and walked away, knowing that my newfound friend was wrong. My mistake had been to react in kind when the right action would have been to keep my mouth shut. This time I had lost, defeated by the fierce, formidable monster in the mirror.

When people ask me the name of the toughest fighter that I ever fought, I tell them it was Rubin "Hurricane" Carter, the old Rubin "Hurricane" Carter, and I won that bout! I knocked him out in the sixteenth round. But that mechanical monster is anything but dead. He's spoiling for a rematch. And I have to stay awake or it'll be me looking up from the canvas.

In prison, I needed to defeat that false monster of personality. I needed to slay the dragon that jealously guarded my essence and liberate myself from the power of Kundalini. When I began to understand the external forces that were shaping my life, I saw that I had to bring all of my many different "I's," all of those different personalities that were not even aware of one another, into one "I." There's a saying, "In the land of the blind, the one-eyed man is king." My goal, then, or my ideal, what I wanted to be, or what I wanted to have, was only one eye. Then I would embody essence. The teachings of Ouspensky quoting Gurdjieff taught that when personality is active, essence must be dormant; when essence is active, personality must also be dormant. The miraculous change that takes place in people—that transformation into essence—comes from Consciousness. But you cannot become conscious unconsciously; it just doesn't happen! Consciousness means double attention, seeing from the earth and above the earth at the same time. This phenomenon is sometimes mistakenly referred to as an "out-of-body experience." Consciousness allows you to discover the true purpose of your life. For me, that purpose became seeking out the perfection in myself, seeing exactly who I was then, what I had been in the past, and become what I could be: real, right, good, and true. A conscious being. Every person on this earth is born with that transformative power. We lack for nothing. We were all born perfect, which means complete.

Most of what the New Testament teaches is not about going to heaven or hell, although most people will insist otherwise. Institutional Christianity sees heaven and hell as places of reward and punishment, a vacation spa or a trip to prison. These constructs are actually products of sleeping people intended for the consumption of other sleeping people. I am amazed that so many people still believe in them, just as so many people still believe that the earth is at the center of the universe. What religion really teaches is that heaven is here, right now, and that the Spirit is the connecting medium between the higher and the lower worlds. Man cannot enter the Promised Land until he first finds God within himself. Becoming who we truly are, I would tell my fellow prisoners, is a miraculous achievement.

When we find God within ourselves, we learn to trust ourselves. We no longer find it impossible to make decisions. The key to keeping us out of prison, then, was to act only upon this "new vision" of ourselves. When we are not confused and disheartened by difficulties, when we have only one eye—or when we are one with our eye and not filled with inner conflicts—there is nothing we cannot accomplish! I am an alcoholic. How did I become an alcoholic? The physical body will work with anything that you put into it. If you feed it alcohol, it will demand alcohol, and when it doesn't get its alcohol it will kick your ass! You know that it's bad for you. That it can even kill you! But your inner systems are in conflict. Your house is out of order. Alcoholism is no different from any other useless habit or addiction. What you know and what you do are out of sync. The same can be said of moral and ethical conflicts. If you cannot act upon what you know to be real, right, good, and true, then the things you say, the values you profess to believe in, have no meaning at all.

Waking up, then, while possible for anyone, is no easy task. As prisoners, we had to challenge all of our irrational beliefs, all of our treasured thoughts, and all of our insane faith systems. We had to let go of all those illusions that had put us to sleep and tried to prevent us from ever waking up. If we hated somebody or some group of people, for example, we needed to examine that false state of identification that was producing the hatred: *I'm a Christian and I hate all Muslims.* Or *I'm an Arab and I hate all Jews.* Or *I am white and I hate anything black!* Hating another human being, who is the same as you are, is nothing but self-hatred.

We also had to work on our physical bodies, which should have performed perfectly but, as a result of our conditioning, became sick, disorderly, and break down altogether. We use higher energies for lower functions, like watching sporting events, or playing sports ourselves, or buying a new car, or going shopping. It leaves us spent. We don't have the necessary energy for vital functions like remembering ourselves. Functions that nourish body, mind, and spirit. If we fail to conserve energy, it is because our primary focus is upon diversions, searching for that least line of resistance, or expressing our negative emotions. If we complain continuously about the weather, our jobs, the police, politics, or family, if we waste energy by identifying, then the day will soon arrive when this three-storied chemical factory, our bodies, minds, and spirits that should generate surplus energy, runs into a deficit. We become depressed, bored, tired, and groggy. Depression is a chemical imbalance, yes, but its treatment requires much more than simply taking a pill.

To resolve our energy problems in prison, we first had to put our houses back in order. Or, rather, we had to understand first that our houses were out of order. The human organism, as I learned from Gurdjieff, consists of seven separate and distinct functions, Instinctive, Intellectual, Moving, Emotional, Sexual, Higher Emotional, and Higher Intellectual, that operate on different levels using different kinds of energies. The mind, or our Intellectual function, which uses the lowest form of energy but is accustomed to running the house, must not be allowed to be an overpowering and unrelenting force. It must simply be what it was created to be: an avenue of awareness by which we clearly perceive all things. We had to understand that the constant internal dialogue that was always going on inside our heads was actually a destructive and undermining habit. Mind had taken over the house and imprisoned our Spirits in the basement. Essence is knowable only if we are not slaves to the egotistical mind. To know the difference between ego and essence was not as difficult as we thought. The ego is afraid of death and the loss of control, whereas essence (or Spirit) is not concerned with either of those things.

Just knowing these ideas was not enough to actually change a person, just as knowing I was an alcoholic was not enough to make me quit. My understanding informed me that change only comes about as a result of some kind of shock or trauma that physically, psychologically, or even financially suddenly overturns all that we believed in and all that we have taken for granted. Being imprisoned on a wrongful conviction was the shock that showed Sam and me tangibly how we had lost control and wandered down the wrong road. If we kept going down that road, we might walk into a snarling bear or step on a rattlesnake. We had to understand this with every aspect of our beings. We had to stop, physically, mentally, consciously; we had to back up slowly, turn around, and begin to think for ourselves. Only then would we be ready to enter the wilderness as individuals.

Of course we are all born thinking that we are individuals. That's part of the power of Kundalini—our conditioning, the constant brainwashing by external impulses and the media. "Buy this product and become an individual" amounts to nothing more than "Do what we tell you to do." Be a puppet. Be a slave.

———

I admit that trying to transform a mechanical, egotistical mind into a mind that is conscious is every bit as difficult as it is for an alcoholic or drug addict to go cold turkey. Our minds have been running mechanically from the moment we were born. This kind of thinking has now become a "habit," and a habit is the only thing in this world that will work for you for nothing; just let it get established and it will operate even though you are walking around in a trance.

Now you are going to tell your mind to shut up. The mind is going to say, *Fool, are you crazy? You don't control me!*

First, we have to watch the mind. See what it's doing on its own. Then listen to it. As long as the mind does what it is created to do, the mind is a perfect avenue of awareness. But when the mind starts associating with other functions or uses the energy of other functions on its own, the mind becomes the prison. The egotistical mind is a maximum-security prison of the first order. And we must never do the work of a prison.

When I first thought about the hole in the wall, I doubted, because the unawakened mind knows only doubt and denial. The awakened mind is only for thinking what is true, just as the heart is for perceiving that which is good.

The state of our minds, or the state of our beings, is dealt with in the parable of the sower and the seed in the Gospel of Matthew. Given the time I had spent in the Christian church, I was not unfamiliar with the story. But knowing a story and understanding that story are two different things. The Bible, for example, is written on three different levels: stone, water, and wine; speaking, signifying, and concealing. Most people make no attempt to go beyond the level of stone—the tablets represented by the apparent simplicity of the Ten Commandments. Organized religions do not encourage their congregations to think for themselves. On the level of stone, the Ten Commandments speak to us as children or as savages: "Honor thy father and thy mother"; "Thou shalt not kill!" Even the Ten Commandments can be turned into water, into wine, and into awakening, just as Jonah and the whale can be read as a children's story or as a profound statement about justice, mercy, and human equality.

In the biblical parable, the sower sows his seeds, some by the wayside, some on rocky ground, some on thorns and thistles, and some on rich soil. For me, those seeds now represented absolute Truth; the places where the seeds are sown represent our states of being that allow or prevent us from being receptive to the Truth. Seeds sown by the wayside are blown in the wind and do not get planted at all. That person does not or cannot even hear the Truth. Seeds sown on rocky ground do not take root very deeply. That person hears but fails to understand the importance of what he is hearing. Seeds sown among thorns and thistles are planted, but the growth is choked off. This person understands the Truth but cannot sustain the insights because his mind will not allow it. Some seeds land on rich soil; the Spirit is then open and receptive to a Truth that it could not have previously comprehended. The Truth not only takes root in that mind but grows and flourishes. This person understands the Truth and can act upon the Truth from the level of good.

What I mean here by Truth, the whole Truth, and nothing but the Truth, is available to us not in some courtroom or church or synagogue but only through unconventional means. Truth comes to us indirectly, through fable, through fairytales, myths, legends, and artistic expressions. It cannot be literal because the language of the higher mind is symbolic.

———

The Truth comes to us in many different forms. Sometimes it comes to us in the form of another human being, someone we might have failed to notice had we not been awakened to possibility. One day, while completely preoccupied in my "prison laboratory," a letter arrived. The guard pushed it into my cell like always: "Letter for you, Mr. Carter." But it was not to be just another letter like the other ones on the floor beneath my bed. Something about this one letter, maybe the childlike handwriting, maybe the vibrations I felt, compelled me to open it. I picked it up. I looked at it, then put it down for a moment, looked at it again, and then opened it. I pulled out a piece of three-ringed loose-leaf paper, on it what appeared to be the handwriting of a little child: "I read your book. I think you are innocent. We need more people in the world like you."

The letter was from a sixteen-year-old boy from Brooklyn named Lesra Martin, telling me that he was living with a group of people in Toronto, Canada, who were teaching him how to read. *The Sixteenth Round* was the first book he had ever read. A nice letter from a place I knew nothing about. *Lesra*, a misspelling of *Lazarus*, one who has risen from the dead, writing to *Rubin*, a misspelling of *Reuben*, "behold a son." I connected the two names together in my mind: "Behold, a son has risen from the dead!" I showed the letter to Sam, and he asked me what I would do about it.

I pulled out the old Underwood and began to write back. As you may know, my being awake to the importance of that letter began the process that would eventually result in my exoneration and my release from prison. One might say that it was a mere coincidence that my spiritual awakening and my lifeline from the outside world happened simultaneously, but I prefer to see such an occurrence differently. On this level of life where we live, breathe, and exercise our beings—this level of unconscious human insanity living under the law of accident—nobody does anything. Everything just happens along a chain of reactions. On the level of the higher mind, however, there is doing. Doing is magic! Doing is action self-directed. It was no longer a question of *if* I was going to be released from prison but *when*.

Had Martin and the Canadians come to me before the time they actually did, all that passed between us would never have taken root. Notwithstanding the fact that Martin was a black person, too, my mistrust of white people would have made any response to a group such as theirs impossible. Now, I could see them as part of a different kind of existence, part of an inner circle of humanity. On the worldly level, I needed them if I was to walk free, and I think they needed me as a cause for their idealism. There were thirteen of us, Lesra included. They became my small army for justice, and luckily they had the money for a long, drawn-out battle. *The Sixteenth Round*, the letter in the bottle, had been answered in the way I most wanted.

Sam Leslie and I, reflecting back on our previous learning and experiences, used to talk about whether it was possible for black people to fully trust white people, Americans or Canadians. We both began to see in the most concrete way the meaninglessness of these false distinctions, of borders and boundaries, of nationalities, of skin color.

The Canadians would go through reams and reams of testimony on my behalf, helping me to reorganize and visualize my case from a fresh perspective. We drew up a chart, graphing the many changes in witnesses' testimonies, unraveling a knotted, twisted skein of yarn. When we were able to analyze the entire judicial process from 1966, we found numerous contradictions. Every time a witness testified again, his or her statement became more and more damaging to

John Artis and me. When we went back to the beginning, back to the very night of the crime itself, all of the original testimony was in our favor. The goal of those who ran the judicial system had never been to unearth the Truth, but to whitewash their reputations at our expense. We had been wrongly convicted, sent to prison, and kept there year after year. Truth would become a burning fire in the eyes of those who allowed it to happen.

———

Coming into contact with the power of Truth forced changes at every level. I began to grow my hair. I cut off my beard. Nobody knew who I was anymore. Rubin "Hurricane" Carter had disappeared. When I appeared in federal court and sat in the bullpen, I heard people ask, "Where's the Hurricane?" And I heard another say, "Don't worry. He's coming." And there I was sitting right in front of them!

That was the very moment a miracle occurred! The laws of a higher world intervened on the lower one. The federal court, represented by the Honorable Judge H. Lee Sarokin, intervened in the state court proceedings through the writ of habeas corpus, and the higher principle, the principle of Truth, was triumphant. After freeing myself from the universal prison of sleep, I was released from the actual prison of brick, steel, and mortar, humiliation, and degradation.

The federal court ruled that "to permit convictions to stand which have as their foundation appeals to racial prejudice and the withholding of evidence critical to the defense, is to commit a violation of the Constitution as heinous as the crimes for which these defendants were tried and convicted."

The day of Judge Sarokin's decision, I wanted to avoid the press and the media. So we asked a young man who looked like Lesra Martin to come to the proceedings. I was wearing a sheepskin coat and he had on a blue windbreaker. People on the outside, having not seen me in many years, did not recognize me—no bald head, no beard, no glaring eyes, no mean stares—all they could see was the sheepskin coat.

Afterward, waiting outside, there was a limousine and an ordinary sedan. In Judge Sarokin's chambers, the young man who was supposed to be Martin exchanged coats with me. When we came out of the courthouse, the would-be Martin, now wearing the sheepskin coat, climbed into the limousine followed by hundreds of reporters and camera people, who actually knocked me out of the way. I stood off to the side, then got into the sedan driven by Kathy Swinton and was driven away.

It was a personal moment in which I wept tears of joy and relief. I looked back through the rear window on all that was, thinking that the young man in the sheepskin coat might just as well have been the old Rubin "Hurricane" Carter, and waved good-bye to my former life. The end point of my prison journey, through the hole in the wall, was to find in the darkest recesses of the world—in prison—the flowering of the human spirit. It was to be my responsibility now to carry the work I had done in prison out into the world. Never again would I enter a prison as anything but a black angel!

———

Every year now I go on a pilgrimage to a place called The Way, a community center located in Swainsboro, Georgia, a small town on the road between Savannah and Macon. Many of the wrongly convicted, when finally freed, make helping other people the main focus of their lives, and The Way is where Sam Leslie gives back to the world the work he did inside the prison. The aim of the center is to speak the Truth in harmony with beauty, moving humanity to freedom. Sam is living out his dream, helping others change.

In Swainsboro, the white folks live in the city, and the poor black folks—not exactly an enlightened group—live in the forest surrounding the city. There's a place called the Branch nearby, a particular section of trees where they used to lynch and hang black people. These illegal public hangings were a form of weekend entertainment for Southern whites—men, women, and children. A 2004 book of graphic photography entitled *Without Sanctuary*, by Hilton Als, John Lewis, Leon F. Litwack, and James Allen, provides evidence of this appalling and inhumane carnage, this terrible crime against humanity in America's past. They hanged so many people at the Branch that it actually changed the migratory pattern of the buzzards; for so many sad years, those buzzards were able to feast on the dead bodies hanging in the trees. Even today, the buzzards still come back to those same trees where their ancestors feasted, waiting for some more "strange fruit," as Billie Holliday sang it, some more black meat.

The first floor of Sam's house is a tavern and restaurant with a great big TV screen, but the community center across the road was intended as something more than just a place for entertainment. The poor black folk in Swainsboro had for years asked the city fathers for a place to get together—a community center—and had always been disappointed by the lack of response. Sam saw a way, if you will forgive the expression, to kill two birds with one stone. When Sam finally decided that he would actually build the center himself, he called and shared his dream with me. He promised to build it with his own two hands. He gave his heart, his sweat, and all of his considerable skills to this venture, while I provided the financing. Roughly circular in design, the outer part of the center has a large hall for weddings, family entertainment, and dances. The place closest to the geometrical center, the heart of The Way, is an inner sanctum, a quiet place where some of Gurdjieff's ideas are displayed on wall panels, such as:

Only a man who can be silent when it is necessary can be master of himself.

Man is becoming a willing slave. He no longer needs chains.

To many of the people of Swainsboro, The Way is an oasis that rose out of a desert of poverty and despair.

Sam Leslie is laid back, observant, and wise, so much so that I call him the Sphinx. Sam will talk to any interested person who asks questions about "the work," but he never pushes this knowledge upon them.

It took great courage for Sam to build The Way. At that time he was swimming against the current. Black people there were steeped in Jesus and living in the most degraded conditions. They didn't know a better life was possible. Most of the men just hunted, drank, and fought one another in the woods. The women had all they could do to keep alive any sense of community. People laughed at Sam when he was building the center, much as people laughed at Noah building his ark. What did those people know? They are the same people who will always be there to belittle a dream. But slowly and carefully Sam showed them that the lives they were living were not the only lives possible for them. Now these people are coming to The Way, hundreds of them. If they want to change, he will help them do it.

When you have been in prison, you tend to lose the knack for small talk. It's not that idle conversation is uninteresting or nonsensical, but in a place where the struggle for life is so extreme, such talk is a luxury that a sensible person cannot afford. Letting your guard down is just not healthy. After twenty years of incarceration, I'd sooner be silent.

But Sam, now he's a different matter. He is one of the few people with whom I can still converse for long periods. Sam flew to Australia with me when I received my first doctorate (in 2003) and then returned with me to Toronto for a follow-up ceremony. It was the longest we had been together since prison, ten days that felt like a tall, cool glass of water in the desert.

———

Erich Fromm wrote that "man's main task in life is to give birth to himself." This work of the Spirit is echoed in all of the great religious traditions. In essence, we move from a place where our growth has been restricted, out into the wilderness, where we come to understand that most of what we think is mere illusion, where the very opposite of what we thought to be the Truth turns out to be correct. The image of the Israelites crossing the Red Sea comes to mind, of a whole people beginning the process of awakening after generations of slavery. But because collective human behavior cannot be conscious and does not really change, spiritual renewal must be an individual journey. On this journey from whatever prison or confinement we faced, the Spirit guides us through the wilderness and subjects us to temptation, so that all that is useless for our self-development is put behind us and all that is true can grow. The greatest temptation we are faced with, then, is the urge to quit before we reach our goal. Preferring "the devil we know" and fearing the unknown, the mind in its state of sleep prevents us from going the distance. Very few will ever reach the Promised Land, but there is no way to the Promised Land except through the wilderness.

6

Taking "the Work" Out into the World: Turning Water into Wine

When I rode away from the courthouse on November 8, 1985, that was my new date of birth. Everything that had gone on before was now no more. The pugnacious prizefighter, the person who married Mae Thelma, the father of Theodora and Raheem, the old Rubin "Hurricane" Carter, was now gone! It was unthinkable for me to ever return to Paterson or to any of my old haunts in New Jersey, because, even after twenty years, I would still be only what people remembered, that boisterous, aggressive, and violent prizefighter. In their eyes, I would be either a former middleweight boxer or a convicted racist murderer, an object of fear, scorn, and even pity.

At the end of the Gospel of Matthew, Jesus talks about this phenomenon when he says, "Even a prophet has no honor in his hometown or among his own family." Or to use a different metaphor: New wine has a very delicate bouquet. You have to put new wine into new wineskins. You must not put new wine into old wineskins because the acids of the older wine will overpower the flavor of the new and even destroy the wineskin itself.

Now that I was free from prison, I had to do everything in my power to stay awake, to prevent my former self or selves from ever reemerging. So I avoided any environment where there would be little acceptance of what I had become. Here was an opportunity for me to re-create myself, to put my Spirit into action, to find a great purpose for my Spirit to act upon to achieve something better in the world. What I needed, first, was a cause to set fire to my Spirit, a cause that would allow me to become what I could be. No more a prairie chicken with his nose to the ground—but an eagle.

Because I had spent so many of my years inside a prison, I was, in the ways of the world, like a newborn babe. I had no idea what my cause was going to be, only that my life outside prison would be committed and devoted to the work. To staying awake no matter what it cost me. I knew, too, that I had to speak the Truth. Since I thought I had gained a measure of Consciousness, I wanted to help others achieve a similar Consciousness, especially through awareness of our interconnectedness. That was my long-term goal but not something I could yet accomplish.

In the meantime, since I had firsthand experience of the difficulty of getting anybody to listen to the voices of the wrongly convicted, I would become their public face and voice and try to free them from prison, one by one. The other alternative for me was to go up into the mountains like Zarathustra and avoid this level of unconscious human insanity altogether, but that course of action would not be true to the work as I saw it.

Before I came to Canada, the place to which many former slaves had escaped via the Underground Railroad, I was trapped in a legal battle with the state of New Jersey, a battle that lasted for two and a half years. During that time, I was confined to the continental United States while my lawyers and I fought off thirteen different appeals of Judge Sarokin's courageous decision. There's a saying in the legal community: "A good lawyer knows the law, but a great lawyer knows the judge." Before the federal court hearing took place, I read all ninety-six of his published opinions and tailored my briefs in a similar fashion. He wrote colorful prose in a witty, humane style, completely out of step with the dry legalese used by most of his colleagues. His reputation for having his clerks read every single petition also impressed me. Here was a judge who actually believed in the Truth, in protecting innocent people, and in judging "wisely and fairly," another anomaly in a system that incarcerates enormous numbers of people and places tight restrictions on the granting of habeas corpus petitions. Judge Sarokin was attacked both in the courtroom and in the media, but his legal work was sound enough to withstand all thirteen attempts to derail it, all the way to the Supreme Court of the United States under Chief Justice William Rehnquist during the Reagan administration.

I wonder how many careers had been built upon my high-profile conviction. I looked around and saw those who had been connected with the case—police officers, prosecutors, and judges—being promoted up the ladder. The police sergeant became the chief of detectives. The prosecutor became a judge. The judge became an appellate court justice. The governor became the chief justice of the New Jersey Supreme Court. The prosecutor in Essex County who helped seal the deal became the governor of the state.

For twenty-two years, I had been trapped in New Jersey appealing to the very same people who had climbed that ladder and were controlling everything. My decision to seek redress in the federal court was based upon my knowledge and understanding that I could no longer receive a fair hearing in the state of New Jersey.

After the state lost their thirteenth appeal, they gave up on overturning Judge Sarokin's decision in the federal courts. But that did not mean that they would give up on prosecuting my case, because, along with trying to protect their reputations, they were also worried that I would sue them for my wrongful imprisonment, estimated to be worth many millions of dollars. To keep that from happening, the prosecutor of Passaic County moved to try my case for a third time. The nightmare played out in my mind all over again with the same people trying me, the same false witnesses testifying against me, the same agonizing verdict—"We find the defendant Rubin Carter guilty on all counts"—and the same iron gates closing around me. There was simply no way I could win in the state of New Jersey.

Since I would have chosen to die or be killed rather than become a prisoner again, I went to my lawyer, Myron Beldock. I told him to speak to the New Jersey attorney general and convey to him my guarantee that I would not seek compensation for the years I had spent in prison. Freedom from prison meant more to the new Rubin Carter than any financial settlement, no matter how large the sum. It was only then, in February 1988, that the New Jersey state attorney general told the Passaic County prosecutors to drop the indictment and close the case.

Going to Canada early in 1988 seemed at least a "temporary solution" to the problem of where I would make my home. I was determined never to live in a country that had the death penalty! Why not live in Canada, where the people who had helped me seemed to be so enlightened and compassionate? So the Canadians and I continued to live together, moving from a large apartment on Wellesley Street in Toronto to a suburb called Woodbridge and eventually to King City in 1989. During my stay with them, which was to last until the end of 1993, I had to earn money to replace the huge sums expended in getting me out of prison. That was my personal debt. I had to return them to the same financial status they had enjoyed when they first met me. My job in the rural community was to take care of the horses. I also made paid public appearances at schools, libraries, law conferences, and business conventions, speaking about my ordeal. Every cent I earned during this period went into the community pot. It was good to be out in front of empathetic and loving Canadian and American audiences. In fact, both jobs were very pleasurable for me, especially working with the horses; it gave me time to be by myself, to be at one with everything. Living with thirteen people in one house, no matter how large the house, makes being alone a rare occasion. Ordinary life is so hectic that nothing of "real value" can be accomplished in terms of working on oneself.

In that same year, 1989, while still living with the Canadians, I was asked by Professor Charles Ogletree of Harvard Law School to be the keynote speaker at an international conference on wrongful convictions at Harvard University. What a tremendous honor this was for me, a grade-eight dropout! This event represented my coming-out-to-the-world party, bringing the work into life. At that conference were Judge Sarokin, Stephen Bright, Larry Marshall, Jim McCloskey, Barry Scheck, and many, many others, a who's who of wrongful conviction workers and organizations. A report on the conference appeared in the *New York Times*. James Lockyer, the distinguished Canadian trial lawyer, and Kirk Makin of the Canadian newspaper *Globe and Mail* discovered through reading the report that I was living outside of Toronto. They found me up in King City and persuaded me to join the Justice for Guy Paul Morin Committee, which actually took very little convincing. At that time, the committee consisted of a mixture of people inside and outside the legal community, along with Joyce Milgaard, the brave advocate for her son, David, about whom I write later in this chapter.

The Guy Paul Morin case altered the direction of many lives, among them Christine Jessop, a sweet nine-year-old girl from Queensville, Ontario, who was, on October 3, 1984, cruelly kidnapped, raped, and murdered; the Jessop family; Guy Paul Morin, the man who would be wrongly accused and convicted of her murder; the Morin family; and my own life as well. Our destinies were linked for a purpose.

The Morin Committee, two years later, became the Association in Defense of the Wrongly Convicted, an organization to which, as CEO, I devoted fifteen years of my life. Our mission (and my life's work) was to free from prison or save the lives of wrongly convicted people and, in so doing, to tangibly demonstrate the meaning of compassion.

By providing "second sight" into cases of wrongful conviction, AIDWYC used the light of Truth to overcome state violence and judicial intransigence. When Truth is stretched all out of proportion, you can usually see right through it. AIDWYC put the Truth above distortions of the law. The innocent walk free not by the law of accident but because they are innocent. I think it's worth repeating Einstein's dictum here, that "no problem can be solved from the same level of consciousness that created it." Whenever the Truth triumphs, higher laws are acting on a lower level. The release of the prisoner has all the appearances of a miracle. And it does happen—but, because the courts and many judges are not primarily concerned with "the facts of the case" or the innocence of a defendant, and because unambiguous DNA evidence is not always available, it does not happen always.

Because of my experiences as a jailhouse lawyer and my being conversant with the ways of the courtroom, I asked for the court records of Guy Paul Morin's trial. As I read the transcripts, I began to smell the same odor in Canada that I thought had been confined to the swamps of New Jersey, the pervasive stink of a wrongful conviction. I knew from experience that the obstacles to releasing Morin would be so formidable that any slackening in the committee's determination would lead to certain failure.

It takes hard work to overturn the decision of a jury, twelve people who have given of their time and energy and have agreed upon a serious matter, supposedly of their own free wills. No one who participates in the conviction—the police, the prosecutors, the judge, or the jury—wants to be found to have been in the wrong. Once a conviction has been entered in a criminal trial, the fundamental issue of actual guilt or innocence becomes subordinated if not lost altogether. The prisoner is presumed guilty until proved innocent. The case now turns on technicalities. Did the trial, especially the decisions of the judge and the handling of evidence, conform to constitutional requirements? At this stage of the process, it is presumed that the convict is guilty. The jury's verdict makes that a given! But, as you will see from some of the cases in this and the following chapters, even at the original trial the accused is no longer accorded the presumption of innocence. The presumption is now accorded to the prosecution.

I knew that the public at large wanted very badly to believe in Morin's guilt. First, they had a justifiable need to feel that someone should pay for nine-year-old Christine Jessop's death. Second, they wanted to feel safe, because a child murderer should not be on the loose to commit more crimes. Third, they needed very badly to believe in the system, that those who are arrested by the police must have done something wrong: *The system must be right! Where there's smoke, there's fire!* The problem with this thinking and lack of proper scrutiny is that the police and the prosecutors may delude themselves into accepting compromised or manufactured evidence in their desire to appear as heroes to an impatient public.

In the case of Guy Paul Morin, I read that he had been accused in 1985 of the rape and murder of a child. Because of the slow pace of justice in Canada, he was not tried until 1989, and even then he won a jury's verdict of acquittal. The fact that he was again being tried and imprisoned set off alarm bells for me. The prosecutors had appealed the acquittal to the Ontario Supreme Court. That's when I became aware that double jeopardy in Canada's legal system has limitations. The appeal was based on the trial judge's instructions of reasonable doubt to the jury, which the higher court found to be in error (although members of the jury claimed to have understood his instructions perfectly).

During the first trial, the prosecutors enlisted the help of an undercover police officer, Gordon Hobbs, who planted himself in Morin's cell. He claimed that while Morin did not exactly confess to the crime, he used stabbing gestures to describe Jessop's death. Using the police officer was a way to get around any negative impressions created by the other two jailhouse witnesses, Robert May, who said Morin actually confessed to the crime, and a Mr. X, a convicted child molester, who claimed to have overheard Morin confess to Robert May. (In 2007, Justice Michael Brown of the Ontario Superior Court, while sentencing May as a dangerous offender in a totally unrelated case, described the Crown's star witness as a "psychopath and an incorrigible liar with little prospect of rehabilitation.") Witnesses like May are used when the case against the defendant is either weak or nonexistent.

To obtain Morin's conviction in the second trial, the prosecutors reused Hobbs's testimony while trying to establish that Robert May and Mr. X were testifying without incentives. The prosecution, which failed in the first go-around, created a new theory for a new jury to believe. Every element of the crime was brought into line to convince this new jury that the prosecutors' theory was more believable than the story being put forth by the defendant.

The most troubling piece of evidence in the case was the attempt by the Crown to establish when Christine Jessop's parents had returned home. Between the time Christine was dropped off by the school bus and her mother's return, there was a window of opportunity for the abduction to take place. In the original trial, the time frame attested to by the Jessops made it impossible for Morin to have committed the crime; Morin had a corroborated airtight alibi as to his whereabouts at that time. His first acquittal rested in part on this alibi.

However, under intense pressure from the police and prosecuting attorneys, the Jessops became confused, admitting by the second trial that they might have returned home later than they first thought. The story now being put forth by the prosecution gained credibility with this new jury.

What happened in the second trial of Guy Paul Morin was that the jury was deceived into believing the false story. Morin was described by the prosecutors as abnormal; in fact, he had been diagnosed with mild schizophrenia. Of course he must be guilty! He had used the term "very innocent" when describing Christine Jessop to the police; he was "weird"; he lived with his parents; he tinkered with cars all hours of the night; he kept bees; he played in a band; he had no friends; and to clinch it all, he lived next door to the Jessops! These prejudicial innuendoes together with the Jessops' revised testimony, the perjury of the witnesses, and the misuse of forensic evidence led this time to a conviction. The prosecutors were vindicated, their reputations salvaged, and Guy Paul Morin went back to prison.

After reading the transcripts of the first trial, I agreed to go see the young man at the Don Jail in Toronto, where he was being held temporarily. Before the second trial, the Justice for Guy Paul Morin Committee was attempting to get bail for the defendant, not usually granted to an accused child rapist and murderer. In fact, it had never been done before. When you try to obtain the release of any person from prison, you have to be concerned with more than just his physical freedom. I had been locked up in prison for more than twenty years with criminals, murderers, rapists, people who have done the foulest deeds. I know that many people in prison belong in prison, since we have yet to devise a suitable alternative to incarceration. I also know who belongs there and who does not. I wanted to see Morin for myself. I wanted to talk to him.

That day in Toronto was wintry and the Don Jail only a few degrees warmer than the outside. Prisoners think it is deliberate that jails tend to extremes of heat and cold. At that time, the Don Jail was a dark, overcrowded, vermin-infested hellhole. You could have sworn that the curses and screams and cries of pain were coming from the many ghosts, among them children as young as twelve years old, who had been hanged there up until 1962.

Morin came out and sat down behind the bulletproof glass. We stared at each other for a few moments. He was shorter than I was, with dark hair and a handsomely chiseled face.

"Gee, Mr. Carter," he said. "You have beautiful eyes!"

This childlike sensitivity, and how that might be interpreted by the guards and other prisoners, prompted me to say, "We've got to get you out of here! You're in serious, serious trouble!" I concluded that there was far more danger to him in prison than to any individual on the outside whom he might supposedly assault.

Much to our relief, we were able to get bail for him because he lived with his family and they agreed to keep watch over their son. When Morin was sent to Collins Bay Penitentiary in Kingston after the second trial, we had to enlist the aid of another prisoner to see that he would be protected. Capital punishment may no longer exist in Canada, but convicted child molesters and child killers, even those kept in protective custody, face the threat of capital punishment every day of their lives in prison. We began a series of vigils at Collins Bay, vigils that sometimes took place during snowstorms and sleet. Once again, during the appeals process, the committee was able to procure his release on bail. I never lost confidence that Guy Paul Morin would be exonerated. And of course, three years later, because of DNA technology, he was.

Justice Fred Kaufman, who conducted a thorough inquest into the case, said that the problem with the prosecutors was their "tunnel vision," their belief in Morin's guilt that "so pervaded their thinking" that they were not able to look objectively at the evidence. This tunnel vision, in which all of the exculpatory evidence is either dismissed or ignored, leads to another phenomenon called Meyer's Law, which, stated succinctly, is that if the facts don't fit the theory, change the facts!

Neither the prosecution team nor the police—or the jailhouse snitches in the Morin case—have been held accountable for their role in convicting an innocent person. Not a judge, not a prosecutor, no one, in fact, has ever been held accountable for that young man's imprisonment. Yet I remember nights sitting up with the Morin family, his mother, Ida, his father, and his sisters, trying to hold that family together from the pain, the hurt, and the deep despair of losing everything. The family almost went bankrupt trying to defend their son.

I believe that anyone who *knowingly* acts to convict an innocent person should be convicted of a criminal act themselves. This evil does, indeed, take place. But you would be hard-pressed to find politicians, judges, or attorneys who would describe it as a crime. But what is it to send an innocent person to prison if not kidnapping, forcible confinement, torture, and, in the case of capital punishment, conspiracy to commit murder? In the Morin case, the objectivity of the prosecution team was compromised. It made no difference to me or to Guy Paul Morin that the prosecution team had deluded themselves into believing that Morin was guilty. The conviction was only made possible by the use of unsavory witnesses and the falsification of the facts. As Morin says, "I know I was innocent, my lawyers knew I was innocent, but it didn't seem to matter."

I know it makes people uncomfortable when I call the actions of rogue prosecutors around the world "criminal." But shoplifters are called criminals, so why is someone who *knowingly* destroys the life of an innocent human being not considered to be a criminal? From the standpoint of morality, the worst thing a person can do is to participate in the hurting or killing of innocent people. We feel enormous revulsion when we see or hear about bodies of bombed, burned, or murdered children being carried through the streets; we say we loathe the killing of innocents. Yet when these acts are done in our names, or in the name of freedom and democracy, why are we so quick to forget them or write them off as collateral damage? Most people, even our worst enemies, do not harm the innocent intentionally, or if they do, they will say that the reason is for a greater good, like public safety or jihad, freedom, or ethnic cleansing. When a single innocent person is tortured or thrown into jail and subsequently cleared of wrongdoing, the accountability is borne by the taxpayer in the form of financial compensation. A life has been taken—off the street—and forced to stagnate in prison until the rot of injustice is so bad we can no longer stand the smell. But those who perpetrated the injustice are free to continue plying their trade as always; they tell us that what they did was a mistake done with the best of intentions. Sometimes that's true, but not always.

The Guy Paul Morin case contains many of the telltale signs of a wrongful conviction. The first is the total absence of any hard evidence. The second sign is witnesses who, after conferring with police, change their testimony. The third indication, and one of which I hope we will see less in the future, is the testimony of jailhouse snitches, informants, and stool pigeons—people whose words should never be believed. Protest it as they might, prosecutors have almost always offered some kind of deal to spout their lies in a court of law. Finally, Guy Paul Morin was the victim of a false and prejudicial character assassination. The prosecution, in other words, had to search for reasons why this particular person committed this crime, even if the allegations were false.

When the Justice for Guy Paul Morin Committee transformed itself into the Association in Defense of the Wrongly Convicted, I came to understand the new purpose of my life. Now I had a home base and an "army" for justice. I had already become a member of the board of directors of the Southern Center for Human Rights in Atlanta, the Alliance for Prison Justice in Boston, and Death Penalty Focus of California. I was also working with Larry Marshall and the Center on Wrongful Convictions at Northwestern University and Jim McCloskey of the Centurion Ministries of Princeton, New Jersey. These connections and our international efforts brought AIDWYC to the attention of groups beyond Canada's borders.

The American projects showed us the way to build a Canadian organization. The Centurion Ministries was founded in 1983. Its mission is "to vindicate and free from prison those who are completely innocent of the crimes for which they have been unjustly convicted and imprisoned for life or death."

Stephen Bright from Atlanta is probably the world's leading defense lawyer in capital punishment cases, a man who channels his outrage into courtroom brilliance. When Bright represented black defendants in the South, he would begin the proceedings with a motion to have the Confederate flag removed from the courtroom. Even if the motion was denied, he sent a strong message to the courts that the proceedings were not going to be business as usual.

Thankfully, such a motion is no longer needed inside courtrooms of the Deep South, but the attitude behind the posting of the Confederate flag is still the same. The defendant gets the message, albeit more subtly, that what really counts for him in that courtroom is the wood of the flagpole and the rope. Stephen Bright understood something that should be fundamental in the legal profession: you don't keep a person alive by being a "defense" attorney but by being an offensive one.

Perhaps the best known North American group is the Innocence Project located at the Benjamin N. Cardozo School of Law at Yeshiva University in New York City. Created by Barry Scheck and Peter Neufeld in 1992, it deals exclusively with cases in which DNA analysis can exonerate a wrongly convicted person. DNA testing has been able to free over 250 people from death row or from long prison terms. It is safe to say that as of now, DNA analysis is the primary tool in overturning wrongful convictions.

One of the more proactive and courageous innocence projects is the Equal Justice Initiative in Montgomery, Alabama. Bryan Stevenson, its director, founded this project to defend poor people convicted of murder. Most of its clients had ineffective or nonexistent legal representation. To give just some idea of the scope of the problem of wrongful convictions, there are now over forty of these groups operating in the United States alone, many of which I helped establish and launch.

The first job of all of these groups is to identify deserving cases. Although they have been accused of being bleeding hearts who hate police and prosecutors and think everyone in prison is innocent, that is far from the truth. The people who form these innocence projects are tough, hardworking professionals who know that most people convicted of crimes are guilty. But they also understand that since no justice system is perfect, mistakes will be made or corrupt law enforcement officials will railroad innocent people into prison. In fighting these cases, the attorneys must examine every bit of the original case to find possible flaws in the evidence. They must look at statements by witnesses, taped confessions, notes by the police, and all of the forensic evidence. Often private investigators are required to find and question witnesses. These tasks take time and a great deal of money. Although some lawyers do pro bono work as a part of their profession, resources are limited. Thousands of deserving cases are not even considered, or if they are, the average of ten to twelve years it takes to even be heard can exact a terrible toll on a prisoner's Spirit.

AIDWYC was one of the more successful innocence projects in gaining an international profile. As executive director, I went to the White House in 1999 when Bill Clinton was president and asked him to intervene for two of our clients. Nguyen Thi Hiep and her mother, Tran Thi Cam, both Canadian citizens, were arrested in Vietnam after heroin was discovered inside some decorative screens they were taking back to Canada. One method of shipping drugs is to use other people, innocent people, as "mules," a technique that we were certain had been used in this case. The mother, seventy-four years old, was sentenced to life in prison. The daughter faced imminent execution by firing squad because she refused to confess. President Clinton agreed to intercede with the president of Vietnam to delay the execution and give AIDWYC and the Crown attorney's office an opportunity to go there and prove their innocence. We knew that another Vietnamese woman, this time in Canada, had been arrested and had told the same story about drugs having surreptitiously been placed inside her baggage. Because of Clinton's intervention, the execution was postponed, but only temporarily. All the time protesting her innocence, Hiep was gagged, blindfolded, and shot, becoming the first Canadian citizen ever killed for a drug offense anywhere in the world. The irony of this execution was that, at the very same time, Vietnam released over twelve thousand criminals from detention to celebrate the end of the Vietnam War.

Eventually, AIDWYC raised funds to fly the women's family to Vietnam. We met Nguyen Thi Hiep's father, Tran Hieu, and the Canadian ambassador, Cécile Latour, and together we were successful in having the mother released from prison and brought home along with her daughter's remains. What I learned from this case was that quiet diplomacy, the method used by the Canadian government to protest against the impending execution, is often the wrong way to proceed. The Vietnamese government was able to hide what they were doing, while an international outcry might well have gained Nguyen Thi Hiep a stay of execution. In my time with the organization, AIDWYC won more than it lost, but losing often meant losing a life. That can be a devastating experience. Defending innocent people from the consequences of a wrongful conviction is an awesome responsibility.

To participate in the release of even one of these people is extraordinarily rewarding. But to think that you have made a significant dent in the numbers if you help to free 5, 50, or even 550, is an illusion.

The best way I can approach what an innocence project is meant to be is to talk about different levels of observation and meaning. The criminal justice system, which operates on defective reasoning or logic, is purely mechanical. Defective reasoning is nothing more than superstition or willful ignorance, believing what we are told in the absence of hard evidence. Logic, in which we draw conclusions from available evidence, is the highest level we can attain as sleeping people. Most people think of themselves as acting in a significant way on this level of life, but there is more "reacting" than acting here, in the same way that we react to sporting events and to the seasons and to calendar holidays and other external influences. That's what holidays are, mechanical alarm clocks. Christmas is coming, so we have to be nice to each other, and when it's over, nothing has changed. Christmas is the mechanical alarm clock thrown into the lives of sleeping humanity to wake us up for a period of time before we fall back to sleep. For one brief moment, we recognize each other as the precious beings that we are. That is the so-called "feeling of Christmas" that people talk about.

As executive director of the organization, I wanted AIDWYC to be able to rise above the level of mechanical meaninglessness and bring the love of Truth and respect for life into the court of last resort. The spirit of flight, the flight of the eagle, is the life force that compels us to great action, being what we are and becoming what we could be. The life force is an intense fire that stirs within us and moves us to right action. It never seems possible to me that those who deliberately promote falsehood can defeat those whose basic principle is Truth, and yet they sometimes do.

In this work, it is not only proving or disproving trial error that is at issue. We like to think that we are dealing with the whole human being. But what if the prison has destroyed that person who was innocent of a crime? I go to see every client that we take on while they are still in prison or on death row to tell that person,

"We know that you have suffered. We know that you are innocent of the crime. But you've got to understand that you've been damaged by the prison. We won't get you out of here if you're going to go out and act like a fool. That would be a slap in the face to every other wrongly convicted person in the world. It would be a mockery of the time and energy and effort it takes to get you out of here. You've got no money, but you've got people out there believing and trusting in you and working for you—many, like me, working for nothing but the look on your face when you walk out of prison. So now you have an obligation. I'm giving you the wake-up call! You have an obligation and a responsibility to every other wrongly convicted person to not go out there and fuck up, to not go out there and become a recidivist."

Prison destroys. It contaminates. Not just prisoners, either. The employees—guards, social workers, psychiatrists, doctors, wardens—all are contaminated. It is no surprise that there was such a hue and cry about brutality toward POWs in Afghanistan and Iraq, but you don't need to go to Iraq to see the brutality of prisons. Go to any prison in the United States or in Canada and you'll see it. Our penal institutions do not exist separately from the prevailing culture of sadistic violence.

———

Here in Canada, before Morin, there was Milgaard. David Milgaard was a young man who, in 1969, was wrongly convicted of the rape and murder of Gail Miller, a nurse, in Saskatoon, Saskatchewan. At that time, Milgaard was somewhat of a hippie, a rebel, and a hell-raiser and into petty crime. He admitted that on the night of the murder he had been driving around with friends looking for someone to mug. So many wrongful conviction cases bring me face-to-face with my old self. It does not help your standing with law enforcement officials to have a criminal record. They may well choose you to arrest instead of the guilty party. They figure you have it coming anyway.

Milgaard was a very good-looking young man and managed to retain those youthful good looks even after years in prison. The inquiry into his wrongful conviction began in January 2005. During his trial and his whole time in prison, he protested his innocence of the rape and killing every step of the way. As I have said with respect to my own situation, there is no place for innocence inside a prison. Those who maintain their innocence in prison lose their chances for parole, work release, clemency, or a pardon and may be subjected to horrors beyond comprehension. The prisoners at Stony Mountain Penitentiary saw Milgaard as a choice morsel. He was beaten and raped repeatedly. He tried two times to escape from this living hell and managed on one occasion to get to Toronto where he was shot in the back while being apprehended by the police. But what Milgaard always had upon his return to prison, what every innocent person so desperately needs, is a tireless advocate, in this case his mother, Joyce, who played the same role for her son that Martin and the Canadians had played for me. Of course she had to endure the same hateful stares and whispers that the Morin family suffered through. This future AIDWYC member, also known as the mother of AIDWYC, knew that her son had been far from perfect in his behavior, but she also knew that her son was incapable of raping and killing a woman.

Milgaard's lawyer wrote to then–minister of justice Kim Campbell to have the whole case reviewed. He laid out a litany of problems: contradictory testimony, recanted testimony, another suspect who had not even been considered, and scientific evidence supporting Milgaard. Joyce Milgaard, in a personal follow-up visit to the minister of justice in 1990, was rebuffed. In a now-famous scene caught on tape, Campbell said, "If you want your son to have a fair hearing, don't approach me personally. I'm sorry." This dramatic moment viewed on television turned the public against the government; not that the public actually awakened, but its fickle attention was finally captured. Campbell had treated a mother disrespectfully, and all mothers could identify with that. It helped also that the murdered victim's family decided that Milgaard was probably not the killer, that even in their unending grief they were able to be clearer in their thinking than Canada's minister of justice.

It is now known that the real murderer was Larry Fisher, a serial rapist who, in a horrible coincidence, lived in the basement of the same house where Milgaard had gone to visit his friend that night. While the evidence pointed to the house and the possibility of Milgaard's guilt, the DNA evidence later proved conclusively that the sperm found inside Gail Miller's body belonged to Fisher. Milgaard was given a ten-million-dollar settlement, up until then the largest wrongful conviction settlement in Canadian history, to compensate for the loss of twenty-three years. What is still most significant in this case is that Joyce Milgaard, and not the Saskatchewan police, eventually put the pieces together that would free her son. She was the one who saw that Fisher's string of rapes had been dealt with in Regina and that the Saskatoon police simply would not look outside their own jurisdiction. Their target was David Milgaard, and they had more invested in being right the first time than in the actual Truth.

It was Joyce Milgaard along with AIDWYC who were able to pressure the federal government to come through with Milgaard's massive compensation. Frustrated by an unwarranted delay, Joyce Milgaard began to make plans for a "tent city" on the front lawn of Parliament (that I was set to join) when the money was finally released.

When Milgaard emerged from prison, he could not adjust to life on the outside. He was angry, humiliated, ripped to pieces inside. This was a case of a wrongful conviction where no one would listen and where the individual, unable to defend himself from predators, was traumatized. Joyce Milgaard called me after her son's release from prison asking me to talk to him, but he could not sustain a conversation. I could understand. In the prison hierarchy, he had been on the lowest level, that of pedophile or rapist. The difference between Guy Paul Morin and David Milgaard was in AIDWYC's stepping in to find people in the prison to defend Morin. Milgaard's conviction had taken place over two decades before the creation of AIDWYC. He needed his mother outside the prison to look after his interests, but she was not able to protect him on the inside. In my own case, I was able to protect myself inside the prison and was fortunate to have individuals on the outside—Thom Kidrin, Lesra Martin, and the Canadians—who believed in me.

Milgaard has never recovered from the ordeal of prison. Even Morin was traumatized by his relatively short stay behind bars. Morin's family would threaten to send him back to prison when he was out on bail because he had become erratic and rebellious. They were actually on the verge of revoking his bail, but we prevailed upon the family to refrain from doing something that would make matters even worse.

Being in prison is all about experiencing and withstanding suffering. Milgaard and Morin each found himself inside the shoes of another person, living the life and enduring the living death of that guilty person. If you wind up in jail undeservedly, there's not even the idea of justice to console you. You did no crime, yet you do the time—of someone else.

Victor Frankl, in *Man's Search for Meaning*, talks about suffering as a gas that permeates a room. Gas in an empty chamber will fill that chamber completely and evenly no matter how small the quantity of gas or how large the chamber. That is what makes poison gas so lethal and death so inescapable. Suffering in jail is not measured as big suffering or little suffering, just the fact of suffering that permeates a human being to his very core. David Milgaard, who spent twenty-three years in prison, and Guy Paul Morin, who spent less than a year in total, were both betrayed by the system, suffering disillusionment and devastation. As Milgaard said, "The most important point I can make about my very long experience is that it has not been a good one. There is no justice in being locked up behind bars for something you have not done."

Canada might just be the most inquiry-loving country in the world. The Canadian people are rightly outraged by injustices, but their outrage is channeled into and muffled by these many inquiries. Governments spend millions of dollars on somber investigations and wonderful recommendations are made for more disclosure by prosecutors and the like, but nothing ever changes, nothing except that somebody may retire and a lot more lawyers get rich.

In a Manitoba inquiry dealing with the wrongful conviction of supposed wife-killer Thomas Sophonow, the Winnipeg police were also accused of tunnel vision. The special commissioner, in an echo of the Morin case, wrote the following.

> *Tunnel vision is insidious. It can affect…anyone involved in the administration of justice with sometimes tragic results. It results in the officer becoming so focussed upon an individual or incident that no other person or incident registers in the officer's thoughts. Thus, tunnel vision can result in the elimination of other suspects who should be investigated.…Anyone, police officer, counsel or judge can become infected by this virus.*

With all due respect, I view this statement as putting forth a bad analogy. The thing about this virus is that while the various workers of the justice system appear to have the disease, the suffering and the consequences of that virus are borne by someone else. It is the same as saying that you have cancer, but the tumor is growing inside someone else's body. The statement is also a whitewash of those who pursue wrongful convictions. There is a major difference between tunnel vision, which appears as an error, and malicious prosecution, a crime involving the obstruction of justice and destruction or suppression of evidence, activities in which the police and the Royal Canadian Mounted Police (RCMP) have sometimes engaged in to protect themselves or achieve unwarranted convictions. Milgaard did not sue Saskatchewan for malicious prosecution but for wrongful conviction, because to have charged malice would have slowed his compensation indefinitely. For this reason, the Milgaard inquiry of 2005, run by Saskatchewan Justice Edward MacCallum, stated at the outset that malice would not even be considered. How could it then be a real inquiry? Like most of these inquiries, it was geared to result in an analysis of error, letting off the perpetrators of a gross miscarriage of justice. In the words of Joyce Milgaard:

> If there was the most important point of all, I guess I'd like to know why, when Fisher was caught, he went through the system in Regina. Nobody knew about it. How did they manage that and why? I mean that doesn't make sense. You've got a serial rapist and don't tell anybody about it? You don't tell the victims? There was a cover-up in no uncertain terms.

———

The first of Canada's three M's, Milgaard and Morin being numbers two and three, is Donald Marshall Jr., a Mi'kmaq from Nova Scotia. As I have said, I find a little piece of me in every wrongful conviction—in Canada, none more so than Marshall. He spent eleven years in prison based on who he was, an aboriginal in Canada, never mind that he happened to be the son of the grand chief. During his long ordeal in prison, which began at the age of seventeen, he contracted a serious illness that forced him to have a lung transplant. He left prison a gaunt man near death, but for a period of time after his operation he became his old chunky and muscular self again. I could barely recognize him when I met him outside a Toronto hospital in his healthy state.

Marshall, Milgaard, and Morin appeared at the first conference AIDWYC ever held, along with a small group of other wrongly convicted people (Michael "Subway Elvis" McTaggart, for one) who were never in the limelight. The highlight of the conference was a panel discussion I hosted, where all of us wrongly convicted souls told our stories. I wound up calling the panel "The One Hundred and Twenty-three Club" to recognize the total number of years we spent in prisons on wrongful convictions. While leading the group, I became aware early on that Marshall was weeping steadily, like the trickle from a stone Madonna. The weight of all of these stories coming one after the other was so heavy that his grief soon became contagious. Everyone in the room, panel and audience, was crying before too long.

AIDWYC took up Marshall's claim for compensation that was to amount to three hundred thousand dollars Canadian plus a monthly stipend for life. During the appellate court hearing before the Nova Scotia Supreme Court, the justices stated that Marshall was "the author of his own misfortune," despite the fact that all he did was take a walk with a black acquaintance who was stabbed to death by a deranged man. They put blame on him despite the fact that the Nova Scotia justice system took all of five months to charge, convict, and sentence Marshall to life in prison. "Incompetence fueled by racism" was the final assessment of the inquiry into this legal travesty. Because of Marshall's background, his status as a Native Canadian, people did not believe him. As with Milgaard, life on the outside had sometimes been difficult for him, but in his case it was less his emotional state than his ongoing health problem. After surviving a double lung transplant in 2003, he died in 2009 of the same ailment contracted while behind bars.

———

Steven Truscott's case might have laid the foundation for overturning wrongful convictions in Canada except that his exoneration had yet to occur four decades after the killing of twelve-year-old Lynne Harper. At the time of the murder and rape he supposedly committed in 1959, Canada still had the death penalty for children. Truscott, at the age of fourteen, was sentenced to be hanged. After four months of mental torture, his death sentence was commuted to life imprisonment. He was released in 1969. Not until 2000, when the CBC newsmagazine program *the fifth estate* uncovered the trail of shaky evidence used to convict him, did Truscott feel he had the support to clear his name. AIDWYC became involved with the case at the same time.

The two children had been together earlier that day, but Truscott testified that Lynne Harper had been picked up by someone in a car. One of the problems was that the killing took place in the area of a military base outside Clinton, Alberta, and it was unthinkable that someone associated in any way with Canada's military might have been involved in the killing of a young girl. Truscott became the prime suspect, and the case, as with many wrongful convictions, was tailor-made to fit him. Supposedly the most damning evidence came from a pathologist. He had testified at the time, testimony which he later retracted, that the contents of Lynne Harper's stomach indicated the "precise time" when she and Truscott had been together, a precision which other forensic experts said was impossible. Although science at that time did not have anywhere near the capability or the tools it has now to determine criminal culpability, the jury trusted the pathologist.

Another problem with the Truscott conviction was the use of child witnesses. All witnesses, adults as well, are subject to credibility problems. Child witnesses and their testimony are easily manipulated by the power of suggestion and authority. While a prosecuting attorney is technically not allowed to lead a child witness in the courtroom, the police and prosecutors have no such difficulty in doing it outside the courtroom. The child's imagination then becomes the putty; the story he or she has been told becomes the new truth that the prosecutors have molded.

After serving ten years in prison, Truscott, at twenty-four, was released on parole but had to assume a pseudonym in order to construct a new life. In the eyes of the law, he was still a murderer. After the *fifth estate* program, he decided to clear his name, literally and figuratively. Why should he be made to carry shame for who he is? The shame is Canada's. Why shouldn't his children have the right to bear his real name? In 2001, Truscott, along with AIDWYC, filed an appeal seeking a new trial. Justice Fred Kaufman, chosen for the work he did on the Guy Paul Morin inquiry, conducted a nineteen-month review, and the finding that there had been a miscarriage of justice was handed over to the minister of justice, Irwin Cotler. The Truscott family had great hope in this new minister. In 2004, Minister Cotler, instead of ordering a new trial, referred the case to the Ontario Court of Appeals. The problem with that disappointing decision was that Truscott had to remain on parole during the three years needed for the appeals court to hear the case. Government officials, maybe under pressure to protect reputations, usually take the path of least resistance. More than twenty judges and six separate courts dealt with this one case. Had Cotler ordered a new trial, the Crown would have been forced to drop the case for lack of evidence. Steven Truscott would then have been exonerated and his name cleared.

Truscott is a fine human being. When you face a state-sponsored execution at such a tender age and are able to survive that ordeal, you may develop, along with your new lease on life, a large quantity of inner strength. Just like me, he was not going to let anger and bitterness mar that gift of life that was returned to him.

All of the time that it's going on you're thinking, they're going to realize that they made a mistake and you know, they're going to let me go. But it just never happened that way.

On August 28, 2007, the Ontario Court of Appeal finally acquitted Steven Truscott of the killing of Lynne Harper. Forty-eight years after his original conviction. Just imagine what it meant for him to wait forty-eight years for justice!

———

Maher Arar is a Syrian-born Canadian citizen, a computer software engineer, who in 2002 was kidnapped by the United States on his way back from Tunisia to Montreal and flown to his native country for interrogation. During Bill Clinton's presidency, the United States had developed a secret program called "rendition," as reported by CBC's *The Current* and some U.S. media outlets and now part of common parlance. Rendition, which was the focus of Arar's huge lawsuit against the Bush administration, allowed the CIA, under the direction of the president, to have supposedly suspicious persons arrested on foreign soil and then sent to third countries for the purpose of "contracting out" interrogation by torture. According to international law, this practice is illegal. As confirmed by the Canadian commission of inquiry headed by Justice Dennis O'Connor, the RCMP participated in the rendition program in its treatment of Arar by spreading unfounded and malicious rumors about him to American officials. After enduring two weeks of secret interrogation in the United States, Arar was then flown to the Middle East by private jet. Dispatches to Ottawa from Canada's ambassador to Syria, Franco Pillarella, indicated no interest in having Arar freed, only in having Arar's interrogators share information. Torture may be forbidden to Canadian troops and, until October 2006, to American troops as well (although what constitutes torture is left to interpretation), but it was deemed OK to have other countries do it for us—even to our own citizens! Arar spent ten and a half months in a Syrian black hole; his cell was so horrifically small that he actually preferred the torture.

Arar's case has global significance. He was suspected of having links to Arab terrorist groups, but the only evidence that has ever been presented for that accusation was guilt by association, that is, he spoke to someone who supposedly had links to Middle Eastern terrorism. Arar was never charged. At the time of this writing, hundreds of people are still being held around the world under security certificates, meaning they have no right to know why they have been incarcerated. On February 23, 2007, the Canadian Supreme Court unanimously struck down security certificates and re-established habeas corpus rights for foreign nationals in Canada.

The Arar Commission was set up in 2005 to investigate the case, but the initial stage consisted of secret hearings from which even Arar's lawyers were excluded. The published results of the commission were redacted in the name of national security. An inquiry into the Arar affair and yet another inquiry into the torture and detainment of the other three men were not needed. What should have occurred is a trial, but we haven't yet tried RCMP officials for suspected crimes against our own people, international or domestic. The words of RCMP Superintendent Michel Cabana to AIDWYC lawyer Marlys Edwardh were self-incriminating: "If what you're trying to elicit from me is whether or not in our mind the possibility of ill-treatment toward Arar had occurred, of course that was in our mind.... Unfortunately, in the mandate we're given, sometimes we have hard decisions to make." Two things occur to me when viewing this statement. The first is that torture was justified to combat the fear of terrorism, although the fear of terrorism in Canada is greater than its reality. The second is the phrase "our mind," which implies that when one wears a uniform, individual thinking and moral responsibility go out the window. Even with the resignation of Commissioner Giuliano Zaccardelli in December 2006, the RCMP and the Canadian government were more interested in the suppression of Truth than in accountability.

Arar's release and the O'Connor inquiry were made possible only through the work of Arar's one brave and tireless advocate, his wife, Monia Mazigh, who was able to enlist the help of Amnesty International. She had to be brave, because the forces aligned against her were even more formidable than the roadblocks faced by Joyce Milgaard. In January 2007, however, Arar received a compensation package from the Canadian government worth $11.5 million Canadian, clearly a recognition of wrongdoing by Canada itself, although not by any individual. As of this time, the American government still keeps Arar's name on a "no-fly" list.

In this and similar cases, the traumatized tortured person must sit back and watch those responsible for the torture resume their lives unscathed. The internal inquiries into RCMP wrongdoing protect the names and reputations of the wrongdoers, the people who spread outright lies, unfounded allegations, and misinformation to foreign governments and credulous newspaper reporters looking for a good story.

Such cases as these should concern everybody, not just Muslim Canadians or Muslim Americans or Muslims in general, because it demonstrates that since September 11 your legal rights and your human rights are only there at the discretion of your government. How can you feel safe if these rights can be arbitrarily removed? When do you begin to fear your own political masters more than the external threats they say you need to fear? Countries cannot maintain their value systems or their constitutions when they sacrifice fundamental values to expedience, to terrorism, or to war.

In this regard, the Military Commissions Act of 2006, proposed by Bush and passed by the U.S. Congress, is possible only in an environment of complete unconscious human insanity. This bill denies the writ of habeas corpus to foreign nationals, permits certain forms of torture, and sets up military tribunals that admit both hearsay evidence and evidence obtained through coercion. The law also grants immunity from prosecution to U.S. officials for having participated in the torture of those captured before the end of 2005. The profound and most disturbing question from before the Second World War must be asked and answered yet again: "When will they come for you?" In denying the writ of habeas corpus, that one precious right that saved my own life and is the cornerstone of democracy, I consider the passage of the Military Commissions Act of 2006 to have been the low-water mark of the American republic.

I had already lost my enthusiasm for dealing with Canadian foreign affairs by the time the case of William Sampson, a dual Canadian and British citizen, presented itself in 2003. The underlying principle in his case was that a confession elicited by torture can be given no weight whatsoever. After enduring months upon months of torture, Sampson, along with a British citizen, Alex Mitchell, and a Belgian, Raf Schyvens, confessed on international television to being part of an alcohol-smuggling ring in Saudi Arabia that had car-bombed and killed another British citizen, Christopher Rodway. The Saudis portrayed this bombing as a mob hit, a battle for control over the illegal liquor trade, and Sampson as an Al Capone–type ringleader. John Manley (and later Bill Graham), the Canadian minister of foreign affairs, gave no tangible support to Sampson. The minister would later say in justification that if Canada had accused the Saudis of torturing the prisoner, as Sampson had alleged, then the Saudis might go ahead and execute him.

Canada's typically weak response motivated AIDWYC to go to Ottawa to visit the Saudi ambassador, Mohammed R. al-Hussaini al-Sharif, at the Saudi embassy. By that time, Sampson had been in prison more than two years, awaiting execution—a possible beheading. The ambassador insisted that Sampson was guilty. To us it was always a strange-sounding story. The ambassador referred to Sampson's prison behavior as proof of his guilt. He wouldn't eat. He was unruly. He would not obey. He was urinating on himself and throwing feces at the guards. I informed the ambassador that the kind of behavior the prisoner was exhibiting, behavior that might well be called resistance, was more likely to come from an innocent person rather than a guilty one, especially one waiting two years to have his head chopped off at any moment. The ambassador appeared sympathetic, so we asked him for visas to be able to go to Saudi Arabia, visit the prisoner, and speak to Prince Saud al-Faisal, the foreign minister. By this time, the case had gained international publicity; AIDWYC joined a host of other groups to demand a new investigation into the bombing.

For their own reasons (Prince Charles is said to have intervened personally with the late King Fahd) the Saudis released Sampson without exonerating him, flying him back to England while we were still awaiting our visas. Shortly thereafter, I received a phone call from Sampson's father, James, saying that his son wished to talk to me. When I called England, the person who answered that phone was a very angry man. He was talking about all the heads that should roll on account of his imprisonment. Did I ever understand where he was coming from! The bouts of unadulterated fury! But all of his rage, like mine, would have been counterproductive if brought to bear upon his case.

The first thing he needed to understand was that he was never alone, despite the feeble response of the Canadian government. I told him about how hard his father had fought to try to get him out. I let him know about the other people who understood his predicament and who did everything in their power to help him. And I told him that he just could not come out in a rage and let all those people down. That was the reason he needed to isolate himself from the world for a long period after his release. There's no telling what the man would have done in that bitter and self-righteous state.

We talked several times over the next few months until he calmed down and started to make constructive plans about his life.

We discussed how he could deal systematically with the injustice of what had happened. Later on, we met in Toronto. Sampson apologized to me for something I had known but had never mentioned before. In his blind rage, he had referred to his prison guards as "sand niggers" or just plain "niggers" over and over again. Looking back on his behavior, he felt humiliated to have stooped to racial slurs. Of course a person in that state of mind, one who is being tortured, cannot be held accountable for racial epithets. He had survived because of his rage; it was his food and his sustenance, just as I had survived on my rage for the first decade of my imprisonment. Still, he felt bad, I think, because while in my presence he saw a human becoming and not just a faceless member of a group.

William Sampson's candid admission did show me, however, that Africans in America are still the universal object of fear and the butt of everyone's anger. An Arab becomes a "nigger" in our minds when we become hateful toward Arabs. A nigger! A nonperson! Someone you can kill without a thought! An Emmett Till, a fourteen-year-old Chicago boy who, while visiting relatives in Mississippi in 1955, was murdered, mangled, and tossed into the Tallahatchie River for whistling at a white woman! That irrational fear of black-skinned people has not gone away. It lurks below the surface, waiting to emerge when people anywhere feel hard done by, when in their tribal rage they feel someone must be made to suffer for the wrongs done to them. Hated even when we are not there to be hated, and not even in the Unites States of America!

Early in 2005, Sampson and his codefendants were cleared by a British inquest into Rodway's death. Despite a series of requests to the Saudis for any evidence they might have about the great liquor conspiracy, none was ever produced. And how could they produce evidence when the case against Sampson was built upon nothing but fantasy? Sampson said, "It is hoped that [the inquest verdict] will give pause to those politicians who do nothing more than wring their hands when those that they pretend to represent are abused."

The government of Canada has never spoken with nor apologized to Sampson. No mystery there! In 2009, former Canadian diplomat Richard Colvin accused the Canadian government of ignoring reports of torture of Canadian detainees by the Afghan government. The Harper government responded by calling Colvin a Taliban dupe.

Sampson won a lower court victory (since overturned) in Great Britain when the court ruled that individual victims of torture had the right to sue their own governments. Had he attempted redress at the time of his leaving the Saudi prison, he would probably have discredited himself. Little can be accomplished when your state of mind is reactionary and enraged; victims of injustice and victims of crime share this propensity. When one is angry, you can't "think right," eat right, sleep right, or feel right! The first victory, then, as it was in my own case, has to be a victory over the angry and bitter self. The moral weight Sampson was to generate arose from his transformation, his transformation a result of the control he gained over the angry persona that had taken control of him. Now, whenever he speaks about governments that refuse to protect their citizens, people pay close attention. His ultimate goal is to have every politician the world over respect the Vienna Conventions outlawing torture, just as my goal is to assure that no policeman, no judge, and no prosecutor can incarcerate a person they know to be innocent without paying a large price themselves. Both of these goals involve a long, uphill struggle with no guarantee of success.

————

In all of this work and the work on myself, I was learning something very basic about freedom. I was free from prison, just as I was free from hunger, free from pain, free from poverty, and free from violence. But "free from" is about as far as freedom goes. Freedom itself is just another one of our illusions. There is no state of being free, and for very good reason. Everything in this universe is connected—everything! Freedom for most people implies separation, but my waking state informed me otherwise. Everything in this universe, everything on this earth, is connected. The speed of the cat is born in the bird. As humans, we are no more separate from the things that go on outside of us than we are separate from our own bodily functions. This is Afghanistan. This is Israel. This is America. This is Russia. This is Africa. Being awake means seeing and feeling and being a part of everything on this earth. When somebody is facing execution, I know it. I feel what that person is going through, waiting to be killed: the sordid ritual, the humiliation, and then the death. When bombs fall and where the innocent are made to suffer, I feel their pain and suffering.

I was not free in other ways as well. After leaving prison, my physical freedom felt like a burden. My obligations to the Canadians weighed heavily upon me, and I, like other recently released prisoners, was more than a little apprehensive about going out on my own. The prison had provided for my basic needs for twenty years. The Canadians had given me all that and more—basic sustenance and gifts—and these things engendered in me the mentality of a child. How could I leave this new family that was being so nice to me? They had even bought me a Jeep pickup truck to work the farm. How cruel and ungrateful then it must have seemed when I used the Jeep as a "getaway car"!

Sam Chaiton and Terry Swinton were two of the Canadians who helped to free me from prison. I wrote a book with them, *Lazarus and the Hurricane* (published in 1991), and promised them my share of the royalties. After the successful sale of the book, TV appearances, the sale of the book's movie rights, the temporary transfer of Canadian copyright for *The Sixteenth Round* from myself to Chaiton and Swinton, and my speaking engagement fees, all of which amounted to over two million dollars, I considered my financial debt to the Canadians to be paid in full. They had done for me everything they could do, but, clumsy as my efforts might have been, I needed to make my own way in the world. That meant committing myself to the work of Consciousness and freeing the innocent from wrongful convictions the world over.

The evening I left, in the winter of 1993, the snow was coming down hard. In my mind, I thought that I would drive back to the United States and stay again for a time with acquaintances, but my plan was not clearly formulated. I left with only the clothing on my back, starting all over again. Would I go to Georgia to be with Sam Leslie? I was running away from home without any directed purpose, running away just to get away but with no clear destination in mind. The snow became so bad that any idea of even getting to the border became impossible. With my one eye and the snow blanketing the roads, I was lucky to get from King City to Toronto.

This snowstorm turned out to be yet another blessing in disguise or, perhaps, even a directive from the universe. When Jonah attempted to escape his duties by hopping a boat to Tarshish, a storm came up, preventing the ship from reaching its destination. He was forced against his will to go back and preach to the Ninevites. I remembered that Lesra Martin was attending the University of Toronto at that time and had moved into a flat on Brunswick Avenue, so I went there and froze outside in the Jeep until he got home. What a way to begin a new life, I thought, sitting out in the snow freezing my butt with only $150 to my name. But that was the very place, small as it was, where I was meant to be. Martin put me up for a month; I slept on the floor while his bed was up in the rafters. If we were to stay together, and that is what we decided to do, we needed larger "digs." Bruce Smith, a former CFL football player from the Toronto Argonauts, had become a well-known realtor; he helped us find the house on Delaware Avenue, the house that was to burn in the fire in 2004.

At this time, and not a moment too soon, the people at AIDWYC gave me the financial means to stand on my own two feet. Because everything I had earned since my release from prison had gone to the Canadians, Cal Bricker, who was working for Labatt, and Lisa Pomerant, a lawyer, approached other AIDWYC members and informed them that I needed help. We had already decided that AIDWYC, for four years an amorphous organization helping the wrongly convicted, needed a structure, a board of directors, an executive assistant, and an executive director, the role that I was asked to fill. As the public face of AIDWYC, I had done some early fundraising through speaking engagements and law conferences, so there was enough to pay me $2,833.33 a month for six months.

Thereafter, I was able to make my own living through public speaking engagements, many with Martin, all the while pursuing my new and true vocation of freeing the innocent.

Until 1995, when Martin left for law school in Halifax, we saw ourselves as scourges against injustice, a "dynamic duo" who would awaken the world to the problems of wrongful convictions. The stories of my miraculous release from prison and of Martin's equally miraculous rise to success from the Brooklyn ghetto were compelling. The themes we took up—daring to dream, doing the impossible, going the distance, believing in yourself, justice, literacy, and education—were easy themes to sell because we had lived them. We had walked the walk! AIDWYC's rise to prominence coincided with the growing public awareness of my odyssey and of people being made conscious of other wrongful convictions. The issue of wrongful convictions in Canada had a very low profile up until the Guy Paul Morin case. Yes, there had been other wrongful convictions here, like Donald Marshall and David Milgaard, but no, there had never been a systemic way of dealing with them or an organization dedicated solely to that purpose. Now, with AIDWYC, I had a smooth-running vehicle to take the work out into the world.

7

The Rewards and Responsibilities
of a Conscious Life:
The Way of a One-Eyed Man

Man becomes what he perceives himself to be. That is why the food of perception is the most important food of all. Three kinds of food go into nourishing the three-storied chemical factory that we are: the food and water we put into our mouths, the air we breathe, and the food of perception. If our food of perception is of such a low quality that all we see and are subjected to is ugliness, violence, depravity, and degradation, then we humans will also reflect ugliness, violence, depravity, and degradation in our behavior. We become vindictive savages. We believe that human beings are beasts or clumsy earthbound birds, meant to scratch and claw in the dust. That belief is a reflection of our own states of being and not what humanity really is. The most important of our perceptions, then, is how we perceive ourselves or what we perceive ourselves to be. When, from the love of self, we dare to dream and dare to conceptualize a world of beauty and dignity, that vision will also be reflected in our behavior. We will then behave in noble ways, and our spirits will soar. The world we have constructed and the world we will construct in the future is the product of the way we see ourselves—our minds made visible.

Hamlet said that "Denmark is a prison." I say that America is a prison! A penitentiary with a flag! America already has the largest prison population in the world, and, as if that were not enough, there are now fences being erected north and south of its borders—a real fence on the Mexican side and a virtual fence on the Canadian side—shielding America from unwanted immigrants and terrorists. Great Walls of America! However, those who build fences to keep the barbarians out are also walling themselves in. It should not be forgotten that by sealing themselves off from the rest of the world, the ancient Chinese cultures eventually stagnated.

America is also exporting its prison mentality. The United States has established prisons around the world that are beyond the rule of law, where those suspected of committing or planning crimes against America can be held without charge, tortured, and murdered. The prisons both at home and abroad reflect the perceptions of those who conceived and built them and the universal prison of sleep in which we live—prisons within prisons. If the American republic continues to function, as it now does, by instilling fear in people and degrading human lives, then the entire country, those who run its institutions and those who live within these institutions, is living a lie. With the passage of the Military Commissions Act of 2006, American justice has become an oxymoron, although I fervently wish that the Obama administration will see fit to restore our basic fundamental rights.

There are forty-plus innocence projects bravely operating in the United States today, individuals struggling to awaken their fellow citizens to the problems created by wrongful convictions. Wrongful imprisonment and degraded prison environments not only destroy individual lives but affect all other citizens as well, morally and psychologically, just as war and killing have an equally devastating effect on the psyches of all citizens, not just on the soldiers who must fight in the wars. We are interconnected, very much so, even if we are conditioned to live in ignorance of this reality. For every unjust and barbarous action on this level of life, there is always an equal, opposite, and corresponding reaction. More injustice, more barbarism, more vindictiveness—that's the law!

When an individual sits in prison for a crime he has not committed, his very soul becomes a battleground. The state says that he is a criminal, and society says he deserves to suffer or perhaps even die. How does this person maintain a perception of himself as being not only innocent of a crime but also a decent human being? It is possible, just possible, to do so, but it takes an extraordinary amount of work. Most prisoners, to say nothing of most people, are not in a position to do this kind of work. Nor are they even aware of their need to do so.

Back in 1975, Clarence Chance and Benjamin Powell were convicted, both through perjured eyewitness testimony and the collusion of police officers, of shooting an off-duty sheriff's deputy in California. The problem for the state was that these two men were not even in California at the time of the killing, but they did happen to be black. As far as unscrupulous prosecutors and vast segments of the American public were and still are concerned, one black man to kill or incarcerate is as good as another. When it comes to the killing of a police officer, the haste to convict is greater than any single crime. Chance and Powell luckily escaped execution, and after seventeen years in prison, both men were exonerated. Professor Charles Ogletree invited Powell, fresh out of prison, to the same Harvard conference where I was the keynote speaker in 1989.

Full of justifiably righteous anger, Powell wanted his voice to be heard. Knowing what I did about the volcanic temperament and the damaged self-image of a freshly released prisoner, I would have told the professor not to extend the invitation at that time, but Powell was already on his way from California. As you would expect of someone who had been incarcerated for seventeen years, Powell had great difficulty organizing himself and even getting on the plane. He arrived two days late on a morning flight but had not taken the time zones into consideration. Seeing that the conference was breaking up, Powell began to cause a ruckus. He was about ready to tear up Harvard Law School, flailing around, swearing, and instilling fear, but you also had to have compassion for someone who was completely out of his element. I told Professor Ogletree, "Tree, you got to let this man talk." Without a moment's hesitation, the professor created a panel and gathered up as many people as he could to attend the session. Judge Sarokin moderated that panel and made it his business to keep the focus on Powell and not the penal experts who had been hastily summoned to sit alongside him. That experience validated his having flown in from California to tell his tale; you could see the joy and the relief on his face and everyone else's.

I stayed up all night with Bennie Powell, and we talked together right into morning. He needed to be "tenderized" just as I needed it back in 1976 when I left prison on bail for my second trial and, even later, when I spent my years with the Canadians. For me, it was a slow process of being pulled back into the world after twenty years of having my rough edges ground down and of being able to stand up for Truth. I needed to tell my story. When others listen to your story and stand up and applaud at the end, your experience is shared and the pain somehow diffused. Like a merchant, you have emptied your store of experience to create room for more to come. You sell what is unnecessary for your personal growth to purchase what you need to wake up. And you are no longer suffering all by yourself, nor do you think that your suffering has been in vain. Powell may have moved on from unconscious rage in that one long day and night, but he needed to do a lot more work on himself if he was to survive on the outside.

A short time after the conference, Powell engaged the late Johnnie Cochran in the matter of compensation. Well before the O. J. Simpson case, Cochran was detested by various district attorneys and police establishments because of his ability to get large awards for the wrongly convicted. Cochran had actually been a very fine prosecutor himself before he went into private practice, so he knew where the system was most vulnerable: in the pocketbook. He managed to get Powell and Chance a considerable sum of money, somewhere in the neighborhood of two million dollars each. This money was going to provide a means for both defendants to get their lives back on track. Money can help a lot, don't get me wrong, but Bennie Powell needed more than just money. He was seriously damaged goods.

Soon after the conference, I received a collect call from Bennie Powell, who had returned to California. As I have already said, a released prisoner, if he wants to transform his life, is best advised to avoid his old stomping grounds. The old ways are always much stronger than the new. I knew as soon as I heard the operator's voice that the call was coming from a prison. Powell was in serious trouble, arrested for raping a German woman.

Lesra Martin and I tried to contact his lawyers, but they refused to talk to us. We then went to California ourselves to visit Powell in prison. Myron Beldock, my former lawyer, was able to put us in touch with Barry Tarlow, who, as a highly influential attorney, was able to open up some doors for us. Tarlow put us in touch with one of Clarence Chance's lawyers, and he in turn facilitated a meeting with Powell's defense lawyers. Because of our connection with Tarlow, they allowed Martin and me to interrogate them on every aspect of the case as though we were prosecutors and they were the defendants.

Through these legal contacts, we gained access to Powell at the prison. This time, he was beside himself with grief and regret. Those seventeen years of pent-up desire and rage and bitterness had turned him into a hateful monster. His release from prison had set in motion his desire for revenge. That's what his crime, the rape of a white woman, amounted to. One victim's revenge for his own sufferings always creates another victim.

As in this case, not all exonerations have happy endings. Bennie Powell was convicted of the rape and sent back to prison for fifty years. You can bet your ass that if you have miraculously escaped the system on a "wrongful conviction" and you trip up and do something criminal, anything at all, the authorities will come down on you to the fullest extent of the law. If you, like Powell, commit a felony like rape, you'd better be resigned to the fact that you will probably die in your prison cell. On the other hand, Clarence Chance grabbed at the brass ring. He dared to dream! He bought his wife and family a beautiful home and is living a productive life.

At least both individuals are still alive. As you know, many states in America, including California, retain the death penalty, a remnant of frontier justice. In my mind, no matter how sanitary or solemn they try to make the process, it brings back the carnival atmosphere of lynch mobs. Killing someone is a violent act, and, as Sister Helen Prejean points out in *Death of Innocents*, the wrong person may be killed.

One of my duties at AIDWYC was to speak out against state-sponsored executions both in the United States and the rest of the world. The death penalty had always been a personal nightmare for me. I used to dream about it as a young person, recurring nightmares of being seated in the electric chair with the current streaking through me. If you believe in past lives, a subject about which none of us can be absolutely certain, I must have been executed in one of those lives. When people on death rows are waiting to die, it is easy for me to feel exactly what they are going through: the torture of waiting, the helplessness, the pain and humiliation, and then the gagging death, the obliteration. The death penalty is dead wrong! I narrowly escaped it myself in this life. The emotions behind executing people are entirely negative. The expression of these emotions rarely leaves the individual satisfied. In fact, intense anger can be exhausting. The closure that families seek cannot be attained by watching the suffering and the death of another human being. What was wrong for the killer to do is also wrong for the avenger, be it a vigilante or a state apparatus. In another example of action-reaction, that violence begins to permeate the whole of society. Those who promote the death penalty are acting against the higher calling of the human Spirit, which is why people, even the victim's closest relatives, are usually left feeling uncomfortable and deeply unsatisfied when the dead body is bagged and carted away.

The death penalty, as Sister Helen Prejean also points out, is an instrument of vengeance unequally applied. The poor cannot afford to defend themselves, so their legal representation is often substandard until after sentencing, when skilled help may come far too late to save them. Worse still, the Antiterrorism and Effective Death Penalty Act passed by Congress in 1996, along with recent legislation in American states such as Virginia, which has imposed strict time limits on the filing of appeals, has stacked the deck against the wrongly convicted. Of course people are frustrated and grieving and angry when their loved ones are murdered, but you cannot ask for a perfect punishment, which is death, to come from an imperfect system run by sleeping people. It may seem an easy way to dispose of a problem, but we actually create more problems than we solve, not the least of which is the possibility of killing yet another innocent person. But as was mentioned before, killing, even legal killing that defines the death penalty, just feeds into the overall atmosphere of violence and into the perception that human beings are naturally violent. Increasing numbers of American lawmakers and citizens are beginning to recognize the irremediable problems posed by state executions.

In the United States, nine executions took place in January 2004, and another nine were scheduled for February. AIDWYC was called upon to stop one of them, Kevin Cooper, in the state of California. He was scheduled for execution on February 10. On January 13, I received a call from Lanny Davis of the prestigious San Diego law firm Orrick, Herrington, and Sutcliffe, requesting that I come to California, join up with Death Penalty Focus of California and the Campaign to End the Death Penalty, and try to save his client's life. At differing but coordinated press conferences, Jesse Jackson, Denzel Washington, former Illinois governor George Ryan, actor and activist Mike Farrell, the attorneys representing Kevin Cooper, and I pointed out that new evidence called the case into question and that the defendant deserved a stay of execution and a new trial. You should have heard the hate coming from people's mouths, especially from the victims' friends and extended family. "I know he did it!" they were saying. "I know he did it! We need closure on this! He needs to die!" Even the newly elected governor, Arnold Schwarzenegger, was seeking closure. I was saying to myself, *Everyone can understand why you are in pain, but you can't possibly know that Kevin Cooper did it. You were not there. You are only going by what the police and the courts have told you. And what the police and courts have told you is very much in question right now.*

The hate just kept spewing out thicker and thicker with strong tribal overtones. A gorilla, supposedly representing Cooper, was hanged in effigy in San Diego. I went back to my hotel room that evening and began to write in my journal. "Ignorance and evasion of reality is causing America, whose name once inspired the world to freedom, to die. The line of destruction has overtaken and surpassed the line of construction."

The history of the crime itself began in 1985 when Kevin Cooper, an escaped convict living in an abandoned house in a rural community, was convicted of murdering Doug and Peggy Ryen along with their ten-year-old daughter and her eleven-year-old friend who happened to be spending the night on a sleepover. This crime was bloody and ghastly, all the victims suffering multiple wounds. Three different murder weapons were used: a hatchet, a buck knife, and an ice pick. The coroner, Dr. Irving Root, testified that he would have a difficult time envisioning that one person alone, using three different weapons, could control and kill four people in one minute. The coroner later changed his testimony to mesh with a one-assailant theory presented by the investigating officers. The Ryens' eight-year-old son, Josh, who had his throat cut but miraculously survived the attack, was, at the time, able to tell the police that the crime had been committed by three white or Hispanic assailants. While recovering from his wounds at the local hospital, Josh viewed a photograph of Kevin Cooper on television. He let it be known unequivocally that neither Cooper nor any other black person was the assailant. At the trial, however, Josh recanted his original statement and identified Cooper as the murderer, proving, if nothing else, the malleability of child witnesses. Moreover, another man, a convicted felon with a violent criminal history, confessed to the crime while in prison, telling his cellmate that the Ryen murders were an Aryan Brotherhood "hit" gone wrong. While that source was considered to be unreliable for the defense, at least he provided a possible motive for the crime, something that the prosecutors and the police were never able to establish for Cooper.

One week after the murders, according to a defense investigation, a woman named Diana Roper contacted police to report that her boyfriend, Lee Furrow, came home wearing blood-spattered coveralls on the night of the Ryen murders. Roper, believing that Furrow might have participated in the killing, gave the coveralls to the police. The police allegedly destroyed the coveralls without submitting them for DNA testing and without contacting the defense team to advise them of this evidence. In addition, Roper told police that Furrow was wearing a beige T-shirt on the night of the murders. A half mile from the crime scene, the police found a beige blood-stained T-shirt that was determined to have Doug

Ryen's blood on it. Roper also said that Furrow owned a hatchet that was missing from his tool belt after the murders.

To be fair, one piece of the evidence implicated Cooper, an "inconclusive" DNA match of "one drop" of his blood found with other blood at the scene of the very bloody crime. However, even that piece of evidence was suspect, since various pieces of evidence had been released in 1999 without a court order and may have been tampered with. The defense was seeking an "EDTA test" to determine whether or not there were blood preservatives (EDTA is an anticoagulant) in the drop of blood found at the crime scene. The presence of preservatives would have determined that the blood came from a test tube in a crime lab instead of directly from Kevin Cooper. In other words, an EDTA test would answer the question if this blood might have been planted there by the police. In addition, blond hairs were found clutched in the hand of Jessica Ryen. The jury was never apprised of this fact, nor were the hairs ever analyzed. What I am pointing out here is that where the death penalty exists, enormous pressure is exerted to ignore or to explain away any exculpatory evidence and to end the story, to seek closure. Angry citizens believe that it is somehow unfair when a condemned person uses every means at his disposal to fight for his life and causes a delay in his execution. Although I know that execution is wrong under any circumstances, I nevertheless support the statement from the Ninth Circuit Court of Appeals: "No person should be executed if there is doubt about his or her guilt and an easily available test will determine guilt or innocence." These words are a departure from the usual procedural restrictions that supplant questions of guilt or innocence. Doubt, the mere shadow of a doubt, should always be the legal cornerstone whenever a person's life is hanging in the balance.

Kevin Cooper's execution was stayed at the very last minute by one dissenting judge in the Ninth Circuit Court of Appeals. The intravenous tubes had already been inserted into his arms. I sat down in my office that night and wrote Judge James R. Browning a thank-you note.

> *Your Honor (and I mean that very sincerely), while reading and absorbing your dissenting opinion [which was to become the opinion of the higher court in* Cooper v. Woodford, 04-70578*], I had the feeling of listening to an old-fashioned lover of liberty, the kind of man Americans love, one man alone who speaks the Truth, mocking the enemies of freedom, justice, Truth, beauty, achievement and joy. The kind of man who fights for you if you are right and against you if you are wrong. One cannot be for justice and not against injustice. The Truth can only hurt a lie. Good will only hurt what is bad. You, sir, are a good human being and we all thank you for that.*

Because of Judge Browning, Kevin Cooper is still alive today.

––––––

While on the subject of the death penalty, I had occasion in 1998 to come into contact indirectly with then-governor George W. Bush. I was a member of a Canadian delegation opposing the execution of Joseph Stanley Faulder, an indigent Canadian citizen living in Texas who had been held incommunicado on death row for twenty-two years! His family in Canada had been searching for him continuously and had concluded that he must have fallen off the face of the earth. All that while, he was on death row in Huntsville, Texas. He had been wrongly convicted, I came to believe, of murdering a wealthy socialite whose son was a Texas prosecutor. This prosecutor, *the son of the deceased*, personally hired a private attorney for seventy-five thousand dollars to do the job of ending Faulder's life. Hired guns had once been part of the scene in Texas, so why not hired prosecutors? The execution was scheduled to take place on December 10; AIDWYC had only gotten involved in the case a month earlier.

On a four-day whirlwind tour, we held press conferences and were scrummed by the media in Austin, Houston, and Huntsville, while the good Governor Bush shunned us altogether. We met with Victor Rodriguez, chairman of the Texas Board of Pardons and Paroles, with Margaret Wilson, Bush's legal advisor, with church justice advocates, and with civil rights activists in Austin and Houston. Looking back, it was a good thing that Denzel Washington had graciously provided me with his own security team, five burly men. The atmosphere in Texas had become poisonous and hostile, even dangerous.

In 1975, during my own wrongful conviction campaign, the city of Houston had hosted a benefit concert for me with Bob Dylan, Joni Mitchell, Joan Baez, Stevie Wonder, Isaac Hayes, and others at the Houston Astrodome. The mayor presented my wife and daughter, who had attended on my behalf, with the keys to the city. Paying homage to that previous time, the new mayor of Houston allowed us to speak to the city council on Faulder's stay of execution. It was one of those rare acts of courage by a politician who was willing to take the heat for the sake of a principle.

We were finally able to get the case back into court, which is no mean feat in Texas, the state where Governor Bush presided over the executions of 152 prisoners, some of them with severe mental handicaps, while commuting just one death sentence. Taking as long as a half hour to decide whether to kill them or not, Bush said he "anguished" over these executions. Only fifteen minutes before he was to be executed, the Supreme Court of the United States granted Faulder a stay of execution.

Governor Bush went on television that night and told the people, "We got some Canadians down here trying to tell us how to run our system. You kill somebody in Texas, we kill you!" The good governor had been "too busy" to meet with the Canadian delegation, probably because an execution had been carried out at 6 P.M. every night that week and he didn't want to break the pattern. Faulder's stay of execution had spoiled the lynching party.

On June 17, 1999, the thirty-third anniversary of my own wrongful conviction, Joseph Stanley Faulder was finally executed after an ordeal of having survived six previous attempts. As you might imagine, by that time he actually welcomed his death. Texas and George Bush were both torturer and executioner. Texas needed to take an eye for an eye, even if it might have been the wrong eye. The Canadian government, although willing to protest, would not take the United States to the International Court of Justice, would not sue the United States and the state of Texas for the violation of holding a prisoner from another country incommunicado for all those years. The Vienna Convention on Consular Relations, Article 36, says that any person arrested or detained in a foreign country has the right to notify the embassy of his own country and obtain competent legal assistance. Faulder's attorney failed to utilize the issue of the defendant's foreign status or to investigate the impropriety of a conviction obtained through bribery of a female codefendant, Linda McCann, and the codefendant's brother.

Faulder had nothing even resembling a fair trial. His court-appointed attorney had to battle the richly paid prosecutor. In the sentencing phase, his death was sealed by the testimony of Dr. James Grigson, at that time the court psychiatrist of choice in the state of Texas. Grigson was asked to testify in all capital cases. The criterion for the death penalty in Texas is the certainty that a defendant will commit another crime, something that scientists say is impossible to ascertain. Grigson decided that if an individual showed no remorse at all for his crime, he must be "incorrigible" and, therefore, likely to offend again. It never seemed to occur to anyone that Faulder showed no remorse because he had not committed the crime. Of course, the lack of remorse is a problem for all wrongly convicted prisoners.

"Dr. Death," as Grigson was known, labeled 100 out of 167 people about whom he testified as incorrigible. A decade before, he had worked a "tag team" with another distinguished colleague, Dr. John Holbrook; together they were known as "The Killer Shrinks." According to Faulder, Grigson never even interviewed him, just handed him some tests to fill out, yet the doctor testified unequivocally that Faulder should be executed. The court never learned that Faulder, at considerable risk to himself, had once saved the life of a woman who had been seriously injured in an automobile accident. Dr. Grigson was subsequently expelled in 1995 from all psychiatric associations both in Texas and the United States. That penalty was a very small price to pay for someone who should have been convicted for crimes against humanity.

Before the execution took place, Lloyd Axworthy, then Canada's minister of foreign affairs, and AIDWYC had arrived at a plan to save Faulder's life for a second time. Axworthy promised that if AIDWYC did all that we could do, then Canada would finally take the United States to the International Court of Justice. AIDWYC sent teams of psychiatrists and lawyers down to Texas, arguing both the facts of the case as presented in court and Faulder's psychological history, which indicated no penchant for violent crime. Canada reneged on Axworthy's promise to go to the International Court. It was rumored that the Canadian government feared retaliation over pending trade agreements. Fear prevents countries from doing the right thing just as fear prevents individuals from doing the right thing. I have learned that fear stops action and that action conquers fear. The government of Canada would not go to the wall for its own wrongly convicted citizen. It was not to be the last time that was to happen.

George Bush was the governor of Texas for five and a half years. I never saw that folksy so-called Christian, either as governor or president, demonstrate an ounce of compassion. His public persona was an "aw shucks," down-to-earth sort of guy, but his actions revealed the ruthlessness of both the man and the people surrounding him. Of course, I am not saying anything here that is not already known. During his undistinguished term as governor, he commuted only one death sentence, Henry Lee Lucas, a retarded person, because he feared public outcry during his first presidential campaign. I spoke out against Bush during his 2000 presidential campaign because of those 152 executions. Why would he hesitate to kill 152,000 as commander in chief? And that's exactly what he did! People say that Bush was tough, that American presidents have to be tough. You tell me what is tougher to do: order the bombing of innocent people or act from moral principles? How many politicians of either party in America, people like Senator Robert C. Byrd of West Virginia or Congresswoman Barbara Lee of California, are courageous enough to stand up and confront the "big lie" and not hand you a whole lot of bullshit covering up their desire to be re-elected? A large majority of them supported an illegal war that sane people all over the world could see was based upon lies. When the war became unpopular, they said that they were deceived by faulty intelligence. But the fact that this president was completely discredited did not prevent a majority of the Congress from rubber-stamping the Military Commissions Act of 2006, the license to torture citizens of the world. Nor did it prevent them from giving near unanimous consent to the immoral bombing of Gaza by the Israeli army before Bush left office in 2008. During the post–September 11 era, the former occupier of the White House, the sheeplike members of Congress, and, with some notable exceptions, the judges in the courts have displayed all of the principles and morality of a spaghetti Western. America, the country in which a large majority of people claim to believe in God, is dying spiritually, sleepwalking into the twenty-first century.

The case of Joseph Stanley Faulder was not an isolated incident. Jose Ernesto Medellin, a Mexican citizen, was also placed on death row in Texas without access to his embassy. Because he was poor, Medellin was given the usual inadequate legal representation. He joined fifty other Mexicans on death rows throughout the United States who had not been given access despite the fact that in 1963 the United States was a signatory to the Vienna Convention on Consular Relations. That protocol works both ways, because it gives

American citizens in foreign countries the same rights to consular representation. The International Court ruled that the Mexican prisoners, and Medellin in particular, deserved new hearings. The Bush administration at first supported Medellin's right to review, a stunning development in and of itself, but, true to form, reversed itself and withdrew from the protocol altogether. They did not want the International Court to have any say over the American justice system, despite the fact that such a stance would have an adverse effect on their own citizens abroad. The U.S. Supreme Court declined to hear the Medellin case in May 2005, a fact that only demonstrates once again that severe obstacles stand in the way of those inside and outside America seeking redress or the right to habeas corpus.

When convenient, some members of the court and those who put them there will hide behind a strict interpretation of the Constitution. They will hold that this document is written in stone. When not convenient, they play fast and loose with the same document by saying, for example, that "enemy combatants" are not entitled to know why they are being held in Guantanamo Bay without specific charges being leveled against them. But those who allow such injustices must also learn to understand that these rulings stem not from legal documents but from reactionary vindictiveness.

Another way is possible, not just by changing administrations, much as we might like to think. Another way is possible only through self-knowledge. Self-knowledge is the first step to Consciousness. Consciousness brings about enlightenment. One by one, we must do the work to become better people. Better people act from love! As Jiddu Krishnamurti said:

Love alone can transform the world. No system, either of the left or right, however cunningly or convincingly devised, can bring peace and happiness to the world. Love is not an ideal; it comes into being when there is respect and mercy, which all of us can and do feel. We must show this respect and mercy to all.

———

Rolando Cruz, along with Alejandro Hernandez, was convicted in Illinois of the 1983 rape and murder of Jeanine Nicarico, a ten-year-old child. At that time, Rolando's persona was that of a tough guy who needed to prove himself. After his arrest, his wife gave up his baby daughter for adoption; the baby died soon after. Ten years after Rolando was sent to prison, his father died. At no point before or after his arrest could he bring himself to show weakness or vulnerability. Earning a reputation on the streets, where vulnerability can get you killed, can do that to anyone.

Under police questioning, Cruz had foolishly implicated Hernandez, thinking he would collect the reward money. Hernandez, also tempted by the reward, had implicated other people, including a made-up person named Ricky. The police, prosecutors, and politicians, needing a swift conviction in a child-murder case, were only too happy to blame both of them, along with a third codefendant, Stephen Buckley. Cruz and Hernandez were convicted while the jury couldn't decide on Buckley because of lack of evidence. (Buckley was eventually released three years after his arrest when the only evidence against him, a shoe print on the Nicarico's door, was completely discredited.) Cruz and Hernandez were sent to the death house.

During the trial, another man, Brian Dugan, was arrested for the rape and murder of a young girl. While being interrogated, Dugan confessed to a number of other such crimes, among them the rape and killing of Nicarico. The police took Dugan out on a "drive around," and he directed them both to the Nicarico home and to the bridle path where the girl's body had been found. DuPage County officials did not wish to believe his confession, but the Illinois Supreme Court did, ordering that Cruz and Hernandez be given new trials. In the retrials, the prosecutor was successful in having Dugan's confession kept out of the courtroom and away from the jury. Why? If Cruz and Hernandez were to get off, the DA's office would look incompetent and corrupt. So what did they do? They tried to put two innocent people back on death row! What difference would it make? They were just Hispanics.

In 1990, Cruz and Hernandez, echoing my own experience, were convicted again, but this time only Cruz was sentenced to death. In May 1992, the Illinois Supreme Court affirmed the convictions. In 1994, Larry Marshall of Northwestern University, counsel of record for Rolando Cruz and a leading advocate for the wrongly convicted, contacted AIDWYC. We held an international conference, "Innocents Behind Bars," in February 1994 and invited Marshall to profile the Rolando Cruz case.

After the conference, Marshall asked me to visit Cruz on death row. In August 1994, Lesra Martin and I went down together, and this tough guy, bad as he appeared to be in some ways, left us convinced that he was neither a pedophile nor a killer. I saw him much as I had seen myself, trapped inside a negative persona, incapable of an emotional response to the personal tragedies he had suffered. He later referred to himself as "a smart-assed kid off the streets." Fear had caused him to do away with anything that had the possibility of hurting him in any shape, form, or fashion—he covered up his Spirit with coldness until he was satisfied that he could neither feel nor love. It didn't help either that he, like me, had a propensity for shooting off his mouth. Now he had to dig himself out from under all that shit! It took a great deal of TNT to accomplish the job.

With intense pressure from individuals inside the United States and Canada and the tireless work of Marshall's innocence team at Northwestern University, another trial was granted the two men. By this time, DNA evidence had proven conclusively that both Cruz and Hernandez were innocent of the rape and murder, but the prosecutors, with their tunnel vision and reputations on the line, insisted on taking them to trial. The judge, after reviewing the nonexistent evidence in the case, stopped the trial in midstream and simply ordered that both Cruz and Hernandez be acquitted and released. They both had spent over ten years in prison, Cruz on death row for the entire time, and were awarded $3.5 million for their wrongful convictions. In 2002, Governor George Ryan gave them a formal pardon. This case, along with the case of the Ford Heights Four (discussed below), provided the main impetus for Governor Ryan's suspension of the death penalty in Illinois.

After the exoneration of Rolando Cruz, a special prosecutor was appointed by Judge Edward Kowal. The prosecutor, William Kunkle Jr., indicted seven individuals who worked within the criminal justice system and who had been responsible for actual torture of prisoners and manufacturing evidence. It may come as no surprise that at the time the charges in two cases were dismissed, and the other five resulted in acquittals.

George Ryan was one of the few political heroes in the fight against execution in the United States. On that score alone, he was nominated for a Nobel Peace Prize. A wide, burly, gentle man with a cherubic face and weighing over two hundred pounds, he left office with a maximum of enemies and a minimum of allies.

Despite the numerous flaws he may have had, a lack of sensitivity and compassion for individual human beings was not one of them. As far as justice was concerned, people were more important to Ryan than procedures. My first meeting with him on the Northwestern campus was cordial and friendly, confirming a prejudice I had in his favor.

The Ford Heights Four—Verneal Jimerson, Kenneth Adams, Willie Rainge, and Dennis Williams—were convicted of the 1978 rape and murder of a white couple. Williams and Jimerson were sent to death row. While the police were given the names of the actual killers and rapists a few days after the arrest of the Ford Heights Four, they refused to follow up. They chose instead to believe the testimony of a seventeen-year-old girl with an IQ of less than sixty who, when she first recanted her testimony, was threatened with jail for perjury. The Ford Heights Four were exonerated in 1996 after DNA evidence excluded them and the two real killers confessed to the crime.

When Governor Ryan placed a moratorium on the death penalty, he referred directly to the Ford Heights Four. He said that if it were not for the unpaid work of journalism students at Northwestern University and others from the same university such as Rob Warden and Steve Drizin, these men would have been executed. The governor, in his written moratorium, labeled as "shameful" the fact that thirteen innocent men had been condemned to death and exonerated "after rotting for years on death row." He also pointed out that there continued to be no culpability or responsibility for these wrongful convictions, that not a single person within the system was dismissed: "All those responsible for the error remain inside the justice system." These are strong and uncompromising words from a politician, and Ryan was bound to pay a price. There is always a price to be paid for speaking the Truth on this level of life.

I was surprised to see Ryan in the California law offices of Orrick, Herrington, and Sutcliffe when I arrived to deal with the Kevin Cooper case. By that time he had completed one term as governor of Illinois and was out of office, unable to run again because he had been indicted in a corruption and racketeering scandal. We had lunch together that afternoon, just the two of us. Considering he had worked for George W. Bush in the 2000 election, he was shocked and angered that the federal government was going to pursue an indictment against him. He felt that this indictment was a response to his decision to clean out Illinois' death row by commuting the sentences of some 160 people and fully exonerating another seven. The moratorium had all been done on his own, in opposition to his colleagues, a majority of the state legislature, and the federal government, so now he was forced to stand on his own. "How could they do that to me?" he asked. And I answered him by saying, "That's what every wrongly convicted person in the world always asks: 'How can you do this to me?'"

George Ryan was convicted on sixteen counts of corruption and is now serving six years in prison. But the good he did has certainly not been in vain. Sometimes an individual, even a deeply flawed individual, acts from inescapable conviction. Irrespective of politics, Ryan just could not allow innocent people to die on death row during his watch. Given Ryan's fall from grace and the increased public pressure to overturn the moratorium, the next governor of Illinois, Rod Blagojevich, might also have been seen as a hero since he continued to maintain the moratorium. However, it now appears as if Blagojevich was every bit as corrupt as Ryan!

———

The highest-profile death-row prisoner in America today is Mumia Abu-Jamal. Now over sixty, he has been facing execution in eastern Pennsylvania for three decades. AIDWYC refused to take up his case because the circumstances surrounding the shooting of Police Officer Dan Faulkner made it appear at first that Abu-Jamal was guilty. The facts on the surface did not look favorable. Before his arrest, he had been part of MOVE, a back-to-nature commune lead by John Africa. Abu-Jamal had been present in 1978 when a police officer in Philadelphia was killed while attempting to evict the MOVE organization. Nine of the MOVE people were arrested and convicted of third-degree murder.

In 1981, Abu-Jamal, a part-time cabdriver, a former Black Panther, and an award-winning journalist, was driving his cab in racially charged Philadelphia. Abu-Jamal saw his brother's car pulled over by the police, so he stopped his cab and got out. Investigators later found the police officer shot dead and Abu-Jamal wounded by the side of the road, a gun inside his cab. No evidence was ever presented that Abu-Jamal's gun was the murder weapon or that he himself had fired a gun. He supposedly confessed to the crime to a security guard while lying in his hospital bed, although no one else, no police, no doctors or nurses, ever heard this so-called confession. His underfunded public defender never interviewed witnesses. Two favorable witnesses who spoke to the press in the early stages of the investigation were intimidated and silenced. Most important, another man, one Arnold Beverly, signed a sworn affidavit claiming that he and another man, not Mumia Abu-Jamal, had shot Daniel Faulkner. Further, he claimed that Abu-Jamal had been shot by police reinforcements when Mumia arrived on the scene.

Four years later came the infamous MOVE bombing. This brutally excessive police action was a tribal incident that every prisoner in America, myself included, knew about before it hit the national media. It brought attention to the long-festering relationship between the Philadelphia police and the black community and, by extension, the relationship between the police and other such communities throughout the United States. Many of the MOVE people, like Abu-Jamal himself, had also been active in the Black Panther Party in the past. The Panthers had been nationally targeted by the FBI, thirty-eight of them murdered and many more sent to prison on trumped-up charges.

In May 1985, MOVE headquarters, which was also their home, was a block of large, well-kept row houses. The neighbors complained because the residents were noisy. Once again, police were called to evict the MOVE organization. When, in understandable fear of possible police violence, the MOVE people refused them entry, a standoff began, resulting in a police siege. To end it, the police decided to drop a large incendiary bomb on MOVE headquarters. The bomb succeeded in setting fire to the house, and when the police refused to allow the fire department to extinguish it, the flames set the whole row ablaze. The final tally of this battle in the unending war against Africans in America was eleven dead, dozens more injured, and sixty-one homes destroyed! Later, the courts, to their credit, would assess thirty-two million dollars in reparations to be paid to the community. To their discredit, not a single individual involved in the police action was ever charged or prosecuted.

From his prison cell, Mumia Abu-Jamal wrote a diatribe on the incident, deliberately bringing back memories of the Vietnam War: "We had to destroy the village in order to save it." You might understand why I call this a tribal incident as opposed to a racial one if you reflect upon the total destruction eight years later of the Branch Davidian compound in Waco, Texas. Race is only one difference, and it is no more important than belief. Sleeping people will focus upon any difference to dehumanize their supposed enemy in order to destroy them.

I see Mumia Abu-Jamal as a political prisoner, a perceived enemy of the state, but that is clearly an unpopular point of view in eastern Pennsylvania. His guilt at the time of Falkner's murder was a foregone conclusion to everyone but his most radical supporters. The judge in the case, Albert Sabo, being a member of the Fraternal Order of Police, functioned as a part of the prosecution. In my view, he should have stepped down from this trial, but the district attorney thought otherwise, because he had already sent thirty-one other people to death row (twenty-nine of them nonwhites). Sabo also sat on the appeal. The ability of the prosecution to portray Abu-Jamal as a Black Panther made it impossible for the jury to accept any other version of him. The Black Panthers, assumed to be fanatics and murderers by most white people, were feared and loathed, although an objective analysis of what they actually did, as opposed to what they said, belied that criminal characterization.

As AIDWYC refused to become involved in the case, I had to pay for my own flight to visit Abu-Jamal in March 2000. On the next day, I was to fly in a private jet to the Academy Awards in Hollywood, where I hoped in vain that Denzel Washington would receive the best actor award for his portrayal of me in *The Hurri-*

cane. What I remembered most about that night was the striking contrast between the two places: the intense and brilliant Abu-Jamal philosophizing, laughing, crying with me, daring to dream on death row, and the surface glitz and glitter, the red carpet, the limousines, the hotels, the posh dresses and suits, and the "empty eyes" of Hollywood!

I go into prisons expecting to see angry people. Abu-Jamal was an exception. I often get an uncomfortable feeling inside those stone walls, especially when the prisoner is on death row, bound and shackled behind the glass, but in this instance the glass just seemed to melt away. I met this person face to face, bearded, with dreadlocks, eyes glowing like coal embers. His sharp wit and intellect set him off from a Rolando Cruz or a David Milgaard or a Kevin Cooper. Abu-Jamal had weight. Attached to the chain around his waist was a wooden yoke on his arms that prevented him from closing his hands together. We began by staring straight into each other's eyes, checking each other out for about five minutes, steadily and unflinching. Then we both started laughing, laughing on the rim of hell! Even there, in that place, dreams were alive. Mumia Abu-Jamal was daring to dream from death row, daring to dream that he had a shot at life and, therefore, a shot at freedom.

He was asking himself, as most prisoners often do, *How did I get here?* We did not speak of innocence or guilt, although he shared a few of his regrets. We were both very much aware that the conversation was being recorded, so they may have heard something about the indomitable human Spirit or the love of humankind, so many different things, although I do not remember the exact words we said. I do remember his insisting that he was not going to die in prison. He believed in the higher laws that would set him free. And I knew that to be true as well.

Communicating to the outside world on every level was nothing new to him. Abu-Jamal had broadcast from death row for a time on National Public Radio. Politics, religion, and the prison system were his usual subjects. The authorities, responding to an angry public who felt outraged that a death-row prisoner should be given a public forum, closed the program down. His written words, a clean, open, incisive prose, came from the prison in newspapers and were entered on a variety of Web sites. The U.S. federal government quietly ordered prison authorities to shut down prison newspapers and radio stations and to restrict access to the Internet so as to deny people like Abu-Jamal the ability to speak out at all.

If I can venture an opinion on Abu-Jamal's case, I would like to think that the man I met did not commit that crime, in the same way that even the angry Rubin "Hurricane" Carter of 1966 did not fit the circumstances of the Lafayette Bar and Grill murders. Had I shot four innocent people, killing three, and white people at that, I would not be here today. No way after doing something "insane" like that would I have suddenly become sane again and let the police just stop me and take me in. But then I've never been a cold-blooded killer either. The eyewitness testimony and the forensic evidence in the case of Mumia Abu-Jamal are so conflicting and so compromised that his execution would amount to nothing more than an assassination, and yet the state moves inexorably toward that conclusion.

Late in 2006, the United States House of Representatives voted overwhelmingly to ask the French government to intercede against Saint-Denis, a Parisian suburb, for naming a street after Abu-Jamal.

The congressmen were behaving like a herd of sheep, most of them knowing little about either the crime or the man aside from the fact that a police officer had been murdered. Nor did they seem to be aware that Abu-Jamal's case was coming before the U.S. Court of Appeals for the Third Circuit based upon racial bias and improper instructions to the jury. Of course the French town refused to bow to this interference, citing the fact that Mumia Abu-Jamal had been the first person to be granted honorary French citizenship since Pablo Picasso.

The backdrop for many of these cases is the history of denial of human rights for Africans in America. The civil rights movement is a misnomer and always has been. Human rights are a worldwide problem, but the leadership of America has always bridled at the interference of outside states and agencies in what they label "an internal matter." Civil rights are said to be a domestic problem to be solved by the elected governments and courts of the United States. Malcolm X saw right through that deception.

———

Public pressure after the killing of Wanda McCoy in 1981 led to the arrest of her brother-in-law, Roger Keith Coleman, a Virginia coal miner. Because of inexperienced legal representation and a thorough violation of his constitutional rights, he was convicted of McCoy's murder and sentenced to death. This case received an unprecedented amount of media attention. From inside the prison, Coleman was on all the talk shows, *Larry King Live* to *Donahue* to *Good Morning America*, not letting a moment go by without protesting his innocence. *Time* magazine did a cover story that made a strong case for Coleman's innocence.

I spoke with Coleman on the telephone the day before he was to be murdered by the state of Virginia. His clarity, his eloquence, and his presence of mind were impressive considering his tension and the pressure he was under. At one point, our conversation was interrupted by a prison nurse. She was concerned that Coleman had missed his scheduled cortisone shot for his sore shoulder. I said, "Brother, this is crazy! The state is about to take your life, and they're concerned about your health and well-being?" You see, he was barred from presenting his evidence of innocence to a federal court. His petition for a writ of habeas corpus was rejected because of a procedural technicality: in a state that allows only thirty days after conviction to file, his first-year lawyer, arguing her first capital case, filed Coleman's petition one day late! The lateness was caused by the use of the regular, and not expedited, mail. In March 1992, the Supreme Court of the United States refused to intervene; Coleman was executed.

Just hours before the execution, Governor Douglas Wilder allowed Coleman to take a lie-detector test, telling the prisoner that if he passed the test he would be granted clemency. The governor was bowing to public pressure inside and outside the state of Virginia. Lie detectors can be indicative of guilt or innocence, but they are, in a word, unreliable, especially if given in stressful situations. Coleman failed the test, giving the authorities the clear consciences they needed when putting him to death. Imagine how well you would do on a lie-detector test at the moment your life was hanging in the balance! What a contrast between Governor Wilder, who was looking for a way out, and Governor Ryan of Illinois, who decided to do what was right.

In January 2006, fourteen years after the execution, Coleman was finally given the DNA test he had been denied while still alive. Governor Mark Warner, who had the test done in Canada to allay any suspicion of tampering, announced that the test confirmed Coleman to be the killer of his own sister-in-law. I do not fully trust the sample that was sent, since the state had for so long resisted doing the test. Even more important, I still believe that the evidence in this case did not fully support the verdict or the penalty. It is obvious that a shadow of a doubt existed even after his death, or a DNA test would never have been allowed. The execution of Roger Keith Coleman, in other words, was not made more just by the DNA findings. At the very least, his life should have been spared.

———

Steven Crawford, an African American from Harrisburg, Pennsylvania, was fourteen years old when his friend Eddie Mitchell, a newspaper carrier, was found in the Crawford family garage, beaten to death with a hammer and robbed of thirty-two dollars. The garage was located in an alleyway behind the house, accessible to anyone. Nevertheless, the locale and the fact that Crawford was friends with the victim meant that Crawford was to be the only "logical" suspect. The prosecution relied heavily on the analysis of his palm print that was found on the family car in the garage. No one questioned that a palm print on one's family car was anything unusual, but the state of Pennsylvania's expert witness, Janice Roadcap, testified that there was blood in the valleys of the palm print, that the suspect literally had blood on his hands when the print was made. Testimony also indicated that hairs found in the hand of the dead boy were "Negroid" and could have come from Crawford. Of course, in 1974 there was no such thing as DNA testing.

A neighbor provided a good alibi for Crawford's whereabouts during the killing. Crawford had no motive for the crime, and there was no evidence as to where the missing thirty-two dollars had gone. He was given two new trials but was convicted both times on the evidence of the palm print. In 1978, he was offered a deal that would set him free if he confessed to the murder, but he refused. He rejected a similar deal one year later. He would not confess to a crime he had not committed. He remained in prison for another twenty-six years!

Remarkably (or miraculously), right before Crawford's last appeal hearing, Roadcap's original notes were discovered in the lead detective's briefcase, which had been thrown into the trash after he died. Two eight-year-old boys found the briefcase and were trying to open it when the police drove by and noticed the boys playing with the lock. In her original notes, Roadcap had crossed out the words "in the valleys" (of the palm print) and left in only the words "at the ridges." This alteration meant that while there had been blood on the car, there had been no blood on Crawford's hand when he touched the car. It was subsequently discovered that the police had hidden other exculpatory evidence. The so-called Negroid hairs were actually blond! But the state still insisted that he remain in jail.

Finally, in June 2001, AIDWYC made a dramatic move. A team of lawyers from Canada (the Illegals Motorcycle Club, all members of the Canadian Bar Association) rode their big bikes down to Harrisburg. I flew down from Toronto; motorcycles had never been my favorite mode of transportation. After meeting with the prosecution team, we were able to convince them that Steven Crawford, after twenty-eight years of maintaining his innocence, should be freed if any integrity were to be maintained within the system. The judge released him on one dollar bail pending another trial, which, of course, given the lack of evidence, was never held. Crawford was then forty-four years old. To me, he is a hero, just as anyone who rejects their physical freedom to maintain his innocence is a hero. Even more than his innocence, Crawford managed to maintain his self-worth against the dismal surroundings of the prison. What kept him alive throughout his ordeal was his refusal to accept the version of himself offered up by the state and the people of Pennsylvania.

I met Crawford during his incarceration and have maintained a friendly relationship with him ever since. He never showed any bitterness or anger during or after his ordeal, just a quiet determination to clear his name, maintaining the courage to insist he not be released from prison as a criminal. He is one of those people whose integrity jumps out at you. He speaks softly and with great kindness and consideration for the listener. He took a job at a foundation called The Love Ship helping inner-city youngsters in eastern Pennsylvania. He finally received compensation for his ordeal in June 2006.

———

The war on our psyches has many fronts, but it is a war that is fought out primarily in the courtrooms and prisons of the world. From early in our lives, we are conditioned to believe that we are who and what other people think we are. Let's say you are one of those people innocent of a crime but snatched up and taken off the street under threat of death. The process of dehumanization begins right there. They begin by subduing you, slapping handcuffs on your wrists. Then you go to the booking officer, who treats you like a disease or some disgusting object to be despised. Then you are placed in a city jail cell, maybe not even allowed to use a toilet. Your bed is an iron slat fastened to the wall. No sheets. No covers. The next morning, you appear before the court. You are charged. You have not even washed your face or combed your hair. The court-room may be filled with people who know you—family, friends, neighbors, members of the community—or empty, a void where no one will hear you say, "Not guilty."

Back in your cell, you are yelled at and humiliated by prison guards imitating army drill sergeants. If you cannot make bail dur-ing the year or so before you go to trial, you probably feel ready to go to a larger prison, just in the hope that you will have more space. During the actual trial, you hear people talking about you, calling you names, or diagnosing your mental infirmities; you see well-to-do people having secret conversations about your future. No one talks to you. You may as well not even be there. The only individual who is affected by all of this, however, is you! These other people are making a living off you or being entertained or horrified by what they hear you supposedly have done. You cannot open your mouth until they tell you to speak. By the time you get up there on the wit-ness stand to say something, they have put so much shit in front of you, you are afraid to say anything. Who built this case? When did this all happen? Then the judge or jury finds you guilty: "The facts speak for themselves." Then the same judge, this person you thought was there to protect your rights, imposes a jaw-dropping sentence. Triple life! You are devastated.

Then you are placed inside a maximum-security prison and gradually made to feel that this is where you belong. The food and the violence you are fed may be bad enough, but the most poisonous food of all is the perception of yourself that they feed back to you. As far as the world is concerned, you are a guilty criminal. The court has spoken. You try appeals and letter-writing campaigns, become conversant with the law. An innocence project takes an interest in you but then informs you that your lawyer's sloppy work has made an appeal next to impossible. This was the same lawyer that your family hired after begging, scraping together, and borrowing ten thousand dollars—or, more likely, the same lawyer who had been appointed by the court to defend you. You discover that he never interviewed a single witness. During this whole process, your perception of yourself will be altered; any connection to who you might be will be changed into what they think you are—a criminal!

The dominant culture does this to you in an attempt to establish a boundary between itself and barbarism; the manifestations of barbarism are usually called crimes, especially crimes of violence. When you have been convicted of a crime, you are pushed over that imaginary line into criminality and barbarism; if you were not already different by birth, you are different now. But that is also an illusion, albeit a cherished illusion held by the so-called civilized population. What is called a crime is an infringement of existing laws, whereas, in reality, the laws themselves are often equal or greater manifestations of barbarism and violence. Unquestionable crimes seem to escape the field of vision of criminology either because they are not recognized by statute or because they surpass a certain scale. We are told what constitutes a criminal act or a criminal person or a criminal sect, but there is little concept of a criminal state or a criminal piece of legislation. And how could there be, since the definitions of crime proceed from above to below, from those who pass legislation to those who must live under it? Those who are asleep and who think they are civilized enact laws and pass judgments on others who are also asleep and who are seen to be uncivilized.

When, as it is now, the line of destruction is in the ascendancy, the line between barbarism and civilization is not only thin but in many places nonexistent. These two opposing forces can coexist on an equal basis for only short periods of time. Smaller and smaller space today in individual lives is occupied by the principles of civilization. In fact, those very principles of civilization in their falsified forms, be they honor, patriotism, spirituality, or democracy, are now being used for the aims of violence and degradation of the human Spirit. Through our media and our systems of education, which usually reinforce the power of Kundalini, we are being slowly transformed into imbeciles who neither know about nor care about the quest for Truth. That is why, for me, the field of wrongful convictions is of such great importance. It is an attempt to awaken humanity to the fallibility of its cherished institutions and to re-establish the principles of civilization where those things can be done on a manageable scale. If civilization begins anywhere it is with the individual's love of Truth, just as it ends with the mob's collective fear of Truth.

History has shown that if we should presume anything, it should be that those in prison who year after year continue to maintain their innocence, people such as Leonard Peltier, Mumia Abu-Jamal, Maurice Carter, David McCallum, Atif Rafay, and Sebastian Burns, are the very ones most likely to be innocent! Why can't the system be made flexible enough to respond more swiftly to cases such as these? Rafay and Burns have each waited six years for their first appeal. Why can't Truth be allowed to shine its light on cases where governments have decreed time limitations for appeals? Why is procedure more important than Truth? It should be easy to right a wrong. Admitting error should be considered a mark of honor and distinction.

The system of free enterprise in the righting of wrongful convictions, of private individuals giving of their time and energy to this cause, has been remarkably successful. Hundreds of people have been freed in the United States and Canada and elsewhere around the world. Yet we are severely limited. It should not be solely a private sector responsibility to correct the errors of the public sector. Great Britain has instituted a far better system, the Criminal Case Review Committee, which the world would do well to examine and imitate. This committee, set up by the British government, has the responsibility and the power to examine criminal convictions and determine their validity. It has also been given the power to review forensic evidence and to interview witnesses.

The Canadian government, through its countless inquiries, appears to recognize what the American government cannot seem to accept: that its justice system is hugely flawed. American judges, under public pressure and relentless scrutiny, have made it more and more difficult for prisoners to get their cases to the appellate level. There must be a way for innocence to survive within the system, aside from the heroic struggles of individual souls and their advocates. I have to hope that President Barack Obama and his administration will find a way to reverse the course of injustice in America, that they will take this historic opportunity to right the wrongs of a punitive and essentially vindictive system.

This wrongful conviction business is hard work. It takes everything you've got and then some, but those who undertake this awesome responsibility have the advantage of being connected to a higher source. I came to understand that the harder I worked, the longer I worked, the more focused the work became, the more the seed of ecstasy in my head would vibrate in tune with something far greater than the business of a courtroom. I wondered about this music I was hearing.

One night in my office on Delaware Avenue, the same fullness of ecstasy I had experienced inside Trenton State Prison, and several times afterward, overwhelmed me again. I heard what sounded to me like a great rush of wings. Unlike my earlier experience of the hole in the wall, which at the time was purely emotional, this one was both emotional and intellectual, the heart and mind in harmony, thinking and experiencing at the same time. My desk chair began to shake. My first thought was that Toronto was experiencing a major earthquake. I held tight to the arms of that chair. Suddenly, I felt the chair being picked up, moved across the room, and planted, actually planted in the floor, defying all laws of common sense and gravity. At the same moment, my visual perspective of myself changed. I saw myself outside of myself, a double attention that is the purest form of self-remembering, standing on top of the world. I couldn't see my feet because they were planted in the earth up to my ankles. When I looked down, I saw the planet earth below me. I was standing in space, in silhouette, looking down at the earth as if from an airplane descending. I could see in four dimensions. I could see myself looking at myself looking at the earth. I could zoom in and bring the earth closer to me, or I could push it away. I saw antlike beings scurrying from place to place. Where I was standing there was nothing. No light. No darkness. No sound. No weather. No hot. No cold. No time. Nothing! All fear was gone.

There was nothing there to fear. I saw the goings-on of the earth, explosions taking place all over, strife, grief, fear, hatred, war, all on display for me, the world of mechanical beings, of sleeping people, wind-up toys, like the Christmas windows at Macy's. And I could see all of this at once. I was but a little child again. I had broken the law, but they couldn't touch me for this one—because I was not there. I was of the earth but not on the earth. And oh, how I laughed! How everything became so clear. How hate had put me into prison, how love had busted me out!

The way of the one-eyed man is to perceive humanity from above, not from below or across the courtroom floor or the council chamber. Not as liberals or conservatives, Republicans or Democrats, blacks or whites, Christians or Jews or Muslims, or any of those artificial states of identification that divide us. We must begin to see that while attorneys, politicians, and citizens violently debate, while armies clash, we are all on the same earth. To conceive of another world, of another kind of life, we must wake up and embody that world! Peace cannot come from war. We cannot win the peace. We, as our wise ones have said, must be the peace. When we have perceived of ourselves in a new light, we will see the world in a new light: from above, where the Truth is, where love is! Then we will understand what Thomas Jefferson meant when he wrote: "We hold these truths to be self-evident, that all men are created equal." When we feast upon this new vision of ourselves, innocence will be reborn.

8

Why I Left the Association in Defense of the Wrongly Convicted: Acting Upon the Truth

In the year 2004, I resigned in disgust as cofounder and executive director of the Association in Defense of the Wrongly Convicted. Why did it come to that? My departure was a ghostly reverberation from the murder of Christine Jessop and the trials of Guy Paul Morin, the person who was wrongly accused and convicted of the crime.

For thirteen years, I was the executive director of AIDWYC. I was one of the midwives of that organization. I loved it. I nurtured it. I educated it with the love of Truth. The organization stood for justice and Truth in the face of error, injustice, deliberate falsehood, and state violence. Freeing an innocent person from prison or rescuing that person from execution is an unadulterated act of goodness. Being involved in work of this nature is humbling and ennobling at the same time, what I can only describe as "conscious work." Ralph Waldo Emerson said it best: "It is one of the beautiful compensations of this life that no one can sincerely help another without helping himself." What better work could there be for a former prisoner who had himself been wrongly convicted?

So why did I resign? In 2004, Ontario's recently elected attorney general, Michael Bryant, appointed Susan MacLean, one of the original prosecutors of Guy Paul Morin, to the Ontario Court of Justice. I reasoned that it was time for the organization to take a firm stand against that particular appointment and, by extension, against the flawed system of judicial appointments in Canada. MacLean was the only original prosecutor who pushed to have Morin tried twice for the same crime. As was mentioned earlier, he was acquitted by a jury at his first trial, but because Canada's Charter of Rights and Freedoms has no absolute provision against double jeopardy and because MacLean was so certain of Morin's guilt, he was tried again. The second time, the new prosecution team, of which MacLean was a part, was determined to get a conviction; their tunnel vision necessitated that the facts of the crime fit their version of events. At the second trial, Morin's conviction was the result of perjury by jailhouse informants and the manipulation of forensic evidence. After that egregious wrong, Morin was taken from his family and the quiet life he lived and sent to prison.

Now, one of the perpetrators of that egregious wrong, Susan MacLean, was going to the bench. In my mind, something here was not right. In Ontario, a judicial vacancy is advertised, candidates apply, and a shortlist is submitted to the attorney general by a screening panel. Neither ordinary citizens nor members of provincial parliament are allowed to question people who will potentially be making life-altering decisions. We simply have to trust that the screeners and appointees are going to act in our best interests. As to the past behavior of Susan MacLean, we had no idea if probing questions were asked. I can only say, unequivocally, that none of the people who suffered from wrongful convictions served on any of the screening committees. The task of choosing judges in Canada is given over to the class of people who most benefit from the laws as they are now written.

My colleagues at AIDWYC, who had worked side by side with me since the inception of the organization, may have also disagreed with this judicial appointment, but they wanted to put the situation behind them. I thought they were choosing expedience over the risky course of speaking the Truth. That is the fashion these days in most instances when we are dealing with the malfeasance of those in power: "Let's just put it behind us and move on." We used to call that "sweeping it under the rug," a phrase that at least acknowledged that the wrong was being hidden. How many burglars or drug dealers would be able to tell a judge, "Let's just put my crime behind us and move on"?

When Susan MacLean was appointed to the Ontario court bench in January 2004, my first instinct was to go public with a press conference. Surprisingly, AIDWYC's board of directors refused my request, so I asked and received permission from them to write a letter in our name to the attorney general. After a vote was taken and passed on this measure, Melvyn Green, a board lawyer who had opposed the idea of writing a letter (and would be appointed to a judgeship in 2005), then asked to take part in its drafting, a request that for obvious reasons I denied. "Why," the letter asked Bryant, "out of the thirty-five thousand lawyers in Ontario, 2,400 of whom are exceptional Crown attorneys, would the screening panel shortlist this particular person, and, why would [Bryant] choose her from the final six to become a judge?" The attorney general, knowing he was under no obligation to justify any appointment he might make, refused to answer the letter, effectively giving AIDWYC the cold shoulder. His office lacked the courtesy to even acknowledge that a letter had been received.

I learned about Bryant's brush-off when I returned home from a holiday in Jamaica. At that point, I again wanted to hold a press conference and go public with our concerns about the appointment. This time it would come down to a vote. We needed to have a conference call to set up the vote since some members of the board were in Europe at the time. We were able to contact fifteen out of twenty, more than our usual quorum. Discussion, mediated by Cal Bricker, took place; the argument boiled down to whether or not Bryant could be held accountable. The board voted 9–6 to proceed no further on the MacLean issue. How could I be bound by that vote? I took it as a vote of non-confidence and continued to insist that we needed to speak out. They said, "Rubin, you can speak out, personally, but you cannot speak for AIDWYC." I said that if as executive director I could not speak out on an issue such as this, an issue that shook the organization to its very foundations, then I was in the wrong place.

I looked behind me and was surprised to see that no AIDWYC people were coming to my support, not even the five who had voted with me. Up until then, I had failed to notice that the board was composed primarily of lawyers, fifteen out of twenty to be exact. They had now become "lawyers" instead of the friends I once knew, the friends whose families I knew (I'm godfather to James Lockyer's son), and who had always shown me respect, kindness, and hospitality. It appeared to me that these lawyers were not going to hold the top lawyer in Ontario, Attorney General Bryant, accountable for his decision. Up to that point, we had fought the battles and reaped the rewards and publicity of AIDWYC together. But now it seemed that they were not prepared to go public against the very office that might one day appoint them to the bench. It appeared to me then that AIDWYC was becoming part of some old boys' club.

As the public face of AIDWYC, I was going out all over the United States and many other parts of the world opposing death penalties, petitioning governors, meeting with presidents, taking abuse from people frustrated because a person they thought was guilty would not be injected, gassed, fried, or locked up indefinitely. The lawyers at AIDWYC who were so willing to fight against judicial abuses in Vietnam, South America, Saudi Arabia, Japan, and even in the United States of America, could not bring themselves to criticize the unaccountability of judicial appointments in their own backyard.

I gave the organization an ultimatum: either we go public in our protest before MacLean's swearing in, or I would call my own press conference and resign. Since, as I said, the prosecution of Guy Paul Morin was the original reason why AIDWYC even existed and since Susan MacLean was part of that prosecution team, we could no longer be true to ourselves if we let this appointment go without comment or protest. Being true to yourself is the essence of moral, ethical, and conscious behavior. How could AIDWYC maintain its integrity if the board of directors, for what appeared to me to be opportunistic reasons, had joined the mass of sleepwalking humanity? AIDWYC would then have to pretend to be what it was not.

In opposing my ultimatum, Brian Greenspan, a member of AIDWYC's board of directors, gave his own ultimatum: that if AIDWYC did go public, he was going to resign. I could understand his position: we'd had a vote, and that was the end of it. Further-more, he insisted that Michael Bryant was going to be the best attorney general in Ontario's history. On March 8, the day of Susan MacLean's swearing in, AIDWYC did go public on the MacLean appointment, but Greenspan's resignation was not forthcoming. Three other board members accompanied me to the press con-ference. In my view, the three did not come to protest MacLean's elevation to the bench but to apologize to the press for having to be there. *This is Rubin Carter*, they appeared to be saying, *and you know how he can be.*

Nevertheless, we had made it known, at least officially, that the organization opposed MacLean's appointment to the bench, and so I thought our work would go on as usual. The public statement had to be enough for me, even if the backing for it was unenthusias-tic. A slight shift occurred within the organization. What appeared to me to be a grudging acceptance of what I had done was reflected in a statement by then-president Peter Meier that we had "come down on the side of the angels." I knew that we could not seek the removal of MacLean, that such an outcome, however desirable, was plainly impossible. Nevertheless, she was placed on notice that her work as a judge would face scrutiny.

But then I found out that my work was being sabotaged. A lec-ture that I was to have given to an international group of journalists was cancelled by Peter Meier without my knowledge or consent. The article that I wrote on Bryant's appointment of Susan MacLean for our quarterly journal, an article in which I made unequivocal statements about her suitability, was altered, defanged you might say, without my knowledge or consent. At that point, I took an indefinite leave of absence from AIDWYC, hoping that my colleagues would wake up and see the dead-end road toward which we were headed. They were attempting to silence their own spokesperson. The individual who altered my writings, James Lockyer, then submitted to me his letter of resignation, acknowledging that he had "doctored my article" without my knowledge or consent. In that letter, he offered an apology, blaming his conservative nature for what he had done. I was moved by his letter and felt vindicated in having taken the leave of absence. But it soon became apparent when I read his letter at the next board meeting that Lockyer had not really resigned. In fact, he acted as if he hadn't even written the letter! Both he and Greenspan must have assumed that I would not accept their resignations. I felt, however, that both of them had to resign and perhaps return to the board at a later date.

Their refusal to resign reminded me that three years earlier there had been an attempt to merge AIDWYC with the Innocence Project at Osgoode Hall Law School (York University) run by the late Diane Martin. Win Wahrer, AIDWYC's director of client services, and I had threatened back then to resign if that were to happen. Although Martin was a champion of the wrongly convicted, we were concerned that AIDWYC's community-based membership would drown inside a large university setting. The board had backed off that plan. But now, in the dead of night, fifteen lawyers emerged from the Trojan Horse to destroy in my heart what we had built together. The ideals and the integrity of the organization no longer seemed to matter. I had come to the painful realization that I no longer belonged in AIDWYC.

I had to leave despite the fact that AIDWYC receives administrative funding from the Law Society of Upper Canada to the tune of one hundred thousand dollars a year, that AIDWYC has a screening system for cases that really works, and that it was home to some of the most brilliant and capable lawyers in Canada, including Lockyer and Greenspan. As for the money, some of the lawyers wanted to use it to compensate themselves for a portion of the time they were giving to clients. This was yet another issue on which we differed, my belief being that since membership in AIDWYC was voluntary, the work should also be voluntary. I wasn't getting paid either. I resigned officially on Friday, August 13, 2004, choosing that unlucky day as an expression of my deep sorrow.

I had to leave despite the fact that AIDWYC has saved so many lives. Even in early February 2004, while the dispute over Susan MacLean was heating up, I went down to California and took part in saving the life of Kevin Cooper who, as mentioned before, was scheduled for execution on February 10.

AIDWYC was created to help free innocent people and to hold accountable those who deliberately perpetrate and those who benefit from wrongful convictions. The appointment of Susan MacLean to the bench made it appear to me that she was being rewarded despite the fact that she participated in the conviction of an innocent person. After DNA evidence completely exonerated Morin, MacLean still insisted that he was guilty. As a result of considerable pressure, according to *Globe and Mail* justice reporter Kirk Makin, MacLean broke down in tears two days later and finally apologized for questioning the basis of Morin's acquittal.

Because of my personal experience behind bars and knowing what it takes to survive, I have come to understand both the dangers of disregarding factual Truth and of not being true to one's self, that which we usually call hypocrisy. People like the Morin family are made to suffer when Truth is treated as a barrier or an inconvenience. By refusing to actively oppose this particular judicial appointment, I began to think that AIDWYC had become a hobby or an extracurricular activity for most of the board members, something they might put on their resumes when it came time for them to be appointed to the bench or to run for political office. In my mind's eye, the passion for Truth, the Spirit that drove AIDWYC, was gone! What is left when the Spirit goes out of anything? Nothing but an empty shell of its former self.

It may help to put a human face on these abstractions. Guy Paul Morin was a young man who was thrown in jail because of overzealous police and prosecutors. His family—his mother, father, and sisters—was devastated. I sat up crying many nights with them, trying to neutralize their pain and suffering. They were pushed nearly to bankruptcy. They had to endure hateful or pitying stares from their neighbors and read accounts in the press that their son was a murderer and a sexual deviant. They will never recover from the trauma of that experience, yet the prosecutor of their innocent son was elevated to the bench! And, of course, the real killer of Christine Jessop is still free, because the authorities failed to follow up on other leads in the certainty that they had their man. The Morin and the Jessop families are still suffering.

It is the everyday nature of the legal profession to choose expedience and compromise, to seek deals, rather than to stand up for principle, for that which is real, right, good, and true. If some aspiring lawyers enter law school with ideals, far fewer of them will leave that way. They learn that idealism is for fools and losers. They train their minds to be committed to words, to precedents, to best the opponent in the courtroom game, to win. That is the function of a courtroom, however frustrating it might be to an outsider or to a defendant. Most wrongful convictions occur because of the ineptitude of appointed or overworked defense counsel, even while the guilty may escape punishment because of their lawyer's superior skill. What does Truth have to do with it? Truth is a stranger to a court of law and would not even be recognized if it sashayed through the courtroom and took a seat in the judge's lap.

AIDWYC maintained its integrity and credibility by rising above the law, by making Truth its first principle, by foolish idealism. In not fully opposing the attorney general's appointment of Susan MacLean, I felt that the board was throwing that integrity and credibility out the window. That was my integrity and credibility too. The only way for me to maintain my integrity and credibility, short of Greenspan and Lockyer resigning, was to fly out the window myself. Unfortunately, there was no King Solomon to adjudicate and award the baby to the rightful parent. Rather than start an internal or a public struggle that would have jeopardized the ongoing cases of the wrongly convicted with whom AIDWYC was then dealing, I left, at a great personal loss.

Having departed from the Association in Defense of the Wrongly Convicted after thirteen years, I needed to establish a new school for "the work," and on September 25, 2004, Innocence International was born. This new generation of wrongful conviction services is sponsored by the law school at Griffith University in Brisbane, Australia, where I received my first doctorate of laws in 2003. It functions as a global service network dedicated to defending innocent people from wrongful convictions and holding those accountable who knowingly convict the innocent and benefit from those convictions. Two ongoing cases deserve mention here, the first being that of David McCallum of Brooklyn, New York, a prototype for all wrongful convictions, a case dealt with thoroughly in the appendix of this book. The second case, sometimes referred to as Burns/Rafay, is one in which many people were very surprised by my involvement. Nowhere in my experience, except perhaps in my own case, have I felt such public prejudice and outrage against two defendants who were unjustly imprisoned for the remainder of their lives.

In 1994, Sebastian Burns and Atif Rafay, then two teenagers and both Canadian citizens, returned home late one night to the Rafay house in Bellevue, Washington, only to find Rafay's family (his father, Tariq, his mother, Sultana, and his disabled older sister, Basma) murdered. They were not just murdered but crushed, bludgeoned to death, wiped out, annihilated with blunt instruments. After making a 911 call and fearing the killers might still be in the house, the two boys ran outside and waited in the street for the police.

Almost immediately the police focused their investigation on the two teenagers. Their alibi as to where they were at the time of the murders was confirmed: they were seen at a movie theater where *The Lion King* was playing. Yet the police isolated them in a grubby motel room. They were persistently questioned, and they submitted voluntarily to blood, clothing, and hair analysis. During this time and up to this very day, the authorities have found no forensic evidence linking the two boys to the crime. In fact, the DNA evidence in the Rafay home pointed to other, unknown persons.

Tunnel vision being what it is, everything the two teenagers did, every normal teenage behavior, including the viewing of rental movies at the motel and returning home to Canada, was seen by the Bellevue police as confirmation of their guilt. The rental movies showed callousness. Leaving for Canada was called "fleeing," despite the fact that Burns still lived there with his family and Rafay had nowhere else to go. The police, the jury, the judge, and a sleeping, credulous public came to believe that the two teenagers committed this bloody crime for Rafay's inheritance, some $350,000, so that the pair could make a film.

The two former high school buddies had been staying at the Rafays' that summer, Atif home from his first year at Cornell University, to which Tariq Rafay was paying $30,000 a year in tuition fees. Sebastian Burns was visiting from his home in West Vancouver. Aside from some of Burns's hair found in the same shower that he had been using for days, other evidence, such as blood spatter that indicated three killers in the house, DNA samples from the blood, and a pubic hair in Tariq and Sultana's bed, pointed to other suspects.

A tip from an FBI informant who had knowledge of the murder weapons before that information appeared in the press, suggested that Tariq Rafay could have been the victim of a hit by Muslim fundamentalists. The manner of the killing certainly fit with a crime of fanaticism or revenge.

Still certain that these two seemingly arrogant teenage intellectuals were guilty of the crime, the Bellevue police enlisted elements of Canada's emblematic and problematic national police force, the Royal Canadian Mounted Police. They bugged the Burnses' home and Rafay's automobile (which produced nothing in the way of evidence), while setting the two boys up for an elaborate sting operation known as Mr. Big. In this scheme, investigators pose as members of a crime syndicate specifically to gain suspects' trust and elicit videotaped confessions.

Because the two boys were believed to be murderers, they were isolated from their West Vancouver community. Burns was particularly vulnerable to a sting because he had always had problems reading other people. He was easily entrapped into stealing cars and laundering large sums of money supplied by the Canadian taxpayer, supposedly on behalf of the imaginary syndicate. Finally, he was "accepted" into the gang, but told that he had to come clean about what happened in Bellevue. If he told the truth, he would be "solid." If he didn't, they knew where he and his family lived. These not-so-subtle threats of violence and death succeeded. They were finally able to get Burns on camera talking about the crime to a person he thought was the boss of the crime syndicate—a Mr. Big! Rafay was swept up into this morass, confirming Burns's statement in order to protect his friend. Soon after the "confession," the fake mobsters shed their disguises and arrested the pair.

The evidence from such schemes is prohibited in American courts as a violation of Fifth Amendment rights against self-incrimination. We believe that the judge erred in allowing the false confessions to be seen and heard in the courtroom, even if, as he said, the evidence was gathered outside the United States by people "who were not in authority." As part of what we have determined to be his erroneous judgment, he held that no coercion had been involved since the boys did not appear to be under duress on the videotape.

Innocence International finds this case of wrongful conviction both appalling and abhorrent. Two young men have had their lives stolen away. While the RCMP has been able to elicit confessions and solve crimes by using Mr. Big, this method is poorly designed to separate the innocent from the guilty. The function of the police is to serve people, to protect them, and to support the scientific gathering of evidence, not to behave like gangsters! If a police officer looks like a criminal and continually acts like a criminal (more than five hundred of these stings in British Columbia alone), where does one draw the line between police activity and criminal behavior?

I became involved in this case after viewing a film entitled *Mr. Big* by Tiffany Burns, Sebastian's sister. In this film, she documents several other cases where Mr. Big had been successful in getting false confessions from both young people and adults alike. Canadians Kyle Unger, Patrick Fischer, Clayton George Mentuck, Jason Dix, Wade Skiffington, and Andy Rose were trapped in this web of deception by their own human weaknesses, by lies, fraudulent criminal acts, and millions of dollars in criminal money. These people, like Burns, believed that they had joined a ruthless gang headed by the notorious Mr. Big or Big Al or some other phony name. They were also warned implicitly that if they were not "solid," they or their families would more than likely be whacked, or killed. Since denials were always met with scorn and disbelief, it is clear to us that the purpose of the sting was less the Truth and more the confession.

I met Atif Rafay at the prison in Monroe, Washington. Under the circumstances, his constant smile amazed me. This slight but brilliant and somehow optimistic young man answered every probing question we threw at him for three long hours. Never a hesitation, never a moment where he visibly attempted to cover up a single statement. After studying this case in great detail, I can say the following without fear or doubt: Sebastian Burns and Atif Rafay were delivered to Calvary by the RCMP; the state of Washington nailed them up on the crucifix; the media stood there and jeered.

Both boys would have been executed had not some of Canada's top lawyers interceded and won a Supreme Court decision preventing Canadian citizens from being extradited to face the death penalty. Allan Rock, then Canada's minister of justice, was all too willing to comply with Washington's request.

We believe that the 2004 convictions of the two teenagers should be overturned and that they must be granted a full and fair hearing as prescribed by the United States Constitution. If a new trial is based upon fact and not character assassination, upon evidence and not prejudice, it will become clear to everyone that Atif Rafay and Sebastian Burns are entitled to exoneration. It will become clear that two teenage boys are no match for seasoned professional interrogators who are determined to get a confession. It will also become clear that the heinous murder of the Rafay family has never been solved.

9

Just Enough:
Home Free

Four monster hurricanes—Katrina, Ophelia, Rita, and Wilma—hit North and Central America in 2005, to say nothing of Charley, Francis, Ivan, and Jeanne in 2004. The singularity of a hurricane is symbolized by its so-called eye, its one eye. It's the Cyclops of storms. Panic, fear, and alarm precede its coming ashore. Devastation, destruction, and loss follow in its wake. But you need not fear this "Hurricane" with his one eye. He has a message for those who care to listen. The immense cataclysmic storm that makes us aware of our feeble existences in the face of the mighty forces that govern the earth and the universe also sends a message of hope, a message of salvation in the face of destruction and loss.

Along the road of life, it appears as if I have lost everything: my physical freedom, my athletic career, my family, my home, and my organization, AIDWYC, to which I had dedicated my unwavering loyalty and energy. But I am telling you here and now that I have not lost a single thing. I have not lost anything because I have not lost myself, which, in the end, is everything! I have remained true to myself over time. It's not as if I have not faced the temptation to pack it all in. While in prison, people said to me, "Why don't you behave? Be ordinary. Obey the rules. Be like everyone else so we can come down here to visit you. Be ordinary, and they will not put you in solitary confinement. Give up your dream to be free so we can come to this prison and watch you rot away."

They meant well. They thought I was going to be defeated. They didn't want to see me hurt. They didn't mean to become the very force that would have driven me to despair and suffocation. They wanted me to be nice, tame, gentle. They didn't believe that I could win, because they could only see the walls surrounding me. But I found a "hole in the wall," and I walked right through it. I had the courage to wake up, become an individual, and remain true to myself over time—true to the work. The only way that can happen is by practicing principles and acting only upon the Truth.

I did not leave AIDWYC because my colleagues were imperfect. They are, like all of us, struggling with their own foibles and weaknesses and illusions. I left because we no longer had the same vision.

For me, AIDWYC was not only a means to an end, the freeing of innocent people, but an end in and of itself: speaking the Truth in harmony with beauty, moving humanity to freedom. AIDWYC was a part of the work, and that work, if it is to have any meaning at all, is the work of waking people up in order to regain our rightful places in the world. We must be true to who and what we are by following our principles. That is why I am here today. On the level of good, the Truth can only hurt a lie. Justice can only hurt injustice. If my colleagues at AIDWYC were going to play fast and loose with the concepts of real, right, good, and true, if the "legal game" and the "money game" and the "prestige game" were to take precedence over the work, then there was nothing left for me to do but leave and create a new school for the work, Innocence International. The greatest evil of all is when good people do not fight for *what they know to be the Truth*. As Shakespeare wrote, "Lilies that fester smell far worse than weeds."

I have an unwavering respect for the worth, the greatness, and the inviolable miraculous nature of each individual human being. When I go out into my garden and put little seedlings into the ground, I know that by themselves, in the earliest stages, they depend upon me for their nourishment, for fertilizer and water, and for their weeding. We human beings, like those little seedlings, if nourished correctly will become rooted, will stand up on our own, blossom, and bloom, lifting our heads in joy to the place from which we come, the sun. We can become so powerful that our light, reflected by our joy, will shine to the farthest star. We must never allow ourselves to forget that possibility, or, if we do, we must find a way to return to that dream of ourselves. We must free ourselves from this universal prison of sleep, this prison of false personality, or we will become calcified in the unreal; we will be nothing more than flies in amber. Humanity will not evolve.

My main purpose in writing this book is to share with you what I have discovered to be the Truth. The love of Truth is the Spirit of man. Given where I was and for how long I was there, I have no business at all being here now. The fact that I am here right now demonstrates that good will prevail. The fact that I am alive and free means that something higher than my feeble self is in operation. That is why the work I do in this wrongful conviction business has been so successful. A lower level must always eventually give way to a higher level. That's the law. This level of life is controlled by the law.

Only in those moments of greatest challenge, of devastation, of despair, will your greatness of Spirit demonstrate itself. You must never give up before you give your Spirit a chance to work its greatest magic, which is nothing more or less than waking up from this level of unconscious human insanity.

If I had the opportunity to change anything at all in my life, I would not do it, because everything in this universe is connected, from the outer galaxies to a tiny drop of dew, and a change in one place would "automatically" produce a change in another place. I love the person I am today. I love myself. The person who went into prison and the person who came out of prison are two different people. They don't think or feel alike. They don't even look alike! In my sleeping state, I was just another highly trained savage—a civilian savage, a soldier savage, a prizefighting savage, who thought he knew it all. But on the level of life at which I now live and from which I operate, there is nothing but good.

This planet earth is a paradise, a fantasy island. Whatever your mind can conceive of and believe in can be achieved. First, though, you must dare to dream. Without the dream, nothing can be different. Once you dream, you change. Your dream becomes your aim, and only with a permanent aim can you accomplish anything. Everything that helps you to succeed is real, right, good, and true, and that which slows you down or saps your energy is wrong. It's a lie! You may have a goal, but you give up on it because you feel that you can't get there, or because your mind interferes with what you have set out to do, or because people have belittled your dream. Without a permanent aim, your sense of right and wrong, truth and falsehood, good and bad, is as aimless as you are. You are lost in the wilderness without a compass.

You must dream about what has not yet come to be and then cause that to come into being. But in order for your dream to bear fruit, you must act now as if you have already attained it. You must act as if you already have what you as yet have not, and you will have it. That's the answer to prayer as well. That is how I willed myself to be free from the physical prison of bricks, steel bars, and concrete walls. I acted like a free man. Even when I was buried six feet under the ground in solitary confinement, I still acted like I was a free man. And yet human beings outside the prison walls, so-called free people, act like they are slaves. The terrible things on this earth that people do to other people—murder, rape, theft, enslavement, war, oppression, deceit, and victimization—cannot be the behavior of conscious people. So it must be the behavior of sleeping people who do not understand anything.

The question is, then, how do we become conscious? How do we wake up? Just as doctors or lawyers or scientists need to learn a new language to operate competently within their chosen professions, in order to wake up we, too, must try to learn another language, the language of Consciousness, a language without contradiction, the language of the higher mind, the universal language of love and Truth, joy and achievement. The saints in heaven are only the sinners on earth who just kept on trying.

We did not know that we were put to sleep by our conditioning, just as our parents were also put to sleep by their conditioning. We had nothing to do with that. None of us did. We were all born with exactly what we need to live as complete human beings, just as everything in this universe is inviolate and perfect. But we were also born into a world of sleeping people, a world of violence, a world where wars, hate, anger, death, destruction, and inequality reign supreme. We now find ourselves not only in the midst of this violence, but actually taking an active role in that violence, calling it citizenship, democracy, loyalty, and honor. Calling it everything that it isn't. We have no idea why we do the things we do other than surviving from one day to next.

To wake up and become conscious, you have to die to yourself, die to the sleeping person you are right now. And you are probably afraid of dying. Up until now, you have lived in fear of many things. The prairie chicken is always fearful. You have to let the prairie chicken die for the eagle to take flight. And what is this thing called death anyway? What is this thing that, as long as it happens to someone else, we revere? What is this thing to which we accord much time, honor, and glory? In reality, death is nothing at all. Nothing has changed. Everything remains exactly how it was. Those who loved you will continue to love you; those who hated you will go right on hating you. Everything remains the same. You have merely passed into another room.

Waking up is exactly the opposite—you are the room, the house in which you find the room, the street upon which the house sits, the city where you find the street, the province or state of which the city is a part, the country to which the state belongs, the continent, the earth, the planetary world, the sun that the planetary world serves, all galaxies which encompass all worlds to the Absolute, which is everything and nothing at the same time. Consciousness, the Alpha and the Omega, has no limitations, and that's why unlimited possibilities exist. But you have to wake up! And that means dying.

One day, a few seasons ago, I had just finished speaking to a group of people at a Toronto high school when a young woman in the audience stood up and asked me how I wanted my life to be remembered. I had to pause a long moment, because I'd never given the question a moment's thought. When I did think about it, I realized that the way people remember me doesn't really matter. What really matters is how I remember myself, the act of self-remembering that saved me from perdition. But given the opportunity, I answered her question like this: I was a prizefighter at one point in my life. I was a soldier at one point in my life. I was a convict at one point in my life. I was a jailhouse lawyer at one point. I was the executive director of AIDWYC at one point in my life—a black angel. Today, I am the CEO of Innocence International. I have been a writer and a doctor of laws. I have been many things and have many things still yet to be. But if I had to choose an epitaph to be carved upon my tombstone, it would simply read, "He was just enough." He was just enough to overcome everything that was laid on him on this earth. He was just enough not to give up on himself. He was just enough to believe in himself beyond anything else in this world. He was just enough to have the courage to stand up for his convictions no matter what problems his actions may have caused him. He was just enough to perform a miracle, to wake up, to escape the universal prison of sleep, and to regain his humanity in a living hell. He was just enough. And so, my young friend, are you.

Just enough.

APPENDIX

Where the Law Silences the Truth: The Tragic Wrongful Conviction of David McCallum

My childhood was stolen from me; I don't have any children of my own. In truth, to a man in prison for a crime he did not commit, every moment is [excruciating]. I can never get used to prison life. In my sleep, I hear voices, some of them long dead, like loved ones. Some voices are like torture, to wonder every day, every hour, whether or not I will ever be free again is a special form of torture. I'm telling you that it takes a daily, hourly toll on your heart and in your soul, particularly when you have to explain to your nephew why they just won't let you out of the house to watch cartoons with him. Just the other day, my nephew asked me why I could not come over to his house to play with him. He did not know that my sentence is twenty-five years to life. I had to pause before I responded to his innocent comments, because I had to gather myself.

—DAVID McCALLUM III

In 1974, while still in prison, I wrote and published my autobiography, *The Sixteenth Round*, and sent it out into the world as a "letter in a bottle," hoping that someone of conscience would find and read it and come to my assistance. Thirty years later, as founder and CEO of Innocence International, I received a letter in a bottle from another person in prison seeking the very same redress that I had sought: relief from a life of living hell!

David McCallum, an African in America and the author of this letter, was arrested in 1985 when Reaganomics, as the war on poor people was then known, would result in a permanent underclass in the United States: out of sight, out of mind, and voiceless. From the first volley, a broadside against the striking air traffic controllers and, by extension, all the American labor unions, to the tightening of unemployment and welfare eligibility, the inner cities became places of extreme tension and daily confrontations with the police. The police were given the power and increased numbers to keep a lid on the ghettos, the prison system began a major expansion, and the poor were forced into low-paying service jobs or lives of petty crime. If anything, this trend has only intensified over the last twenty years; the rich are richer, the poor poorer, and the middle has been squeezed into silent submission. Overwhelming police power, the election or appointment of ultraconservative judges, and restrictions on habeas corpus rights have also resulted in numerous wrongful convictions and abuses.

We at Innocence International got to know David McCallum through his words, specifically his letters, which reveal a fellow human with insight, compassion, and empathy for others. Those letters form a part of this appendix. Just to talk about McCallum in the abstract would only make of him one of the many thousands of wrongly convicted people, a statistic with a story. Behind every wrongful conviction is a story, but not all the wrongly convicted have McCallum's self-taught gift with language.

Over the past two decades in the United States and elsewhere, so-called moral conservatives, some pretending to strong religious beliefs, have become increasingly influential in the sentencing of people convicted of crimes. The very same people who pontificate over the value of a human life sometimes appear to think that the life of a fetus is somehow more important than the life of a fully grown human being. These kinds of people are in an especially deep state of sleep. They may fashion their beliefs selectively from the Bible. They think that the principle of justice is best expressed in the phrase "an eye for an eye." They are unforgiving, unless they themselves or someone from their own families gets into trouble with the law. They fail to see that innocent people are doubly harmed by a wrongful conviction: first, the reputations of the innocent are totally and utterly destroyed, and then they must spend many, many years of their lives being tortured in a prison cell. The fishing net for the less advantaged is widely cast and tightly knit, entangling the dolphins and the small fry along with the catch.

The story of McCallum's wrongful conviction begins on the streets of New York City. Police reports described two black men, one five-foot-eleven with braids and the other five-foot-two, identified as having been responsible for eight carjackings within a forty-eight hour period, the eighth of these carjackings at 5:45 A.M. on October 20, 1985. On the afternoon of that same day, a twenty-year-old white male named Nathan Blenner was kidnapped in Queens, New York (the very same precinct and neighborhood where the other carjackings took place), while sitting behind the wheel of his car in front of his own house. A female witness living around the corner from Blenner was accosted by two men meeting those descriptions within an hour of what we believe was the ninth carjacking of the spree. Blenner was later found murdered, shot in the back of the head, lying facedown at the rear of Aberdeen Park in Brooklyn.

Five days later, two carjackers, identified as Terrence Heyward and Herman Murphy, both twenty years old, were taken in by the Queens police for questioning. They were interrogated by Brooklyn detective Joseph Butta because the murder itself had taken place within his precinct. In the midst of this interview, Heyward identified David McCallum and his friend Willie Stuckey as having a gun "with a body on it."

On October 27, McCallum and Stuckey, both sixteen-year-olds, both from Brooklyn and both black, were arrested and charged with the kidnapping and the subsequent murder. They both gave videotaped confessions, tacitly admitting to participation in a kidnapping while blaming each other for the actual murder. According to McCallum, each was told, "You tell me that *he* did it, and *you* can go home." Their statements indicate that McCallum and Stuckey hopped a train to Queens, entered Blenner's all-white neighborhood, and randomly stole his car with the victim inside.

One year later, at a pretrial hearing, both teenagers were advised by their court-appointed lawyers to plead guilty, a recommendation which Stuckey's attorney relayed to the presiding judge, Francis O. Egitto: "I have professionally told [my client] I don't believe that there is any possibility of him coming out victorious in this trial.... He's informed me that he is not interested in a plea." The lawyers knew about the power of a confession to a jury, false as it may have been.

The judge then told the two teenagers that a guilty plea would result in a fifteen-year-to-life sentence, whereas a trial by jury conviction could result in a twenty-five-to-fifty-year minimum sentence, with emphasis on the word *fifty*. If a young person has committed a major felony and faces a lifetime in prison, it is more than likely that he would follow the advice of his own lawyer who tells him that he stands no chance of winning. But here you have two juveniles, both of whose lawyers are throwing in the towel, and neither one of them would agree to plead guilty.

Why did both teenagers opt for going to trial? McCallum says that common sense told him that if you didn't commit a crime, you wouldn't go to jail. They were both certain of their innocence. They also knew that the videotaped confessions had been beaten out of them. Stuckey, who had never been convicted of a major crime, and McCallum, who had, were on that day playing handball in Halsey Park in Brooklyn, nowhere near the scene of the kidnapping in Queens. Surely, both thought, the truth would come out and they would be set free. Surely this belief was the ultimate proof of their naïveté. If you are not a lawyer or have not gone to school to study the law, then, when it comes to the criminal justice system, you are brain-dead!

During that pretrial hearing, called a Huntley Hearing in the state of New York, when a judge must assess whether a confession was obtained according to constitutional guidelines, McCallum made a very costly mistake. Under questioning from his court-appointed lawyer who hadn't even interviewed him before this hearing, McCallum claimed that he had invented all the details in his confession. The problem for both defendants was that Stuckey's confession had come before McCallum's, and some of the details jibed or dovetailed between the two confessions. During the actual trial, when McCallum changed his testimony to say that the lead detective had *fed* him those details, it appeared to everyone in the courtroom that he was lying. There were only two ways McCallum could have known about the details of the crime: either he was actually at the murder scene or the detective had fed him the information from Stuckey's earlier confession. Stuckey's lawyer, Harvey Mandelcorn, upon hearing McCallum's contradictory testimony, immediately moved that the two trials be severed and that Stuckey and McCallum be tried separately to defend his client's Sixth Amendment right to cross-examination: "What I'm asking this court to do is give this defendant not the minimum fair trial but the maximum fair trial that this country could provide." The judge's reply was terse and impatient if nothing else: "Your application at this time is denied." Judge Egitto then went on to jury selection, a process that took an hour, a brief timeline normally impossible in a murder case. What had actually happened at the Huntley Hearing was that the judge, the prosecutor, and the defense attorneys had hastily concluded that the two defendants were guilty. The trial would be held only because they had a right to a trial, but it would be a perfunctory exercise.

The legal mind works in a particular way. Knowing that David McCallum had hopelessly prejudiced his own case and would eventually be found guilty in the end was all that mattered. The facts of the case became irrelevant and, in fact, were always irrelevant. To lawyers and judges, the outcome of the trial or the verdict is all that matters. Talking to McCallum more than twenty years after the fact, you will begin to understand that a stressed out seventeen-year-old (as he was during the trial) does not give his full attention to any matter. A teenager's mind wanders even in the best of circumstances. Once McCallum said that he had made up all the details, he just continued going down that road. The car was headed full throttle down a wrong-way highway. McCallum had no idea of the significance of what he was putting into the cold-record facts of the trial. This fatal mistake was attributable to the fact that McCallum did not meet with his lawyer a single time before the Huntley Hearing, so he was completely unprepared for questioning a whole year after being charged with the crime.

We know conclusively that neither McCallum nor Stuckey was at the murder scene. The only scene the detective knew about was the one he himself had created from knowing where the victim lived and where his body had been found, from a 911 call in Queens, and by Stuckey's imagination under threat of continued physical abuse. In this framework, McCallum, under the same threat of abuse by the detective, invented new details. The reason for McCallum's providing extra details of the crime is obvious only in hindsight. Since the detective had promised him that he would be released after he explained his role in the shooting of Nathan Blenner, he had a personal investment in making his version of the story more believable than Stuckey's.

One of McCallum's invented details, later referred to in the prosecutor's summation as "realistic," was that Nathan Blenner's arms moved after he had been shot. This description is particularly interesting in light of the fact that Blenner was shot in the back of the head and found lying facedown.

What is very interesting is that the "confession" was and still is the only evidence whatsoever that ties either McCallum or Stuckey to the crime. No circumstantial evidence, no eyewitness evidence, no ballistic evidence, no whereabouts evidence, no DNA evidence—not a single, solitary piece of evidence exists against either McCallum or Stuckey; the killing of Nathan Blenner has never really been solved, but the real culprits are very obvious.

When this case came to my attention, it gave me the strangest feeling that in 1985, McCallum and Stuckey had swapped places with John Artis and me, two other black men whose convictions served only to satisfy the community's need for closure. Artis and I and McCallum and Stuckey had all been arrested in the month of October. Willie Stuckey died in prison in 2001 at the age of thirty-one; whatever disease or injury he died from may just as well be called despair. Artis was paroled after fifteen years because they could see that he would rather die in his prison cell than falsely implicate me. McCallum stays alive today because he will never give up the belief in his innocence and will never stop fighting to free himself.

Two major issues arise from this case. The first, of course, is wrongful conviction, and most of the telltale signs of a wrongful conviction pertain to the plight of David McCallum. The second issue is the sentencing of juvenile offenders in the United States. Only a handful of countries sentence juvenile offenders to life terms. Many adolescents lack the impulse-control expected of an adult. Because they might act first without thinking, they tend to make very serious mistakes, but those who make the most serious mistakes and even those who commit the worst of crimes should not be written off as incorrigibly evil. It does society no lasting good, to say nothing of how expensive it is, to keep anyone of that age behind bars for the remainder of his life. Right now, there are over nine thousand young offenders in the United States serving life sentences, two thousand of whom have no chance whatsoever for parole. Some people would probably be happier if all the recalcitrant teenagers were brought to the gates of the city and stoned to death. That is what one passage in the Bible says to do with them, even the ones who simply disobey their parents. Never mind that most of the Bible is more about mercy and forgiveness than revenge. The Supreme Court of the United States ruled in 2005 that executing children was cruel and unusual punishment and has banned the practice, at least for now. Judges, even before the ruling against executions, have been intimidated by a vocal majority of Americans (more than 65 percent in support of capital punishment) into handing out draconian prison sentences, mostly to teenagers of a darker skin color. Were McCallum guilty of the crime, and I maintain that he was *not guilty*, it is still unconscionable that he would be placed in a prison at the age of seventeen and sentenced to life imprisonment.

The supporters of harsh sentencing have little to say about the problems of the wrongly convicted. I must assume that innocent people are seen simply as collateral damage in the wars against drugs, crime, and terrorism. Nevertheless, the justice system does not feel comfortable with a person who proclaims his innocence. He is a sore toe or a hangnail, something small but irksome, like a conscience, but not really a conscience, because to have a conscience, which is one half of Consciousness, one needs to be awake enough to act upon its demands. The system is weighted against anyone who claims his innocence until that moment when he admits his guilt. The office of New York governor George Pataki and, later, David Paterson wrote to Innocence International saying that David McCallum is eligible for clemency. But as long as McCallum proclaims his innocence and does not show remorse, it is unlikely that he will receive clemency or even parole when he becomes eligible. The confessed rapist or the confessed murderer in the cell next to his will go home before he does.

David McCallum III was born in Dillon, South Carolina, a small working-class city where people appeared to get along well, and where racial tension was not a part of his upbringing. In McCallum's description of its bars and factories, Dillon reminded me of Paterson, New Jersey. He remembers being happy, but he realizes in hindsight that there must have been few opportunities for his three brothers and three sisters to lead fully productive lives. His family moved to Bedford-Stuyvesant in Brooklyn in 1976. How anyone could see this neighborhood, especially in that year, as a place of opportunity is a mystery only partially explained in his unpublished autobiography.

> *This part of Brooklyn had a reputation for being one of the roughest neighborhoods in the entire New York City area. [It was] filled with run-down buildings and vacant lots. The people living in this neighborhood really seemed to be struggling to make ends meet, which is why I had a hard time understanding why we moved in the first place. However, at eight years of age, it was not meant for me to understand, I guess.... When I got*

*older, my mother said that getting off public assistance was one
of the proudest moments of her life. After a couple of days of
living on Hart Street, I could not understand why it smelled so
badly, as if something had died and become a permanent fixture
there. My family did not come from perfect conditions in Dillon,
but compared to Bedford-Stuyvesant, Dillon was like living on
Hilton Head Island.*

Like many young people who migrated to northern cities from
the South, McCallum had to deal with the culture shock. First of
all, his new neighborhood was almost entirely inhabited by black
people; the fact that the McCallum family was intact made them an
exception to the rule of fatherless families surrounding them.

*I moved to New York at a very young age from Dillon, South
Carolina, which is affectionately known as South of the Border
by those of us who were born and raised there. Moving from a
rural community in the South to NYC was a culture shock even
at such a young age. I come from a fairly close family, although
we had our problems like everyone else. To describe my upbringing, it is not too far-fetched for me to reflect back on the many
episodes of the television show* Good Times. *I did not have
much, but I never went to bed hungry and I never went to school
unprepared. If there was one constant in my family, it was my
mother and father's ability to make sure me and my siblings
were all right, even if it meant sacrificing some of their joys in
life. I have three brothers and three sisters, so one can imagine
how much sacrificing they had to do.*

His school, P.S. 304, was a refuge from the daily muggings and robberies that took place in the streets to police indifference. He still remembers his third grade teacher, Miss Archibald, a short Caribbean woman "who put her heart and soul into 'her children.'" The family moved from Bed-Stuy to Bushwick, but the conditions, graffiti, vacant lots, and rampant crime at that time were much the same, with the exception that Bushwick had a large Latino population.

The most troubling aspect of McCallum's youth was his father's being on disability after suffering a work-related accident. The elder McCallum was so frustrated and humiliated by his condition that he became an abusive husband.

> *I used to go to bed at night praying to God that he would deliver my mother to us the next morning....I remember times when my siblings and I were embarrassed to go to school, because if there was one thing that was evident living in Bushwick...it was that everybody was nosy. To me and my siblings, however, my father was a very kind man, but I don't think he could recover from the burden of not being able to work again. There were days when I did not want to go home after school, because I was scared that my mother would not be able to handle it anymore. It was at that point in my young life that I made a vow that I would never lay a hand on a woman no matter what she did or how upset I became.*

When McCallum's mother, Ernestine, "the best mother in the world," got a job in 1980 as a home care attendant, the whole family was energized. She no longer had to be trapped inside the house with an abusive husband, and the family could be provided for without resorting to the indignities of welfare.

As parents usually find to their dismay, a child's peer group is the most powerful force in his or her life. McCallum had to build his reputation on the street where positive role models were few and far between. While young in years, he was tough and able to learn how to survive. He drifted into a life of criminal behavior because that was the shortcut to respect. Like me, he was swallowed up in reputation, "fronting," or building a false persona that was meant to convey an impression of cruelty and heartlessness.

Over the years, I often wondered if my arrest [for Blenner's murder] had more to do with my past transgressions rather than what I was accused of doing. I will admit that my reputation was terrible, and I did nothing to dispel that notion, because I thought it gave me credibility as a thug in my neighborhood....Hanging out on Wilson Avenue was a safe haven for the young kids; I mean we spoke the same and acted the same, even though deep down inside we knew we were "fronting," which is another word for trying to pretend like something we were not....The name Supreme was given to me based on my ever-growing reputation as someone who did not take any shit and because of my size. In the Nation of Islam, the name Supreme means the most highest...although the Nation of Islam did not preach the kind of behavior I exhibited....I believe that I have done more sinning in my lifetime than being sinned against, which is why I have been reluctant to express my embarrassing past to you.

Because I, too, had been guilty of robbing an older woman in the street, one of the most shameful episodes of my life, I can understand the impulse behind McCallum's becoming involved in the same type of crime and the terrible remorse that was to follow.

On this night, we were coming out of a candy store on the corner of Central Avenue and Schaefer Street when we noticed a lady, a dark-skinned woman with a heavy build, walking toward us, apparently on her way to church, which sat directly across from the store. She wore a multicolored dress with different colored ornaments on it. A stranger walking on a dimly lit avenue with no one around, especially in a neighborhood like Bushwick, was asking for trouble. I turned to my friend, Unique, and, as if he read my mind, he said, "Let's rob her." As we fast approached this lady, Unique pulled out his gun and ordered her to give him the pocketbook. "Give me your fucking pocketbook," he said, in a heavy but even-toned voice that would not alert anyone to what we were doing. When the lady hesitated to give up her pocketbook, Unique repeated it again, this time more forcefully, and she handed it over to us. We then ran to Wilson Avenue where we could blend in with everyone else if she decided to call the cops. It was not until we reached Wilson Avenue that it dawned on me what she said to Unique prior to handing over her pocketbook. She said, "Can I please have my Social Security card?" Unique said "No!" and we ran off. When I got home that night, I began reflecting back on the horrible memories of watching as my mother struggled with the welfare system, and how much her Social Security card meant to my family. I felt as though I had robbed my own mother. The way she pleaded for her card actually reminded me of my own mother. You could say that it was a life-changing experience for me, because after that I made up my mind that I was going to really try and do the right thing.

As so often happens, McCallum's reputation and his past behavior overrode his attempt to re-create himself. His picture was on display at the Brooklyn precinct; the detective in charge of the Blenner case must have figured that McCallum would make a very credible suspect, especially since Heyward and Murphy had said that McCallum had a gun with a body on it. Why not follow that lead even if other, more credible leads had been presented?

David McCallum was sent off to Rikers Island to await trial after his arrest for the murder of Nathan Blenner. Rikers is a penal colony that houses over fifteen thousand violent offenders and is located only five miles from downtown Manhattan. It is an integral part of the whole processing machinery in New York State; those sentenced to long prison terms are eventually transferred to upstate institutions, while those who are acquitted or have served short sentences are put on the bus and cross the bridge back into society. But the prison leaves its mark on everyone who comes into contact with it, including the over ten thousand people who work there. McCallum's description of life at Rikers in 1986 is not too far from what you might see today.

The most notorious criminals were kept on Rikers Island. The bus stopped at C-74, which is known to everyone on Rikers as the 4 building. It was for adolescents. The most dehumanizing way to ruin a person's soul was demonstrated in the 4 building's receiving room, where the newly arrived were sent. Inmates were given a bar of state soap, which if used too much, could peel the skin off your body. The new inmates, myself included, were sprayed with a water hose reminiscent of the way slaves were treated. It also reminded me of the little black girls in Kansas who were sprayed with a water hose because they were not welcome to attend school. The corrections officers took pleasure in humiliating inmates.... On our way to the reception area of the building, the long corridors smelled of trouble. It was not out of the question for an inmate to jump out of one of the wings of a housing unit to attack new inmates. Actually, with some of the ambushes that took place, [they had been] concocted by the inmates and the escorting officers because some guys had sexual assault and other unforgiven crimes. If you were in there for killing a cop, the officers would deal with you, but if you were in there for a heinous crime such as rape, the inmates would deal with you.

Rikers was and still is a perfect example of unconscious human insanity thriving in an environment in which the only law is survival of the fittest.

Every day there was something going on. There were racial riots between Puerto Ricans and Blacks that went on and on. There was no end to the madness, and most of it was over nonsense. The majority of the white inmates were either in protective custody or in a housing unit away from the general population. During these riots, fights were so violent that some inmates required over a hundred stitches in their faces. Most of the incidents occurred in the hallways or on the way to and from the mess hall. Believe it or not some even occurred in the visiting room when inmates were with their families. It seemed that everywhere I looked, there was an inmate with a scar on his face.

It's bad enough that a country such as the United States of America condones the torture of its enemies and allows its own citizens to be tortured inside foreign prison walls. But the knowledge that prisoners such as David McCallum, be he one in ten or one in a hundred, are actually innocent of a particular crime and must endure these conditions, the sadism and the humiliation, is a sad commentary on the state of our society. New York itself may have an overstated reputation as a place of justice since, according to the Benjamin Cardozo School of Law, more than 10 percent of DNA exonerations have been in New York State, although it has only 5 percent of the nation's population.

If courts worked the way they were supposed to work, if police officers, prosecutors, defense attorneys, and judges were all held accountable for their actions under the law, wrongful convictions would not occur with the frequency they now do. Prosecutors are obligated to expose everything that is exculpatory to a defendant, even if it means that the accused will escape conviction. The defense is under no such obligation to expose information that will implicate the defendant, and, of course, the defendant is protected by his Fifth Amendment right against self-incrimination unless he or she so chooses to waive it. Ideally, then, the justice system is weighted to avoid wrongful convictions, seen by those who created the system as a worse evil than a guilty man going free. In that protection against possible injustice and infringement upon the rights and security of an individual, we can see the idealism of the founding fathers. But the courts are now less about the protection of the rights of individuals than about clearing the streets. They are about the mechanisms of oppression. Especially in the United States, where many legal officials must attain and maintain their positions by running for office, the law can be about winning and losing or about establishing reputations for toughness on crime.

Protections built into the system have been steadily eroded because of the perception, the illusion fostered by the corporate-owned media, that crime is out of hand. Nowadays, governments even force some lawyers to sign confidentiality agreements, or "Don't-tell deals," if they are to have access to exculpatory material. In this way, governments make it look like they are complying with the disclosure law, while at the same time they shield themselves from the consequences of the disclosure. These agreements make it impossible to publicize the misdeeds of police and prosecutors with respect to certain cases where wrongful convictions have been improperly obtained. Not until the case actually comes to trial (or on appeal) can this material be exposed to the light of day. For this reason alone, some of these cases will never get to trial; the accused will end up accepting a plea bargain. In the event a trial does take place, the years that pass between arrest and trial lessen the effect of the revelation. Confidentiality agreements, then, weaken the effect of disclosure laws. No right of prosecutors or politicians to avoid embarrassment should supersede the rights of a private individual.

Presently, the American system has a small safeguard and protection against executing the wrong person. If a sentencing jury cannot decide unanimously to kill the individual convicted of a capital crime, an automatic sentence of life imprisonment is imposed. Now some members of the United States Congress are seeking to change the law by empanelling another jury if the first one is hung. How these legislators can miss the obvious fact that innocent people have been executed, even with the safeguard in place, only demonstrates once again the unconscious human insanity with which we live.

In addition, our legal systems are weighted toward those with the money to hire expensive lawyers. Both subtly and in ways not so subtle, the system, due to the sheer volume of criminal proceedings, has shifted away from the protection of individual rights and toward the protection of society at large. Although it goes against legal ethics for a lawyer to recommend it, an *innocent* man or woman might opt for a plea bargain because the shorter sentence seems a more appealing option than a possible loss in an expensive trial. Think of the temptation that McCallum and Stuckey had to deal with and the courage it took for them to proclaim their innocence.

The case against them might be better seen if it is placed against the backdrop of other wrongful convictions. The presence of so many telltale signs, along with the retracted confessions, indicates that this case was and still is, almost twenty-five years later, anything but "safe."

The Absence of Hard Evidence Against the Defendants

Forensic evidence, while not enough by itself to attain a conviction, should play a vital role in determining guilt or innocence. You can criticize a case against a defendant for having only a small amount of such evidence, maybe a single fingerprint or a drop of blood, but you have to wonder why the police and the district attorney would rush to convict two people in the face of no hard evidence whatsoever. David McCallum and Willie Stuckey left not a single fingerprint on or in Nathan Blenner's car or on the kerosene can used to burn it, and yet other people did. Nor was any evidence that might have implicated them found at the crime scene. Nor was any evidence found on their shoes or clothing. The gun that was used to kill the victim was never found, nor was the caliber of the bullet that caused the victim's death ever established. Not a single witness ever identified McCallum or Stuckey as being with the deceased. Not a single witness ever saw McCallum driving Blenner's car, although he supposedly drove it around town for two days after the murder. The case was built entirely upon the defendants' forced confessions or, as the court called them, "the statements." Even the judge, who on several separate occasions showed his bias by assisting the prosecutors, stated as much.

> *The case is based solely on the statements. So if the jury believes if they were forced into making the statements…the jury is going to discount the statement. I'm going to so instruct them to do that.*

However, the district attorney must have felt that by themselves the statements might not be able to persuade twelve members of a jury. All other testimony elicited by the prosecution at the trial was an attempt to provide a foundation for their case or to fill in some of the deep holes that remained in the face of the complete absence of forensic evidence. The key for the prosecution was to give the appearance through innuendo and suppositions that McCallum and Stuckey had committed the crime and to shape whatever the witnesses said around the "twin confessions." It was clear that in lieu of the confessions none of this type of testimony, hearsay at best, would have led to a conviction, but two elements were present to make this testimony work. First, the court-appointed defense lawyers spent no time interviewing any witnesses before the trial, so they were ill prepared to cross-examine them on the witness stand. Second, the defense did not take all of the many opportunities handed to them to rebut flawed testimony. I will grant that a confession to a crime is a difficult factor for any attorney to defend against. But if the testimony of the witnesses was shown to be false or suborned, the case against the defendants would have been discredited and the credibility of the prosecution severely damaged.

The justice system does not need to operate this way. Not at all.

In the McCallum case, fingerprints were found on the hood and doors of Nathan Blenner's car and on the kerosene can used to burn it. When it was shown that the prints did not belong to McCallum or Stuckey, the prints were simply disregarded. Since McCallum and Stuckey had confessed to the crime, if another perpetrator was found to have committed the murder, it would have become apparent that the defendants' confessions had been coerced. The need to protect or to cover up police wrongdoing is justice as it should not be.

The Tribal Element

The McCallum case involved the murder of a white person by two black people. It is far more likely that a suspect will be arrested and convicted of this type of crime than if the victim were black as well. This factor in no way exonerates McCallum and Stuckey, but the police would usually have to build a far more solid case before a middle-class white person might even be arrested, if only because the person with more money will have better legal representation.

A jury is less likely to believe a black defendant when he says that a confession was beaten out of him or that the police engaged in brutal violence. The only time the public or a jury is likely to believe a black defendant is when a videotape of the arrest, as in the Rodney King incident, shows the brutality on national television. Finally, the jury is less likely to believe in alibis provided by black people, especially family members of the defendant. In this case, both McCallum's mother and sister provided him with an alibi as to his whereabouts during the murder, but the jury would not buy it because they were McCallum's closest relatives and relatives would lie to protect their own. The jury was also made aware that their stories had inconsistencies. The inconsistencies may have given jurors an easier time in disregarding the alibi.

The False Confessions

In addition to the fact that David McCallum and Willie Stuckey both retracted their confessions, one must also consider the circumstances under which those confessions were extracted. Although there were three arresting officers on record for both defendants, two of the officers conveniently excused themselves while the lead detective carried on the interrogation by himself. And only the lead detective was presented in court for questioning.

To this day, the interrogation of the accused is not usually videotaped, although there are moves afoot in several jurisdictions to require this. What the jury saw on videotape were the results of the interrogations, or the "statements," as the judge called them. (McCallum's took all of four minutes.) If McCallum and Stuckey were slapped repeatedly in the face while their hands were cuffed behind their backs, as they both testified to in court, then the message to them was clear: they were at the absolute mercy of their interrogator, especially when the detective picked up a folding chair and threatened to bring it down upon McCallum's head. Two isolated sixteen-year-old boys could hardly be expected to hold their own against a seasoned professional interrogator.

Before their confessions, both defendants were allegedly read their Miranda rights (that is, that they could remain silent and speak first to a lawyer). During the trial, Joseph Butta, the lead detective, was asked what he actually said to both defendants prior to the interrogation; he needed to consult a card while he was on the witness stand to recall what those rights were. Butta was a veteran police officer but obviously unused to informing defendants of their rights except in the most perfunctory way. Young people who are innocent of criminal wrongdoing will often waive Miranda rights because they believe their innocence will protect them.

Saul Kassin, a professor of psychology at Williams College, Steve Drizin of Northwestern University's Bluhm Clinic, Richard Ofshe, professor emeritus from Berkeley, and Gisli Gudjonsson, a professor of forensic psychology at King's College London, are some of the leading researchers in the field of false confessions. They list a number of factors that are usually present when an accused person falsely incriminates himself. The first is age: the younger the defendant, the more likely it is that he would give a false confession. Education is the second factor: the less education, the more likely the confession. The third factor is isolation: both teenagers were held in isolation. McCallum's mother, told about his arrest by someone in the neighborhood, was not able to see or speak to her son until the following day. McCallum, after denying that he knew anything about a murder, was left by himself for almost two hours until Stuckey was brought into the interrogation room and then whisked away by the lead detective. McCallum was then told by the detective that Stuckey had told him that McCallum had shot Blenner. At that point, and with the use of physical coercion, it was not difficult to get McCallum to reverse the accusation and accuse Stuckey, especially when he was told that if he did so he could go home. The fourth factor in false confessions, then, is deliberate deceit by the police during interrogation, especially the promise that the arrested individual will be released as soon as he provides the necessary information *about someone else*, but that also ties the confessing individual to the crime itself. If the consequences of making a confession are minimized, then it is obvious that a person under severe duress would be more likely to succumb to the deception. That such tactics are legal does not mitigate the fact that interrogations should not be carried on in secret or without reasonable suspicion of guilt.

Indeed, when viewing both confessions on videotape, each defendant talks about the other. Stuckey, a neatly dressed and meek-looking boy, begins by saying, "My friend, Supreme, David..." In other words, Stuckey and McCallum were both made to see themselves as witnesses to a murder and not the perpetrators of a kidnapping. If you are an accessory to a kidnapping and the victim dies, it makes no difference at all from a legal standpoint who did the killing. They are not knowingly confessing, but by placing themselves at the scene they have closed the steel trap around themselves.

In many cases of false confession, the youthful and uneducated person confesses simply to end the interrogation. Then there are cases in which the accused confesses because he has been convinced by the interrogator of his own guilt through the clever use of language. He has fallen into a verbal trap that is created by yes-or-no, true-or-false answers, either of which leads to the same destination. While it is true that the field of false confessions is not yet considered to be a science and that many judges do not allow testimony from these experts, few if any people in the field of law or psychology would argue that false confessions do not occur.

The phrases "wrongful conviction" and "false confession" do not really convey the psychopathology that goes on in a person's mind when he faces the consequences of what the police have done to him or what he himself has said. The first thing he feels is disbelief: *What are they talking about? How could they accuse me of that? Why am I here? How do I get out of this place?* In retrospect, he can only regret not having the presence of mind to react differently to the accusations. He might even blame himself for being in the wrong place at the wrong time, just as McCallum did: "I can say that I wish I hadn't been sitting out on that stoop that day in 1985. I wish I had stayed in the house after visiting my father in the hospital.... There are too many reminders that I have sacrificed nearly two decades of my life, of my freedom, by falsely confessing. I admit, I'm tired."

Here you are, maybe just minding your own business, and a group of police officers comes up to you with guns drawn or prominently displayed. You are being forcibly kidnapped, although they will call it an arrest. Handcuffs are placed on your wrists, and these handcuffs are not fitted to you. They are made small so that you cannot wriggle out of them, and if you happen to have large wrists, too bad. So along with shock, fear, and amazement, you have pain, which is the beginning of torture.

You wind up in the cold, unfriendly confines of a police station, and then you are isolated in a bare interrogation room and made to wait. Waiting is one of the techniques used to make you more pliable, to weaken your resistance. You need something to drink, and you need to go to the bathroom, but your hands are still cuffed behind your back. You hear people outside the door, and you suspect that they are looking at you through a two-way mirror. Pretty soon you're just happy that someone has come in to talk to you, maybe with a promise that you can go home soon. A couple of police officers, good guys, come in and speak to you about a little bit of nothing: "Where were you last Saturday? What time did you leave the house, kid? Just take a guess." You don't know that they are fitting you into their timelines or they are fitting your timelines to the case they are building against you. You are still positive that the whole thing will be cleared up when they discover who you are. After all, you have not committed any kind of crime.

You are left alone again. The cop who arrested you, a broad, ham-handed, and heavy man, enters the room and stares at you as if you were a cockroach. You still need to pee, and you need to drink, and maybe, just to end the ordeal, you agree to answer some questions. You may, as in David McCallum's case, deny you had anything to do with the crime. The detective tells you that your friend has accused you of murder. "What? My friend said that? What did he say to you?" And you hear a story that sounds like something out of a science fiction movie, but somehow you find yourself inside the story, and pretty soon they have you dealing with the "facts" of this story.

Your hands are still cuffed behind your back, and again you deny having anything to do with the murder. Wham! You are hit broadside on your face. The shock of that immediately conveys a terrible message. You are alone and have no means of defending yourself. Wham! Another one. You taste blood inside your mouth. "I don't know what you're talking about!" The detective lifts up a metal chair, getting ready, you think, to smash it over your head. No one is there to witness this assault, no one to stop him. "All right, yeah, I was there," you blurt out, trying to remember what the detective told you that your friend had said. You then tell him exactly what he wants to hear. Then your handcuffs are removed, and you are allowed to go to the bathroom. Now maybe you get a drink or even a pat on the back. Then, with your face cleaned up, you are made to repeat this story to an assistant DA in front of a video camera, all the while with the smiling lead detective at your side. You are his trophy. You think because you have blamed your friend for the killing that you are going home.

But what you have actually done by talking to the police is to seal your own fate. They tried to do the same with John Artis and me. We were arrested at three-thirty in the morning, and I knew the young Artis, nineteen years old, was being questioned in another room. What did I know about him except that I had spoken once at his school and that he was a good dancer? Since I had been involved with the criminal justice system for most of my life and John Artis had never been involved, they assumed that he was the weak link. Artis had no police record. They worked on him. "John, you've always been clean. Carter has a record a mile long. It's always the innocent ones who get hurt." But Artis could not bring himself to implicate me. "My parents taught me not to lie," he told them. "They taught me to tell the truth."

Eventually Artis was relocated to Bayside State Prison, a minimum-security institution in Leesburg, New Jersey, where he graduated from Glassboro State College and was a model prisoner for fifteen years. Every year, a few days before Christmas, the authorities would take him home to his parents in Paterson and ask him to say how I had committed those murders. Every year they made the same promise, "The governor guarantees you'll be home by Christmas." And every year he refused. Artis will always be my hero. How many people on this earth would have done that except him? He was paroled in 1981 because the authorities could see that he was never going to lie for them.

David McCallum may have had a tough exterior and a strong personality, but he was frightened by authority. He had a right to be. You don't play with the police. This is authority that knows how to torture and manipulate. This is authority that learned tactics that are taught at the School of the Americas (now called the Western Hemisphere Institute for Security Cooperation) to despotic regimes around the world. Trained interrogators. Schooled in intimidation, pain, fear, and humiliation. Among the police forces of America are some very fine individuals, no question about it, but some are also the crème de la crème of terrorism and torture, what they call counterterrorism. How else could they have "pacified" a continent full of indigenous people? How else could they have sustained a system of slavery for three hundred years? How else does one make a person obedient to someone else's will? A sixteen-year-old teenager stands no chance whatsoever against professional police officers who are ruthless enough to abandon decency and due process. McCallum has nothing but regret for his confession, his lack of preparation for his trial, and his acceptance of an incompetent lawyer. But that is all the regret of hindsight. All that's left for him now is life in prison.

The day before McCallum was arrested, his father, already disabled, had been in a near-fatal automobile accident from which he never fully recovered. Who was unluckier, the father or the son, suddenly handcuffed with his hands behind his back, thrown into the back seat of a police car, and driven away, not knowing why? Both were completely disabled at the same time. The elder McCallum died in November 2005. David McCallum was transported to Brooklyn, the place of burial, where he visited the open coffin. Unlike me, he was not forced to pay for his escort. In this respect, the prison was merciful. Shackled though he was, McCallum was able to hug his dead father and to promise him that he would never give up the fight to prove his innocence.

> I constantly worry about my mother. I especially worry about my oldest sister, Ella, who suffers from CP and cannot fend for herself. Every time I think of her, my eyes begin to water. I just want to hold her again. I have to further punish myself by avoiding thinking about her, which is impossible.

The Unreliable Witnesses

The witnesses used in this trial by the prosecution were not only unreliable but, to a large extent, irrelevant. The trick for the prosecution was to make these bogus witnesses appear relevant to the jury. The first witness, James Johnson, alias Jesse James, provided a convenient substitute for Heyward and Murphy, perhaps the real perpetrators who the prosecution successfully kept out of the courtroom. Johnson had possession of a gun early in October 1985. Under questioning by the assistant district attorney, Eric Bjorneby, he made a startling confession.

> BJORNEBY: And did you have a license or permit for that gun?
>
> JOHNSON: No.
>
> BJORNEBY: And what did you do with that gun?
>
> JOHNSON: Well I was in the store. I had a fight, right.
>
> BJORNEBY: Yes?
>
> JOHNSON: I got hit in the head with a bat, and I shot off a couple of shots and went to my aunt's house.

The first thing we learn when reading this testimony is that this so-called fight was actually an attempted armed robbery during which Johnson fired the gun after the store owner hit him in the head with a baseball bat. The second thing we learn is that Johnson hid the gun at his aunt Lottie's apartment because he had to go to the hospital to get stitches in his head. Then Johnson testified that his friend, another man named Jamie who happened to know his aunt Lottie, got the gun from her and gave it to Willie Stuckey. But the prosecution never produced the supposed links between Aunt Lottie and Jamie or between Jamie and Willie Stuckey, only a statement from Johnson that Stuckey told him he had a gun and the gun came from Jamie. In this instance, Harvey Mandlecorn, Stuckey's lawyer, elicited the most important and interesting piece of testimony from this witness.

> MANDLECORN: You had it in the store that day, didn't you?
> JOHNSON: Yeah.
> MANDLECORN: And you spoke to Detective Butta last year?
> JOHNSON: Yes.
> MANDLECORN: And he told you if you'd testify about the gun that he'd forget about the shooting in the grocery store, didn't he?
> JOHNSON: Yes.

Here we have another case not unlike my own in which a felon is induced to testify against an innocent defendant in exchange for the dropping of very serious charges: illegal possession of a firearm, firing a weapon in a public place, and attempted armed robbery. Testimony of this type should never be allowed in a court of law. Never! What the prosecution was able to accomplish, however, was to suggest to the jury that Willie Stuckey had a gun—not that anyone ever saw him with a gun. During the interrogation by Butta, Stuckey told him that the gun was hidden at home beneath his mattress. Of course, because Stuckey's story was fabricated, the gun was not to be found there. In fact, the gun was never found. How could Johnson's unsubstantiated testimony have been allowed in any way whatsoever to convict two innocent people of murder?

Two other witnesses, young boys aged ten and eleven, were used to verify that a kidnapping had actually taken place. Neither witness demonstrated firm knowledge of what swearing an oath

291

really meant, yet they were duly sworn in. Using the two boys was extremely risky for the prosecution because they had been fed and rehearsed details of the crime they could not possibly have known, but the defense lawyers, tragically as it now appears, chose not to cross-examine them. Perhaps the two lawyers thought it risky on their part to try to undercut the testimony of nervous youngsters because it would make them appear to be bullying child witnesses. If there is an obvious element in the trial that speaks to the innocence of McCallum and Stuckey, it is contained within the testimony of these two boys, now thirty-plus years of age.

The two friends were playing outside together on Sunday, October 20, when Nathan Blenner was allegedly kidnapped in front of his house. Actually, the only established fact is that the boys, one of whom lived across the street from Blenner, were playing together that day when an incident involving Blenner's car occurred in front of the Blenner house. The boys originally stated that they were outside the house when they decided to go inside and play storm trooper. They claimed to have witnessed the carjacking or abduction from inside the house. Twenty years later, a neighbor, speaking to Oscar Michelen, our pro bono attorney, told the same story. However, she said that the two boys ran inside after seeing two brown-skinned men walking up their street in the direction of Blenner's car. The significance of these accounts only becomes clear when one reads the transcripts of the two boys' testimonies, word-for-word identical and well-rehearsed. The street where these homes were located is a wide residential street, four lanes with a stripe down the middle. If the boys only saw the kidnappers from inside the house (and not out in the street), it was certainly possible that they would be unable to identify them in court; McCallum and

Stuckey were never identified as the two "brown men." If the boys had actually seen the kidnappers while out on the street, then surely they would have been able to identify them. Since they could not and would not identify them in court, the prosecution had to place the boys inside the house for the entire time. Both boys said that the reason they could not see the faces of the abductors was that they were "walking sideways" even though they both testified that the kidnappers walked past the car and turned around. The boys held the key to an acquittal if they were to have said, unequivocally, that McCallum and Stuckey were *not* the two people they saw.

But here is where the boys' trial testimonies (along with the case against McCallum and Stuckey) unravel and where both defense attorneys proved completely ineffective. One of the young boys, who had been told before the swearing in that lying under oath was punishable with jail, began to show signs of stress during the questioning by the DA, Eric Bjorneby. The moment when he began to hyperventilate coincided with his most obvious false statement.

> BJORNEBY: What about their skin color?
> BOY #1: Dark brown.
> BJORNEBY: Now tell us what you saw take place.
> BOY #1: I saw two men walking down the street, and they walked a little past the car and they stopped, looked around. Then they went to the car and said, "Move the fuck over." Then both of them entered the car.
> BJORNEBY: All right. The fellow who was—it's all right, Gregory. You relax for a minute.

(Pause in proceeding)

BJORNEBY: You feeling a little better?

BOY #1: Yes.

BJORNEBY: Who was inside the car, if you know?

BOY #1: Nathan Blenner.

BJORNEBY: And where was he in the car?

BOY #1: In the driver's.

BJORNEBY: At the time did you realize it was Nathan in the car?

BOY #1: No.

BJORNEBY: Was he behind the steering wheel?

BOY #1: Yes.

BJORNEBY: And what was he doing?

BOY #1: He was trying to start the engine.

At trial, it appears as if the boys were persuaded to say (or told to say) that they couldn't see Nathan Blenner behind the wheel. If they could have identified him sitting inside his car, it would have appeared inconsistent that they could not have identified the two defendants. Moreover, the claim that someone inside a house can hear the words "move the fuck over" spoken into a car window across a four-lane street is absurd. Actual words cannot be overheard from across such a wide street *even if the listener is outside the house.* The judge (sometimes referred to as The Court in the transcript) picked up on this discrepancy when the second boy testified and subtly relayed the difficulty to Bjorneby. It is interesting to note how cleverly Bjorneby dealt with the problem and how ineffective the defense lawyers remained.

BJORNEBY: Did you hear them say anything to each
other at that time?

BOY #2:   No, his windows were closed.

THE COURT: Whose windows?

BOY #2:   Greg's.

THE COURT: The porch windows?

BOY #2:   Yeah.

BJORNEBY: So the only thing you could hear was when
he *yelled* at Mr. Blenner? [Italics mine.]

BOY #2:   Yeah.

The momentary problem for the prosecution, which the judge recognized, was that the first child witness had already testified that one of the defendants had said, "Move the fuck over." This detail was most likely fabricated, by whom I am not sure, either by the DA or from McCallum or Stuckey while under interrogation, to make the story more believable. But if McCallum had simply spoken those words and not absolutely screamed them out, they would have been inaudible. In fact, the witness says in answer to what he heard, "No, his windows were closed"—in other words, as would be expected, he never heard anything at all. So Bjorneby, on Judge Egitto's prompting, threw in the word "yelled," and neither defense attorney picked up on the fact that he was both leading the witness and testifying for him. Judging as well from McCallum's description of the way he and Unique had robbed an older woman on the street in a *black* neighborhood, it is unbelievable that he or any other African in America would yell out such a thing on a Sunday afternoon in a white neighborhood and call attention to himself and to what was taking place. In hindsight, Judge Egitto also led the witness by using the word "porch." When Oscar Michelen visited the neighborhood twenty years later, something neither defense attorney, Peter Mirto (for McCallum) nor Harvey Mandelcorn (for Stuckey), thought it important enough to do, he noticed that Greg's house did not have an outside porch, just a small room, or an anteroom, in front of the living room.

Checking the grand jury testimony and the original tape transcriptions of the police investigation, both of which occurred a year before the trial, other contradictions from the two young boys are revealed.

> BJORNEBY: A week ago last Sunday, October 20th, in the afternoon, were you outside your house?
>
> BOY #1: No. Inside where I saw everything.
>
> BJORNEBY: Alright. Well, before you saw everything from the inside, had you been outside?
>
> BOY #1: Yeah.
>
> BJORNEBY: Did you see something that made you go inside?
>
> BOY #1: No.
>
> BJORNEBY: Did you see two boys coming down the street?
>
> BOY #1: Yeah.
>
> BJORNEBY: Okay. That's what I was getting at. And when you ran inside your house, where did you go?
>
> BOY #1: Right to my porch.

BJORNEBY: Okay. And did you look out your window?

BOY #1:   Yeah. To make sure they were gone.

What becomes clear is that the two child witnesses say they saw the abductors, described by the DA as "two boys," out on the street and ran inside the house, from which vantage point they witnessed the actual abduction. I contend here that the term "two boys" might have been recognizable as a racial epithet by the witnesses, but *neither child witness ever suggested that the kidnapping was done by "boys."* Indeed, District Attorney Bjorneby, in the actual trial, usually referred to the kidnappers as "fellows" or "guys," generic terms that deliberately obfuscate actual ages. What is even clearer in the initial investigation a year before the trial is that both witnesses said that Nathan Blenner was, indeed, behind the wheel of the car.

BJORNEBY: Did there come a time when you saw
              Nathan Blenner—?

BOY #1:   Yes.

BJORNEBY: In his car outside?

BOY #1:   Yes.

BJORNEBY: Was that across the street?

BOY #1:   Yeah.

BJORNEBY: And where in the car was Nathan sitting?

BOY #1:   In the driver's seat.

Before the grand jury, their testimony was the same.

BJORNEBY: And did you see Nathan also?

BOY #2:   He was inside the car.

When the two child witnesses testified in court that neither of them could see who was in the car, it is clear that both of them committed perjury and that their stories were too full of inconsistencies to be allowed in a courtroom. I repeat the trial statement for emphasis.

> Bjorneby: At the time did you realize it was Nathan in the car?
>
> Boy #1: No.

Our contention here is that neither boy identified Stuckey or McCallum in court because they were not the "two boys" they saw walking up the street. They began their testimonies, both during the investigation and at the grand jury, by stating that there was a significant, visible height disparity between the kidnappers, that one, the one who went up to Blenner, was clearly bigger than the other. During the trial, Bjorneby, unchallenged by the defense, kept describing one of the abductors as being "a little bigger" than the other one, and the two child witnesses eventually agreed to what the adult kept repeating.

Another witness, Cathy Hank, who was interviewed by the police on the day that Nathan's body was discovered and who was outside that day washing her car, had seen two "black men" walking north on the street, one of whom complimented her car, a Buick Regal like the victim's. The verbal exchange between one of the men and the woman was typical of what might be expected in an area of the city where black people were not often seen.

> Man: That's a nice looking car.

WOMAN: If it's not here tomorrow, I'll know where
to look.

Hank described the speaker as having braided hair, but, as can be seen in the confession video, neither McCallum nor Stuckey had braided hair. She also said that both men had "thin builds" and were of noticeably different heights. McCallum and Stuckey were both the same height—five feet five inches tall, McCallum 160 pounds and Stuckey 150 pounds. In the same police report, Hank also stated that she "would be able to identify the two black males and would view photos." She was never called to testify in this case by the prosecution or the defense. When interviewed in 2006 by Jay Salpeter, a private investigator acting on behalf of Innocence International, Hank clearly remembered that Butta came back and showed her photographs of two black males whom she insisted were not the two men she saw. In clear violation of normal procedures, no police report of this contact exists. Nor was there a follow-up. Whose pictures did she see? We think they were photographs of McCallum and Stuckey. When Butta didn't get the answer he was seeking, he simply abandoned the witness.

When Butta was being questioned in court by defense counsel about Cathy Hank, District Attorney Bjorneby objected and deliberately led the jury to believe that she was washing her car "two hours before" the crime was committed (at 12 noon instead of 2 P.M.). The jury was falsely led to believe that she had really seen two other black men. And yet, at the beginning of Butta's trial testimony, a woman washing "a red car" and the conversation about a "nice car" appears in his transcription of Stuckey's confession. Professor Steven Drizin of Northwestern University's Bluhm

Legal Clinic sees this as an example of what is known in the trade as a "false fed fact." In other words, the detective knew that a woman washing her car had seen two black males on the street. The time in the police investigator's notebook clearly reads that Cathy Hank was washing her car at 1400 hours (or 2 P.M.) and not at noon. Since the witness saw two males who were not McCallum and Stuckey, she had to be made irrelevant.

As already stated, two twenty-year-old men, one described as five feet eleven inches tall and the other as five feet two inches ("AKA Shorty") were picked up on October 25 at 1600 hours in connection with a string of eight such armed robberies in the same Queens neighborhood in a forty-eight-hour period, the last recorded at 5:45 A.M. on October 20, that is, the same day Nathan Blenner was kidnapped. According to the detective's notes, "one had braided hair." Most amazingly, one police officer discovered that the taller man worked at the same hardware store "where the kerosene can that was found in Blenner's car originated."

The two child witnesses came outside and ran to a neighbor's house, and a 911 call was placed. Police involvement began with that 911 call, and yet the call itself was never placed into evidence. We believe that the call may have contained descriptions of the abductors that were at odds with the descriptions of McCallum and Stuckey.

Ineffective Assistance of Counsel

David McCallum's lawyer, Peter Mirto, was seventy-one years old at the time of the trial. Disorganized and disputatious, he was attempting to litigate six other serious cases at the same time. For court-appointed lawyers to make a decent living, they generally have to accept whatever comes their way. Those who run the justice system appear unconcerned that these lawyers may not have time to provide adequate legal representation. What "distinguishes" Mirto in this case—what makes him worse than anyone we've ever encountered—is the fact that he never interviewed his client or the material witnesses before the trial and that he was completely unfamiliar with the facts of the case until he heard them in court. Educators, I am told, call this practice "winging it," although the stakes in court are far greater than in a classroom. It is highly unusual for a defense attorney to waive his opening remarks to a jury and to not even say something generic to them about keeping an open mind and using their common sense. In a murder case, the fact that Mirto made no opening statement to the jury would be almost unprecedented. But, then, how could he—since he was completely ignorant of the police investigation and the grand jury testimony?

Mirto first exhibited his lack of knowledge of the case in the cross-examination of police officer Thomas Kaufer who, at three in the afternoon on October 21, 1985, discovered Nathan Blenner's body in Aberdeen Park in the Bushwick section of Brooklyn. The court had to intervene in an attempt to alleviate the confusion.

> MIRTO: Officer, when you arrived at the scene at
> this area, were you present when finger-
> prints were taken of the car?
>
> COURT: Car?
>
> MIRTO: Were you present when fingerprints were
> taken of this car?
>
> KAUFER: What car?

Mirto: No car was recovered there?

What Mirto *did* know was that a car was involved in this crime, Nathan Blenner's car. What he did not know was that the car was discovered two days later in a completely different part of the city. By bringing up the car at this point in the proceedings and in the wrong context, he not only confused the court and the jury, but he also neutralized what could have been a very strong piece of evidence for the defense—a burnt-out car with the kerosene can still inside, full of fingerprints, and not a single one belonging to Stuckey or McCallum.

Moreover, the jury could see right away that McCallum's lawyer was held in contempt by the judge both personally and legally. Mirto would continuously argue points that either had no relevance to the case at all or back himself into a corner whenever they did. He himself admitted that he needed "to make it appear" as if he was doing his best by his client. Mirto's caseload or other outside activities—he was under active investigation for theft from clients and perjury—did force him to be late to court. On October 23, 1986, he was reprimanded by the court for arriving well into the afternoon, almost two hours late.

THE COURT: You know, Mr. Mirto, I think you've abused
the Court. I think you take liberties with
the Court. I don't think you have the least
bit of respect for your obligations as an
attorney.

MIRTO: Could I give you an explanation?

THE COURT: You have no explanation. You have an obligation to be here when you're supposed to be here. Now please don't make it worse because I was tempted to hold you in contempt, and I'm not going to do it now. So don't press your luck.

MIRTO: Look, please. I don't like to be reprimanded unless there is a good reason for you to reprimand me and I'm entitled to give you an excuse why I'm late. I have five cases in 120 Schermerhorn Street in AP-4. I got there a quarter to ten. I waited until ten-thirty before my cases were called. I walked down here then I appeared before Judge Aiello on another homicide. I waited until he finished his case. I just got through with him and came here.

THE COURT: You didn't get *there* until 11:25. [Italics mine.]

MIRTO: That's right.

By picking a fight with the judge, getting caught in a blatant lie, and not apologizing right away to the court for his lateness, Mirto effectively assured that whatever he said or did in that courtroom would be closely watched and challenged by the court, the prosecutor, and the jury.

One of the most damaging of these arguments occurred around a contradiction in David McCallum's testimony. Mirto was caught by the prosecutor and the judge attempting to distort the record. Mirto made the claim that during the Huntley Hearing McCallum testified "that he was told what to say by the lead detective." Mirto kept flipping through the record in an attempt to find the nonexistent testimony. Even McCallum was embarrassed by this futile and transparent attempt to distort the record that, in the end, only brought more attention to the contradiction.

THE COURT: All right. Now where did the detective tell him what to say? Show me.

MIRTO: Page 96. Page 96.

PROSECUTOR: It's not there.

THE COURT: He knows it's not there and I don't approve of antics like that in my courtroom.

MIRTO: Judge, I wish you wouldn't say that. I take exception to your Honor.

THE COURT: Your exception is noted.

MIRTO: Let's put it on the record. I do take all exception. Don't say that to me. I've been practicing for forty years. I don't distort facts. I'm going—

THE COURT: Well, show me what's in the record.

MIRTO: I'm trying to see it now.

THE COURT: It's been ten minutes already and you haven't found it.

MIRTO: Then you read it, but don't tell me I'm distorting the facts. Don't you ever accuse me of that, no more than I'm accusing you of anything.

THE COURT: You show me in the record that you did not distort the facts.

MIRTO: Again you're saying I'm distorting the facts.

THE COURT: Yes, you did and you know it.

MIRTO: All right.

The ultimate result in the McCallum-Stuckey trial had nothing to do with evidence, testimony, or Truth. As in many of these cases of wrongful conviction, the skill of the attorney and the bias of the judge are what play out in a courtroom. By those accounts, McCallum and Stuckey were doomed to be found guilty. They were going to lose the legal game in a very decisive manner. In his summation, the prosecutor naturally returned to the contradiction in McCallum's testimony. Since Mirto had lost that point so demonstrably in the courtroom, the jury concluded, first, that McCallum and Stuckey were in fact lying and, second, that they must have committed the crime. In the minds of the jury, two had to follow from one; here is an example of why I say that logic, while useful, does not necessitate Truth.

Mirto's summation would be high comedy were not the results so tragic. He made a pathetic attempt to ingratiate himself with everyone in the courtroom except his client. For his client he had these words: "He's not the brightest one. He's not going to be a Harvard Law School graduate or going to St. John's Law School. He's not the brightest one."

For the judge, with whom he battled for the entire trial, he has nothing but praise: "I also like to say that in the many years I've practiced law I always like to commend the judge, and it's rightly so. You have one of the finest judges here, a judge well versed in the law. I consider him a scholar in the law. I'm not trying to fraternize him."

He also attempts to excuse his own lack of initiative in interviewing witnesses by foisting it off onto the prosecution. (But why would the prosecution place exculpatory witnesses before the jury since the only thing that seemed to matter to them was who wins and who loses?) "What about the mystery of the gun? Well [Johnson] says I had it in my aunt's house, Lottie, whatever her name was, Lottie, and she was angry. Why didn't they [the prosecution] bring in Lottie? I don't have to bring her in. I don't have to bring no witness in. The judge told you from the beginning I don't have to bring in a witness." The absence of any defense witnesses, aside from McCallum's mother and sister, even though many other young people had been playing in the park on that day, and Mirto's failure to read police reports or to interview the woman who had seen the abductors while washing her car, speaks to McCallum's claim of ineffective assistance of counsel.

Mirto never even presented another story that might have given the jury an opportunity to draw different conclusions. But how could he? He was completely disorganized: "There are so many papers I can't find it." The entire summation proceeded in a desultory fashion where Mirto would jump from one topic to another and never nail down a single fact. Some of his statements were blatantly false, completely irrelevant, or inappropriate: "The police did a good investigation. See, I'm not knocking the police or the district attorney's office. I'm not going to knock them. The only thing I got against them is his [Bjorneby's] age. I wish I was his age, that's about all. But I tell you this, how about the fingerprints and the police—I tell you the police department is one of the best agencies that we have in the entire city or the entire world. Can't beat them. They're excellent."

Now here's what any decent lawyer would have said during summation at this unfortunate trial: "Ladies and gentlemen of the jury, we have two scenarios here, one of which you have to choose in order to convict or acquit these defendants. The first scenario, the one presented by the prosecution, is that two sixteen-year-old boys who were never identified as the perpetrators in this courtroom or anywhere else kidnapped and neatly executed a twenty-year-old male at random and were careful enough to cover up every single piece of incriminating evidence, including any connection to the gun that killed Nathan Blenner. Were careful enough to leave no fingerprints on the car or on the kerosene can used to burn it and were clever enough to leave other people's fingerprints on both. Were careful enough to have no incriminating evidence from the park on their clothing or to leave any evidence in the park. That these two sinister, calculating youths were then brought into a police station and, of their own free wills, confessed to being part of this crime.

"Or scenario two, that these two friends were picked up by the police separately, police who already knew that two black males had kidnapped the victim. That they were roughed up, intimidated, held in isolation, and told that each could go home if they revealed that their friend was the real killer. Which of these two scenarios, ladies and gentlemen, has the ring of Truth?"

When McCallum, years ago and by himself, tried to appeal his conviction based upon ineffective assistance of counsel, the court ruled his contention to be "without merit." In fact, Mirto was disbarred shortly after this trial, having been found guilty on five charges of professional misconduct. One of the charges should have been "padding his account" with meetings that never took place, such as pretending to have seen McCallum at Rikers Island on three separate occasions or interviewing his mother and sister.

When you, an individual innocent of a crime, are confronted by such willful blindness, and when the judicial bureaucracy keeps sending the message that you are a criminal who has been treated fairly, it takes a special kind of person to hold out and proclaim that innocence for the rest of the world to hear. David McCallum is one of those people.

McCallum is now in his twenty-fifth year of imprisonment. He has lived with constant frustration, humiliation by the bureaucracy, and the fear of violence. The fact that we at Innocence International (and Northwestern University's Bluhm legal clinic) are there for him and that we write letters on his behalf helps him understand that others are trying to absorb some of his pain: "I am grateful and utterly amazed at the attention from the outside world that more often than not forgets those of us within these walls. To those of us locked away in here, there is nothing more important than being remembered, which makes you a very special person, and surely a gift from God." We will continue to fight on and will not relent until the state of New York frees David McCallum and brings this long dark chapter to its just and proper conclusion.

When a person dies in prison, the other prisoners must handle the body and not always with great care. If they disliked the person, they abuse the body. Treat it disrespectfully. Almost every month in these monstrous institutions, someone dies and is taken away to be buried in a pauper's cemetery or in one of the growing in-house prison graveyards. McCallum, probably thinking of Stuckey, feels for a dead man on the prison block and knows that if he dies he will be treated in a similar fashion. Every prisoner feels like that.

There are reminders in this place just how fragile and unfair life can be. Yesterday, a fellow inmate passed on while in his cell. Early in the morning, while an officer was taking the count, he noticed that the inmate was not moving. [A doctor confirmed] that the gentleman had actually died. I did not know the guy personally, but I still found myself quietly mourning his passing....For any human being not to feel a little compassion and sympathy for others and their families, I would say is a person without conscience....I would like to think that every life has value, and for this man to spend his last days locked away in this environment is disheartening.

I am reminded of a similar incident at Trenton State Prison. A young man named Kelly went to take a shower and never returned—alive, that is. He died lying on the shower room floor, blood flowing down the drain. These things happen so quickly, and I'd hate to say how often. That lightning quickness, here one moment and gone the next, is why I am so involved in living every day. Every single moment. Life is beautiful, and we must try to live it as fully as we are able—whatever our condition might be. Life is hard. But it seems that the harder it gets to keep life going, the more beautiful it becomes. If David McCallum has learned nothing else from prison, he surely has learned that. For all the things that life may throw at us, all the indignity, the injury, the horror, we must remember that our Spirits can find purpose and survive even in the worst of circumstances. Of course, they can also drown and be lost forever in hopelessness. The miracle then does not occur at the moment when an "innocent person" is actually released through the iron gates and from the walls of bricks and mortar. The miracle occurs when the prisoner releases himself from the universal prison of sleep, those illusory shackles that we have been conditioned to accept as real, and he, in a moment of great transcendence, rises aloft, pure in Spirit, into oneness.

INDEX

INDEX